TALLULAH

HOLT, RINEHART & WINSTON

NEW YORK, CHICAGO, SAN FRANCISCO

TALLULAH

BY BRENDAN GILL

DESIGNED BY MARVIN ISRAEL

ACKNOWLEDGMENTS

Particular thanks are owed to Susan Simon and
Hugh Beeson, Jr., for helping to make this book.
Others whose assistance has turned work into play compose a
list that runs with pleasing neatness from A to Z, to wit:
James Abbe, George Abbott, Joseph Abeles, Joseph Alsop,
Andrew Anspach, M. J. Arlen, Steven M. L. Aronson,
Brooks Atkinson, Richard Avedon, Mary Louise Baker,
John Behrens, Nathaniel Benchley, Karl Bissinger,
William Bostock, Mrs. Fredson Bowers, Mrs. John Mason Brown,
Leonard Burkat, Sandy Campbell, Kenneth Carten,
The Coffee House Club, Janet Cohn, Marc Connelly,
Katharine Cornell, Sir Noël Coward, Nancy Crampton,
The Department of Archives and History of the State of Alabama,
Drew Dudley, Dorothy Edson, Lynn Fontanne, Al Freeman,
Sheila Fraser, Wilson Gathings, Wolcott Gibbs, Jr.,
Carmine Graziano, Robert B. Hale, Philip Hall, Philippe Halsman,
Claire Haupt, Katharine Hepburn, Al Hirschfeld, John Horn,
Horst, Elinor Hughes, Gail Hurwitz, David Jackson, Mary James,
Walter Kerr, James Kirkwood, Will Lerner, Alfred Lunt,
Raymond Mander, Joe Mitchenson, Robert Montgomery,
Al Morgan, Paul Myers, Edward Naumburg, Jr., Donald Oenslager,
George Oppenheimer, Melvin Parks, Allen Porter, Louis Rachow,
Betty Reed, Rose Riley, Edward Barry Roberts, Cal Schumann,
Donald Seawell, Sy Schechter, William Shawn, Valentine Sherry,
Alan Shulman, Leonard Sillman, Edith Smith,
Benjamin Sonnenberg, Helen Stark, Frank Sullivan, Lena Tabori,
Day Tuttle, Eugenia Tuttle, Harriet Walden, The Walter Hampden
Memorial Library of the Players Club, Thomas J. Watson,
Richard Watts, John Hay Whitney, Dorothy Wilding,
Anthony Wilson, and Jerome Zerbe.

A portion of the text of this book
appeared in *The New Yorker*.

Published simultaneously in Canada by Holt, Rinehart and Winston
of Canada, Limited.
ISBN: 0-03-001026-8
Library of Congress Catalog Card Number: 72-78106
First Edition

Printed in the United States of America

See page 283, which constitutes
an extension of this copyright page.

T his book could not have come
into existence without the help of
Eugenia Rawls, who was Tallulah Bankhead's close friend and
professional associate from the time she played the role of her daughter in
The Little Foxes. With affection and a sure instinct for what must be
preserved in the course of transforming memorabilia into
history, Miss Rawls has enacted the role of a tireless and benign
magpie, providing the means to impose order on the record of
a life that was often notably disorderly.

SHE was a strange one, and no mistake. Her needs were many and outrageous and unappeasable. Sometimes they coincided with her appetites and sometimes not. She despised hypocrisy, and her willingness to let the unconventional episodes of her private life be made public was a way of asserting that she had nothing to hide, nothing of which to be ashamed, nothing for which to feel remorse. Despite her remarkable intelligence, she may have believed this to be the case. The violent scatological energy of her speech and the celebrated speed and frequency with which she shucked off her clothes and prowled about naked, long after her body had grown ugly with age, were intended to convey an impression of untrammeled emotional freedom, and it was not so. The chances she took were extreme and necessary and readily misunderstood. She respected and disliked the theater and gave up her life to it, but the common view of her, which she encouraged, was that she was somehow an undisciplined outsider, a gifted amateur, who drank too much and talked too much and turned cartwheels onstage for want of something more professional to do. The facts were otherwise. During the course of her career she appeared in over fifty plays and twenty movies; she traveled scores of thousands of miles with road companies and in summer stock, by train, plane, bus, and station wagon (she said once, speaking of *Private Lives,* "We have played this show everywhere except underwater"); and she made uncounted hundreds of personal appearances in nightclubs and on radio and TV shows. Year after year, how she worked! Indeed, she may have worked harder than any of her fellow-actresses of the period, though she took care to conceal her drudging. She liked to be thought a party girl and a scapegrace, and she had reasons.

Lynn Fontanne said once of Tallulah that she was the greatest natural talent of her time. Tallulah was also a shrewd judge of theater; better than many actors of reputation, she could tell good from bad and do so instantly. If most of the plays she appeared in were trash, why, most of the plays that most of our best actors appear in are trash, as most movies and novels and poems are trash. She did her best to find roles commensurate with her gifts. At nineteen, she was starring in a play written expressly for her by Rachel Crothers, one of the leading playwrights of the day; in her sixties, she was starring in *The Milk Train Doesn't Stop Here Anymore,* which Tennessee Williams has said he wrote with Tallulah in mind: a cruel enough confession, since the character she played was a harridan in a state of repulsive decay. The contemporary playwrights in whose works she starred make a sufficiently impressive list. Among them, Crothers and Williams aside, are Thornton Wilder, Lillian Hellman, Sidney Howard, Jean Cocteau, George Kelly, Clifford Odets, Philip Barry, W. Somerset Maugham, Zoë Akins, and Noël Coward. The restless life-force with which she was born was always ravenously seeking something worthy of containing it, or, with luck, consuming it, and the search was nearly always in vain. Howard Dietz's remark to the effect that a day away from Tallulah was like a month in the country was clever and just, but even at the moment of laughing at it one couldn't fail to wonder how such a remark must have struck its prompter. What was she to do with the thing she had become? She *was* different, and not alone in respect to her talent and vitality. She flailed about in paroxysms of disguised bewilderment, drinking and clowning and cursing and showing off. She was valiant and silly, and she knew it. But she was not rubbishy, and she knew that too. Out of exceptional qualities, she invented by trial and error an exceptional self, which she flung with a child's impudent pretense of not-caring straight into the face of the world. Caught off-guard, the world flinched and applauded, and it went on applauding to the end. Her death, in 1968, was news important enough to warrant a two-column story and picture on the front page of *The New York Times.* Kings have made do with less.

Even at birth, Tallulah was thought to be different from other babies. Her mother, dying a few days after Tallulah was born, said of her that she would always be able to take care of herself—grim sentence of life to pronounce upon a child. The prophecy passed into the Bankhead family lore; Tallulah was to hear it again and again as she was growing up. Like all such family stories, it may have become a burden too accustomed to seem heavy. In any event, she turned the saying into a joke, laughter with her having many uses. The strength of her character showed itself early. In the cradle, she was already successfully pursuing privilege, by methods that served her all her life. Before she had learned to speak, she found the means, howling and kicking, to make herself the center of attention, and for well over sixty years she never willingly surrendered that position. During the mingled, indistinguishable days and nights of her prime, in London, New York, or Hollywood, wherever Tallulah was was where the party was. Round that rowdy, demonic apparition, now dressed with flapper chic in a frock by Worth, now naked to the last shadowy crevice of pale plump skin, the rest of the dancers circled and drank and fell down exhausted and went to sleep; Tallulah danced on. If the party continued all night and then all day and then again all night, so much the better; her ideal was to leave the house, give a performance in a theater, studio, or nightclub, and come back to find lights blazing, servants abed, the party still under way.

Tallulah's motto was "Press on!" This had begun as an amusing maxim of the London years—the sort of catch-phrase that the golden ninnies of *Decline and Fall* and *Vile Bodies* would shout to one another on the brink of some sick-making social catastrophe—and it became with time something genuine, something worth believing in. She told a friend of her later years that it would please her very much to have the words carved on her tombstone. (In fact, the stone, in Old St. Paul's Churchyard, in Rock Hall, a little town on the Eastern Shore, bears only her name and the dates 1902–1968.) She pictured herself exhorting others from the immobility of the grave to plunge headlong into the intricate, messy thick of things. It was characteristic of her that, while she managed to take in the horror of not being able to move in death, the horror of not being able to talk was past imagining: Tallulah mute was no Tallulah. "Press on!" meant to her, in the words of a contemporary, the baseball player Satchel Paige, "Never look back—something might be gaining on you." In the words of another contemporary, her friend Noël Coward, it meant, "Never apologize, never explain." She had found her way to that stoic credo long before she had found the words to utter it in. Better to make a fool of oneself in the center ring, jeered at by thousands, than not to be inside the tent; there were worse things than failure, and the worst of these things was to be ignored. She was always and at no matter what cost in emotion to herself and others intensely present, intensely to be reckoned with. Impossible for her to remain decorous and aloof upon the sidelines if there was hell to be raised elsewhere. On rare occasions—the inaugural of a President, the wedding of a goddaughter—she would seem to stand aside by choice, but the act of abnegation was so unlike her and therefore so conspicuous that it drew all eyes. She shimmered and burned in the wings, and so they were no longer wings: she had obliterated them.

Imperious and cajoling, Tallulah practiced an infant's tyrannies among adults. The consequences ought to have been deplorable, and many right-thinking people were scandalized that they were not. She flourished and she made others flourish. She was superlatively acute in her intuitions, superlatively reckless, and, in her youth, superlatively ignorant. It seemed natural to her in those days to take the daydreams that clutter and befuddle the minds of schoolgirls and make a program out of them. She assumed that there was no hope so foolish that it could not be realized. Her lack of knowledge of the world made her all the readier to conquer it. She was assured by the greasy-papered, gushing movie magazines on which she doted that unknown girls from small towns became great stars overnight and she believed it. She had, moreover, in her own eyes a certain hereditary preeminence. Jasper, Alabama, might be a small town but she was not an unknown girl. She was a Bankhead of Alabama, and the Bankheads were far from being nobodies. Her father was a Congressman; her uncle and grandfather were Senators. They were big men at home and pretty big men in Washington. Tallulah never doubted that to be a Bankhead was to insure respect wherever she might go, and it was ironic that she was to make her first name so famous through-out the world that even in her twenties her second name had become gratuitous. It was also ironic that she had made her first name famous by means not altogether respectable, which is to say by being incessantly gossiped about as well as by the hardest of hard work. No matter; she had passed into the language and her patronymic had become a witticism by omission. Beatrice Lillie, on being informed that Tallulah was expected at a party, asked, "Tallulah who?" and brought down the house.

Jasper, when Tallulah was growing up in it, was a sandy, leafy town in the thinly peopled piney-woods country that stretches north from Birmingham to the Tennessee border. The town was served by two railroads—the Southern and the so-called Frisco, whose official name, the St. Louis–San Francisco Railroad, had early proved more wistful than descriptive; with its main line running between Memphis and Pensacola, it never pushed farther West than Texas. Jasper in Tallulah's time had a population of two or three thousand people. A number of mines were being worked in the vicinity, including the Bankhead mine, and creeks and fields, fishing and hunting, waited within five minutes' walk of the courthouse square. The town was all uphill and downdale and smelled sweetly of pine and honeysuckle, sourly of box and the chunky soft coal that burned winter and summer in the kitchen grates. Jasper had been grubbed out of forest, and along the streets were stands of sweet gum and oak and hickory and tulip trees. In a big white wooden house called "Sunset," on a knoll on the edge of town, four or five generations of Bankheads and family connections and servants lived in a grand disorder of continuous hospitable comings and goings, and in their midst a girl with large, dark-blue incandescent eyes and long honey-colored hair threw her terrifying tantrums and got her way. "I would hurl myself on the floor and scream till I was purple," she said long afterwards. "My father would run away out of the house, leaving the women in charge." Then she added a singular medical self-diagnosis. "I think I must have been suffering from low blood-pressure."

2 She was fat. She was motherless. She had a sister who was a year older than she, prettier than she, and, being in precarious health during the early years, more pampered than she. Eugenia, named for their mother, Adelaide ("Ada") Eugenia Sledge, was every bit as intelligent as Tallulah; indeed, among the friends they were to have in common, there were some who considered Eugenia the more intelligent, as she was often more exuberant and bizarre in her conduct. (Any list of Eugenia's bizarreries must include her seven marriages, three of them to the same man. Over the years, Eugenia has lived in many countries, under many dispensations; at the moment, she is living in Hawaii and, at the age of seventy-one, is said to be sampling life there with undiminished vigor

and eccentricity.) No one was surprised by the intelligence of the Bankhead girls: the family was known to be brainy. The girls' grandfather, John Hollis Bankhead, enlisted in the Confederate Army in 1860, at the age of eighteen, and was mustered out at the end of the war with the rank of captain. By quickness of mind and unusual energy, Captain John, as he was ever after to be known, prospered in politics and business alike—Tallulah used to maintain that he once owned a con-

Tallulah was born in a tiny flat on the second floor of the ambitious corner building.

trolling interest in the Coca-Cola Company, which was not the case, but money came easily into his hands from here and there. In alliance with Oscar Underwood, his fellow Senator from Alabama, he created a political machine that secured for his elder son William Bankhead, a place in the House of Representatives; for his son and namesake, John Hollis Bankhead II, a place in the Senate; and for Dr. Thomas M. Owen, who married his daughter Marie, a post as head of the Department of Archives and History of the State of Alabama. Alabama was the first state to establish such a department; it did so in part because that inexhaustible busybody Marie Bankhead Owen wanted a suitable place in which to store the family memorabilia. During the thirties, she hornswoggled the Roosevelt Administration into constructing an enormous white marble mausoleum of a building for the Department of Archives; it is a far grander structure than the nearby state capitol, and Dr. Owen's paneled office, which became Marie's upon his death and her immediate appointment as his successor, would not seem out of place in the White House.

Will Bankhead, father of the girls, won a Phi Beta Kappa key at the University of Alabama, where he was on the football team, the baseball team, and the debating team. Upon graduating from the Law School of Georgetown University, he set himself up in the practice of law in Huntsville, Alabama. He spoke and wrote with a Victorian orotundity, well suited to what he would no doubt have called the hustings, and it is sometimes difficult to catch sight of the real man behind the fancy-Dan verbiage. He had once hoped to be an actor and was not above striking poses, privately as well as publicly. Tallulah quotes at length from his diary in her so-called autobiography, compiled by her friend and press agent Dick Maney from recollections she dictated at random into a device she never wholly mastered; the autobiography was published in 1952 and was one of the best-selling nonfiction works of the year. In an entry in his diary for January 31, 1904, the twenty-nine-year-old Will is full of maudlin eloquence and self-pity:

> Six years have flown, and have flown almost with fury since last I wrote herein. The scene then was New York City, the writer a young struggler in the malls of a stupendous city, and his years were far fewer then than now. Today, I write again in Huntsville, placid, tender old town in the shadow of the hills, and I am older far than they, and sadder.
>
> This is my wedding anniversary. Four years ago I took to my heart and to my name,

the tenderest and the most beautiful girl the golden sunlight of Heaven ever curtsied to in caressing. Today out at Maple Hill cemetery, sleeping beneath a white shaft of marble, not as purely white as her soul but meant to typify it, sleeps that blessed dust "dearer to me than the ruddy drops that visit this sad heart," my blessed Gene.

I have often since that greatest tragedy of my life had a purpose to write of her, of our courtship, our joyful married life, of my struggles and her sacrifices, of the coming of the babies, and of the coming of the gray angel to my home, my grief, and all the bittersweet days that came and went; but I have not been able to find the spirit, or the vein in which to set it down.

I am aware that my children will soon begin to make inquiries about their mother, of how she lived and loved and died, as they should and as I want them to. But I know how my heart and my speech shall fail me when the time comes, how my eyes will brine with ever-too-ready tears and my throat throb with a choking pain that ever is attendant upon that cruel retrospection. They will be able to know how beautiful she was by the pictures I have of her, and yet which are so impotent to give an idea of her glorious coloring, the tenderness and yet the spirit of her brown eyes, the beauty of her curls, the fair and rosy skin, her expression when animated or in conversation.

I met her very casually one night at the McGee Hotel in Huntsville, while she was here on a shopping expedition from Courtland. She afterwards told me she had come to buy her apparel in which to marry another man. . . . It was truly a case of love at first sight. I continued my attentions after she went back to Aunt Alice's at Courtland, and often went down there on Sundays to see her—in fact, on the old front porch at "Summerwood" I made my first declaration of love—of a true love that still lives beyond the tomb and beyond the stars.

I have preserved for our babies our love letters—mine to her, and hers to me. If they should ever read them I hope and believe that they will feel and believe ours was a love of tenderest trust and consuming affection. Those letters tell the story of our courtship with a tenderer diction than I now can write—for then joy and beautiful anticipation ran with my pen, while now I write in the shadow of the loss while choked with the anguish of absence.

The wedding took place in Memphis, on Jefferson Street. It was beautiful, the flowers, the dazzling lights, the joyous guests, the dreamful and soulful music, and far and above the beauty of the environment was the matchless beauty of my bride. I have her wedding gown. She wore it only once. I have never had the courage to look upon its silken folds since she went away to God.

Will Bankhead was indeed a sad young man when he wrote those lines, and he was perhaps also a tipsy one. With reason, he had taken to the bottle. He was genuinely bereaved—he didn't remarry until many years later—and his babies had been wisely enough bundled off to the swarming big house in Jasper, to be brought up by his mother, sisters, and assorted hangers-on. The cases that came the way of a beginning lawyer in Huntsville were as meager in substance as they were in payment: slim pickings for the handsome young spellbinder who had once been invited to join a theater company in Boston and who had tasted briefly the exhilaration of a sketchy financial career in Wall Street. Few amusements are available to the chaste and inconsolable save drink and brawling, and Will Bankhead's pursuit of them was such that, by Captain John's standards, he amounted to a family disgrace as well as a public nuisance; he was ordered to join his parents and babies in Jasper, where a strict eye could be kept on him. Even there for a time he was drunken, combative, and suicidal. In one of Tallulah's unpublished and not always reliable tapings, she asserts that he twice took the Keeley Cure, a popular means of arresting alcoholism. Be that as it may, Will Bankhead pulled himself together and by 1916, when, thanks to an ingenious stroke of gerrymandering devised by his father and brother, he was elected to Congress, he had learned how to drink in moderation. Congress then as now contained a notably high proportion of heavy drinkers, but Will Bankhead kept a stern hold on himself; he was mild, charming, dutiful, and accommodating. Far more liberal in his politics than the constituents he represented, he became a loyal servant of the New Deal and saw to it that ample Federal funds were continuously funneled into the impoverished countryside of northern Alabama. Though already in ill health, he was elected Speaker of the House in 1936 and in the Democratic Convention of 1940 he was a candidate for the Vice-Presidential nomination—a position that, despite Roosevelt's having earlier assured Bankhead that the race was open to all comers, by Roosevelt's command went after a single ballot to Henry Wallace. It was just as well for the party that Bankhead lost. On September 10, 1940, while getting ready to address a political rally in Baltimore, he suffered a ruptured artery and was carried to a hospital. Tallulah and her sister flew down from New York to be with him. Tallulah was in rehearsal before resuming a long national tour in *The Little Foxes;* the first performance of the tour was to be at Princeton on the 14th. Tallulah and her father had met at rare intervals in the previous twenty years, but he had remained—and would always remain—the most important figure in her life. Speaker Will in his last days said two remarkable things; they serve to make him a much more vivid presence to us than anything else we learn about him in the rest of his sixty-six years. At the hospital in Baltimore, a doctor examining him inquired, "Where is the pain?" Speaker Will replied, "I don't play favorites; I scatter my pain." Many years after the event, Tallulah confided to her friend Eugenia Rawls, who was acting with her in *The Little Foxes* at the time of Will Bankhead's death, some of the details of her final meeting with her father. "He looked about thirty," Tallulah said. "The doctor came in and he said Daddy had been unconscious. When he regained consciousness, he felt he had to go back to Washington, insisted on being moved. The last thing I did, it was September and hot, his feet were sticking out, and just before I left, I stooped down and kissed his feet, and said, 'Do you love me, Daddy?' and he said, 'Why talk about circumferences?' "

Circumferences—what can that mean? What can it not mean? Tallulah, who had a strong feeling for words, was haunted by "circumferences." Her father had a wry sense of humor (once, during the Russian–Finnish War, when Tallulah was vehemently urging him by long-distance telephone to do something in Congress on behalf of the Finns, he said, "Baby, I can't do anything about Finland, I have the flu"), but surely he was not being flippant on the edge of the grave. Whatever the word meant to him, Tallulah would have liked it to mean that his love for her was so great as to be without bounds. When she and Eugenia were little, it was the accepted fact that Eugenia was their father's favorite; Tallulah spent a lifetime seeking to redress that imbalance, of course in vain—the wounds of childhood are never to be healed. The rivalry between the sisters was intolerable; so was the bond that held them together. It was a favorite family story, told by both of them, that when Tallulah got the croup at four and had a hot mustard plaster applied to her

Eugenia and Tallulah dressed in their Sunday finery and awaiting a treat.

chest, she cried out, "Burn Sister, too! Burn Sister!" Nevertheless, in her will she established a sizable trust fund in Eugenia's behalf; she had helped her out often in life and she would go on helping her out after death. She did her best to forgive Eugenia for being their father's favorite and she did her best to forgive her father for having made Eugenia his favorite. Some day, somehow, he would come to see how precious Tallulah was to him. It was only to be expected that her autobiography, published twelve years after Speaker Will's death, would bear the dedication, "For Daddy." Who else ever offered him a whole book?

It was Will Bankhead who first encouraged Tallulah's interest in the stage. He had a voice, she was to say long afterwards, like Lionel Barrymore's, and his amateur play-acting was in the robust Barrymore tradition. Once in Washington, a few years before his death, he drove Tallulah from the railroad station to the theater where she was starring in *Reflected Glory*. As they reached the stage door, he

glanced about and said, "Oh, Tallulah, if I had only just had one whack at it!" He had had many a whack at it in private, for in the early days in Jasper, instead of reading bedtime stories to the girls, he would entertain them with long passages out of Shakespeare, the Bible, Dickens, Mark Twain, Robert W. Service, and James Whitcomb Riley. He recited the poem "Little Breeches" so often that Tallulah was under the impression that he had written it himself. She boasted of this achievement many years later to her friend John Hay Whitney, and was disappointed to learn from him that the true author of the poem was the grandfather for whom he had been named, John Hay.

When she was four or five, Tallulah's father took her to vaudeville shows in Birmingham, where—a quick study from birth—she readily memorized stanzas of songs that, by her father's standards, were far too racy to be sung by little girls. In the recordings that Tallulah let Maney render into the peculiar English of the autobiography, she remarks: "The first play I ever saw was when I was at the Sacred Heart [a convent in New York], and Daddy came to stay with us for Christmas, and he brought us two little gold watches on a little elastic and he broke them before we got them." (The published autobiography suppresses the mysterious episode of the breaking of the watches. Had Will, a widower, packed his own bags and packed them clumsily? Or had he been drinking again? In a passage already quoted from the tapes, Tallulah speaks of kissing the bare feet of her dying father; in the autobiography, this becomes a kiss on the cheek. Evidently, there were things that the Puritan Irish Catholic Maney could not bear to recount.) During that Christmas holiday in New York, Will Bankhead took the children to see *The Whip,* playing at the Manhattan Opera House. Here is the official Maney-autobiographical version of that adventure:

> *The Whip* was a blood-and-thunder melodrama in four acts and fourteen scenes imported from London's Drury Lane Theatre. It boiled with villainy and violence. Its plot embraced a twelve-horse race on a treadmill (for the Gold Cup at Newmarket), a Hunt Breakfast embellished by fifteen dogs, an auto smash-up, the Chamber of Horrors at Madame Tussaud's Waxworks, and a train wreck with a locomotive hissing real steam. It boasted a dissolute earl and a wicked marquis, and a heroine whose hand was sought by both knave and hero. . . . The curtain hadn't been up five minutes before Sister and I were on the verge of hysterics. . . . When the careening car smashed into the bridge at the start of the second act, we became so overwrought Daddy had to hang onto our collars to keep us from tumbling out of the box. . . . At the final curtain I was a wreck, frantic, red-eyed, and disheveled. I didn't sleep for two nights running. When I did nod, the treacherous marquis intruded on my dreams. Nothing I had ever seen or heard or read had made such an impression on me.

With perhaps one exception. According to a story that Tallulah relished telling, she and Eugenia and some other children were on a picnic one fine spring day in the woods outside Jasper. She heard a whirring in the grass, glanced down to find out what was causing it, and was bitten by a rattlesnake. Daddy rushed to her side: "Quick as a flash Daddy snatched off my panties, and sucked the blood from the wound. Subsequently he was quite ill. He had an abrasion in his gums and the poison infected them." This is a very strange story indeed, on several counts. The rattlesnake was unlikely to be in the grass where Tallulah says it was, it was unlikely to strike so high up on her leg as to require the removal of her panties, and there would have been no blood for Daddy to suck unless he first took care to cut open her skin. Eugenia has told one of Tallulah's biographers that the episode never took place—that their Uncle John had been bitten by a snake at about that time and that the source of Tallulah's suffering was a large carbuncle on her upper thigh, which had to be lanced. In her autobiography, Tallulah seeks to give credence to the story by mentioning that when she sailed for England, in 1923, on her passport under the heading "Distinguishing Marks," she wrote the word "Snakebite." But this, too, is strange. If she did such a thing, why did she do it?

Surely the passport office had no interest in distinguishing marks that, on the persons of most travelers, would have remained altogether invisible.

Will Bankhead's nicknames for Tallulah when she was little were "Sugar" and "Dutch," the latter being at the time a common term for anyone who was fat. His nicknames for Sister were "Nothin' Much" and "Kildee," because she was so tiny. (The kildee, or killdeer, is a small plover, noted for its plaintive cry.) Will Bankhead called Tallulah by her baptismal name only when he was displeased with her, and then only very gently—"Just 'Tallulah' was enough to make me shake." Many years later, when his daughters were among the most notorious international show-offs of the nineteen-twenties, Will Bankhead refused to find any public fault with them. He was a conventional man of his time and place, who knelt beside his bed every night to say his prayers and who never swore or took the name of the Lord in vain, but no matter what scandalous activities Tallulah might be making headlines with, he would say, "Don't criticize my daughter—whatever faults she has are from me."

3 No faults from the mother she never had, beside whose open coffin Tallulah was christened? The mother's contribution to Tallulah's character is worth speculating on, and perhaps all the more so because it came from the far side of the grave. At this distance in time, it is hard for us not to judge harshly the economy of family emotion that led the Bankheads to link a funeral with a christening; a pious Episcopal man of God turned from ushering Adelaide Eugenia Sledge Bankhead out of this

Tallulah's mother on her flirtatious and speedy way from school to marriage.

world to ushering her baby into it. What a bleak welcome it must have been, even if one were unable to take the measure of the bleakness until years later! "I never knew my mother," Tallulah said. "She survived my birth by but three weeks. Her death was brought about by complications arising from my birth, but I never had any feelings of guilt. . . ." Under the circumstances—for who would think of blaming a newborn infant for anything?—to protest that one feels no guilt is to imply that feelings of guilt are reasonable, do indeed exist, and are being purposely ignored. In Tallulah's case, we know that she grew up believing that her father blamed her for the loss of his matchless bride. Hard enough not to be his favorite; harder still to be thought the occasion of what he called the greatest tragedy of his life; hardest of all to feel, like any motherless child, that she had been betrayed, and for this feeling to be a forbidden one. It was Tallulah who had been wronged by Ada, not Ada by Tallulah, but who among the family would dare to accept this version of the events that had overtaken poor Will? *De mortuis nil nisi bonum;* of Ada, the nonpareil ("the tenderest and most beautiful girl the golden sunlight of

Heaven ever curtsied to in caressing"), nothing but rhapsodies. Thus, to the guilt of having as an infant "murdered" her mother was added the guilt of blaming her for a betrayal that only Tallulah seemed to have any awareness of. Ada had abandoned Tallulah—in childhood there can be no graver injury than that. For the mother to have gone off to wherever it was she had to go and not come back: for the mother to have forgotten the child! All the rest of her life, Tallulah was to suffer from the fear of being deserted, of being left alone by day or night, unguarded, unnursed, unloved. She wanted parties never to end and bridge games never to end and conversations never to end. She would turn friends into prisoners, locking their hats and coats in closets to keep them from saying good-bye. Like most of us, she feared the night more than the day, and her fear increased with age; predictably, her means of dealing with it grew more and more unbecoming as they grew more unsuccessful. Drink, drugs, sex: they were for her the means by which to outwit an intolerable prospect, and they did not suffice.

Ada had done Tallulah another and more indirect injustice by dying; she had become at once a figure unchallengeably superior to any living person. It was true that Ada had been a celebrated beauty—Tallulah would quote with pride the opinion of the drama critic Stark Young that her mother had set a standard for beauty throughout the entire South in his time—and she had died at twenty-one. The delicacy of her features, the exquisiteness of her coloring, the flirtatious piquancy of her manner were fixed forever; what would anyone wish to remember about her save that she was perfect? This was the burden Tallulah grew up under and would have been ashamed not to consent to bear. Still, there is evidence that Ada had a number of attractive faults. For one thing, she was, as they say in the South, "spoiled rotten." Her father, who was a speculator and very rich when he was not poor, gave her whatever she asked for; as a small-town girl in her teens, she had traveled abroad and returned to wear on the dusty roads of Como, Mississippi, gowns by Worth of Paris (as her daughter, at a slightly later age and in a more appropriate setting, was to wear gowns by Worth of London). A friend of Ada's assured Tallulah once that her mother had been as mad as a hatter—"at least as mad as you!"—which Tallulah took for a great compliment. A classmate of Ada's at school in North Carolina, visiting Tallulah backstage after a performance of *The Skin of Our Teeth*, said, "Your mother was the most beautiful thing that ever lived. Many people have claimed you get your acting talent from your father, but I disagree. You inherited your talent from your mother. Did you know she could faint on cue? Once she had a crush on a young doctor. Whenever she saw him approaching she would feign a swoon, which would bring him galloping across the campus. When somebody told her that she looked wonderful in black, she appeared in chapel on the following Sunday dressed in widow's weeds, with a prayer book under her arm."

As Will Bankhead noted in his diary, at the time that Ada and he fell in love she was engaged to another man (not the suggestive equestrian doctor but, according to Tallulah, a wealthy Virginia planter). Indeed, she was shopping for her trousseau when Will began to court her. The identity of the bridegroom at the wedding in Memphis changed but the honeymoon dresses remained the same. Having married him, Ada made Will her slave, and how gratefully he accepted his subjection!

Nothing about his mother and sisters—stocky, ambitious, armored like dreadnaughts—had prepared his imagination for such a prize. Her coquetry and extravagances alarmed and enchanted him. She awakened in him sexual feelings that he scarcely knew how to deal with, and perhaps he did as much for her; nevertheless, one wonders whether he would have been able to hold her devotion for long as he slogged away at the law in the languid backwater of Huntsville. Would she have found it amusing to remain faithful to this virtuous, weak young man? (It had taken but a single letter to summon him home from the promise of a theatrical career in Boston.) Delightful to marry at nineteen and have one's pretty babies; less delightful to feel the years rushing past without ranks of new worshipers pressing round. For Ada was a belle, and belles require the refreshment of conquests. Her daughters were to seek that refreshment with an avidity shocking to their contemporaries, and it may be that in this regard, as in so many others, they were unwittingly the rivals of a dead girl as passionate as they but far more innocent than they.

Just as well, then, that Tallulah saw little of her father as she was growing up. She was shuffled at irregular intervals from her grandmother and Aunt Louise in Jasper to her Aunt Marie in Mont-

"Grandmamma" in her role as a Senator's wife. The tiara was not for Jasper.

gomery and back and forth among half a dozen startled schools, and Will in mourning, his mind full of a sainted lost Ada, was rarely before her eyes, silently reproaching her. Tallulah in Jasper claimed to be her grandparents' favorite, though the grandparents themselves maintained that they loved all of their grandchildren equally well. Tallulah Brockman Bankhead—she always signed her initials T.B.B. and not T.B.—had been named for her grandmother and had at least that claim to extra attention. The mother of the first Tallulah Brockman Bankhead, Mary Elizabeth Brockman McAuley, lived with the family in "Sunset" up to her death in 1915, at the age of ninety-three. Mrs. McAuley and her first husband, James Henry Brockman, making their way into Alabama from the Carolinas long before the Civil War, had spent a night at Tallulah Falls, Georgia, already a well-known scenic attraction, and the family story was that they had conceived a baby there, to whom they gave the name of the falls in homage. The baby grew up to become a fitting consort for Captain John, matching him in energy and determination and providing him with five able and aggressive children. (Except for Will, it was a generation of Bankheads notably fat, round-headed, and full of confidence.) Grandmother Tallulah was "Mamma" to her namesake, and she did her best to play a mother's role at a difficult age—she was in her sixties by then—and with a most difficult child. She was a busy woman and not a subtle one and she preferred quick results to lasting ones. Her method of attempting to control Tallulah's continual tantrums was to spill a bucket of water over her; the problem was to have a bucket of water in the right place at the right time, for "Sunset" was a big house and there were barns and chicken coops and grape arbors and three acres of grounds, and Tallulah was apt to throw a tantrum anywhere, which is to say wherever she thought it would cause the most trouble.

4 Perhaps in despair of keeping his girls in school, Will took to telling them that if they knew Shakespeare and the Bible and could shoot craps, that was all the education they would ever need. Still, he had sought more formal knowledge for himself than that, and his poor jest may have concealed a profound unease about the failure of his fatherhood. In his early days as a widower, when he had drunk and sung and brawled and grieved, it must have consoled him to think that however much he disgraced the family name, his daughters were growing up under the strict tutelage of his mother and sisters and would therefore be sure to reach their high level of decorum and respectability. Life turned out to be less manageable than he had hoped. For one thing, his mother was often in Washington, taking care of old Captain John and enjoying the social perquisites of his increasingly important position in the capital. (Captain John was the last Confederate veteran to serve in the Senate. He took full advantage of the fruits of his seniority there. On one occasion, the intractable, dog-faced old man put on his Army uniform—or, rather, a much-expanded replica of the original uniform—and sat silently at his desk in the Senate chamber until his colleagues gave him the toy he wanted: an appropriation for a bust of Robert E. Lee.) For another thing, Tallulah fiercely disliked her Aunt Louise, who ran the household at "Sunset." It became a question between them which would be the first to reduce the other to tears. If Tallulah nearly always had a good time during her visits with Aunt Marie in Montgomery, it was thanks in part to the fact that Aunt Marie was far too busy with her own family and career—she was constantly dashing off unpublishable novels and unproduceable plays, and she later compiled an eight-volume history of Alabama, in which the Bankheads were not neglected—to keep a close watch on Tallulah, and thanks in part to the fact that she believed in Tallulah. She was proud of her from the beginning and she never stopped being proud. On a visit to New York, in 1939, when she was seventy, she said, "I've seen Tallulah in *The Little Foxes*, I've seen the World's Fair, and I've seen a fight at the Stork Club. Now I can go home and tell them I've seen everything."

Montgomery proved a good place in which to practice showing off. If one's family was important enough to have earned certain privileges, then one certainly ought to profit from them. Tallulah, fat and pimpled and far from beautiful, took care to make herself conspicuous. An adolescent dreamer of girls' dreams by night, by day she was an athletic tomboy. Her boisterous physicality caused a stir in Montgomery. No less a person than the Governor of Alabama once tried to prevent her from cartwheeling the length of a street adjacent to the capitol. Perhaps he had caught a shocking glimpse of white panties, or, if Tallulah had already adopted the practice of her adult years, a more shocking glimpse of no panties at all. Tallulah sassily informed the Governor that she had disregarded his admonition because her grandfather had taught her that she was always to finish anything she had started. And who might her grandfather be? Senator John Hollis Bankhead, of

Washington, D.C. Her answer flummoxed the Governor, as Tallulah intended it to. Over the years, she developed an acute sense of pecking orders in and out of politics. She learned how little it takes to make people bleed, and sometimes she could not resist demonstrating her skill at this unpleasing game.

By a coincidence that must have been striking even then, in Montgomery, while Tallulah was growing up, a girl two years her senior was making local history with her beauty and grace and reckless ways. Her name was Zelda Sayre. What was there in the air of the little Montgomery of those days to foster such a trio of idol-breakers as Zelda Sayre and Eugenia and Tallulah Bankhead? A few years later, they would be among those whom Fitzgerald was celebrating when, in *The Great Gatsby,* he wrote, "In his blue gardens, men and girls came and went like moths among the whisperings and the champagne and the stars." How far they had come, those three, and how quickly! They were clever and lovely and racy, and they would do anything on a dare. Men and women fell in love with them almost without regard to their sex. They charged the air around them with expectation: in their presence it seemed always that something wonderful was just about to happen. They were like superb animals, raging to perform. Whatever they did, it would be as if for the first time and as if without effort, a lightly thrown-away success. Effort and failure were for their imitators.

The hoydenish cartwheels and back-somersaults and handstands that Tallulah perfected in the long summer afternoons of Montgomery were later to astonish New York and London, onstage and off. So were the words she learned in youth—the harsh, violent, incantatory slang that, like so much of the language in which we express emotion, has been slowly leaching up out of underground sources throughout the whole of this century. It is a slang that gained general acceptance among whites only during and after the Second World War and was to become a commonplace of American speech by the nineteen-sixties. In the years when, as a well-born Southern girl, Tallulah ought to have been learning French and field hockey and penmanship at some proper finishing school, she was acquiring a mastery of vulgar English that afterwards earned her a fame distinct from the fame earned by her beauty and talent or from that earned by her sexual and alcoholic misadventures. She was, one may say, incomparably foul-mouthed. In the permissive seventies, when children in prams prattle billingsgate, it is hard to convey the effect Tallulah's language had upon most conventionally brought-up Americans of her time. It was an effect heightened by who one saw she was: so evidently a lady, dressed with care in her neat, short white gloves and pearls, standing when older women entered the room, addressing them as "Ma'am," and risking in their presence nothing stronger than an occasional muffled expletive. The real riches of her obscene tongue were enough to turn top sergeants into Trappists out of envy. From the big, lipstick-smeared mouth, especially if she had been drinking, would flow a sewer of explicit invitation, instruction, dismissal. For some, her vile language was disgusting and exciting, for many it was only disgusting, and for close friends it scarcely existed; through long practice, their ears had learned to screen out the tiresome lubricious débris.

Having an excellent if ill-trained mind, what she said was often memorable, and so was the length at which she said it. A witticism that has been attributed to her friend Fred Keating—"I've just spent an hour talking to Tallulah for a few minutes"—gives a sufficient hint of the torrent of words that the simplest inquiry was apt to release. She practiced free association on a titanic scale. The point at which one was invited to enter the maze of her mind bore little relation to the point at which one eventually emerged; the journey was exhilarating and unretraceable and could prove tiring. A newspaper reporter might begin an interview with her backstage after a performance, hoping with luck to be granted twenty minutes of her time, and end the interview many hours later in her hotel bedroom, numb with information about politics, baseball, sexual intercourse, acting, the British Royal Family, mineral deposits in northern Alabama, gambling odds, gardening, breeds of dogs, brands of bourbon, and ballroom dancing. The reporter might also find himself in her bed, sharing a notable dishevelment of sheets and blankets with a dog or two, a cat, a bottle, and one or more lighted and temporarily mislaid cigarettes. Pencil and paper would long since have dropped from his exhausted fingers, and Tallulah would be just hitting her stride.

From childhood, she displayed a knack for malapropisms and nonsequiturs. Having so much to say and being eager that every word of it be rushed into the world as quickly as possible, she would brook no interference—least of all by her own critical faculties—with a free outpouring of ideas. Besides, she enjoyed making howlers. On hearing some novel blunder fall from her lips, she would salute it with a shout of admiring laughter. She retained all her life the literal-mindedness of the very young. At the end of a story, she always wanted to know what happened next. Once, she was told about an actress who got caught in a curtain as it was being hauled up into the flies. Tallulah asked, "How far up did she go?" On another occasion, she was visiting Donald and Eugenia Seawell at their farm on the Eastern Shore. (Donald Seawell was her attorney for nearly thirty years. Eugenia Seawell—Eugenia Rawls onstage—played with her in *The Little Foxes* and *The Second Mrs. Tanqueray*. The Seawells' daughter and son, Brook and Brockman, were her god-children.) Tallulah was taking a nap on a couch in the living room of the Seawell farmhouse when Eugenia Seawell caught sight of Brockman and a friend approaching the house by sailboat. Knowing that Tallulah disliked being surprised by unexpected visitors, Eugenia gently roused her and warned her of the imminent arrival of the two small boys. Silently, Tallulah reached for her handbag beside the couch, took out a comb, ran it through her hair, put on some lipstick, and lay back to continue her nap. Just before closing her eyes, she spoke for the first time. "Why are they coming by sailboat?" she asked.

A friend who once tested with a stopwatch Tallulah's average rate of flow of words per minute estimated that the daily total came to just under seventy thousand, which is the equivalent of a short novel; on a long weekend, she could match without strain the wordage of *War and Peace*. If the quantity of words that Tallulah spoke was astonishing, still more astonishing was the voice she spoke them in. Over a period of twenty or thirty years, it became perhaps the most readily identifiable voice in the world. Thanks to her movie, radio, and TV appearances, its curious sound, at first hearing not positively that of a woman, was familiar to tens of millions of people, and it was a sorry comic who, in the shabbiest small-town nightclub, could not provide an imitation of it capable of being instantly recognized and applauded. The voice was extraordinarily low, sweet, and husky, and the columnist John Crosby wrote of it that it had more timbre than Yellowstone National Park. It seemed to possess its own humid subtropical climate; one felt drawn to it and warmed by it, and birds and animals found it every bit as irresistible as human beings did. Ever an ardent amateur pathologist, Tallulah attributed its low register to the variety of diseases she suffered during the first six years of her life; by her reckoning, these included tonsillitis, whooping cough, croup, measles, mumps, pneumonia, and smallpox. Whatever the cause of the voice, its effects were immediate and uncanny. Audiences sat smiling at it and basking in it, and the lines it spoke, though they might be in the best drawing-room English of Pinero, Maugham, Barry, or Coward, would have proved equally satisfactory if they had been in Choctaw.

Surprisingly, in the light of her reputation as an amorist, Tallulah's voice, unlike Garbo's, Dietrich's, or Marilyn Monroe's, was not erotic. Sensual without being strongly sexual, it stopped short of promising everything for love. Instead, it remained ribald and uncommitted, as if, provoked by some suddenly observed incongruity of mind and body, it might dissolve at any moment into mocking laughter. Humor is the enemy of the erotic and Tallulah was invincibly humorous and even clownlike; she made love for many reasons, but love itself was rarely the chief one and almost as rarely was lust. The voice hinted that when it was at its sexiest it was performing, like Mae West's voice, a parody of the real thing. Tallulah had given her voice little formal training, and although its range was great she often ran out of breath along the way to the first convenient resting place, and a roaring fortissimo might end in an uncalculated hoarse whisper. The mighty Elizabethan line was not for her, as she let the world observe on one unfortunate occasion. The critic John Mason Brown began his review of Tallulah's production of *Antony and Cleopatra* with devastating directness: "Tallulah Bankhead barged down the Nile last night as Cleopatra—and sank."

Tallulah could not sing, but she liked to try, and the sound that emerged was, in the opinion of many critics, more attractive than singing. There are a number of recordings of Tallulah's non-singing, and one senses in them both her pleasure in the music and her nervous scrambling to get on key and stay there. An unexpected note of sadness revealed itself when she non-sang; she was threatened, her wavering voice said, with some unnameable, unbearable loss: Help me, help me. She made a recording of "Bye, Bye, Blackbird" so charged with emotion that it came close to proving a truer autobiography than the one she published. "Make my bed, light the light, I'll be home late tonight"—the words, warbled in a passionate and absurd baritone, were heartbreaking. "No one here that knows or understands me, only hard luck stories they all hand me." She could utter such words in song, not otherwise; they were outside her code of the permissible. Never look back, never apologize, never explain.

To begin with, Tallulah's accent had been unmistakably Alabaman and she could always restore it to its full moonlight-and-magnolia strength. During her long stay in London, she overlaid her Southern accent with hints of the fashionable Mayfair accent that she was herself engaged in helping to invent. A word that was continuously on her lips—"darling"—contrived to display both accents at once. The "r" that had never been sounded in Jasper was not sounded in London; the "a," sufficiently broad at home, in England grew broader still. Having made her first name famous, soon Tallulah was making "darling" famous as well. In newspaper and magazine interviews, it amounted to a trademark and was always spelled as she pronounced it—"dahling," or even "d-a-a-h-ling." The favored word crept up out of the story into the subhead and then into the headline; sometimes it would take the place of "Tallulah" and render it unnecessary. If it was remarkable for a young woman to have made her first name celebrated enough to provide an immediate identification of her in most cities of both hemispheres, it was even more remarkable that she could make a common appellation of affection—one used by millions—so much her own that it could not possibly be mistaken for anyone else's. The world came to know that when it saw the word "darling" in a headline, it meant that Tallulah was in town and in spate, unstoppably showing off.

Tallulah claimed that she called everyone "dahling" because she couldn't remember personal names, or, for that matter, telephone numbers, street addresses, and road directions. Once, in London, she purchased a car and found it so hard to make her way accurately from one point in the city to another that she had to hire a taxi to drive ahead of her and lead to her destination. (It occurred to her eventually—when it came to money matters, she put off taking thought as long as possible—that it would be more economical to ride in the taxi as a passenger and dispose of the car.) There is something mysterious about Tallulah's failing to remember names and numbers, because she had an exceedingly good memory. She could be line-perfect in a play after two or three readings and would remember whole passages of plays many years after her last performance in them. She appeared to forget nothing she read, and she read continuously and omnivorously— books, magazines, newspapers, and, failing them, labels on bottles and cans, messages on matchbook covers. Nor would she forget people, though she forgot their names. Once, she met a man who happened to mention to her that he was color-blind. Many years later, she arrived at a party where the man was among the guests; Tallulah had been drinking, but she immediately singled him out in the crowd and, spreading her bright skirt wide, called to him, "Dahling! I'll bet even *you* can tell that this is red!"

5 For Tallulah, 1917 was the year after which nothing would ever be the same. A year or so earlier, her father had married a good-looking Jasper girl, and in 1916, with the creation of a new congressional district in Alabama, he had been elected to the House of Representatives. He and his bride and his mother and father occupied adjacent quarters in a big apartment house in Washington, D.C.

Tallulah moved in with her grandparents and Eugenia lived with the newlyweds. Eugenia herself was a newlywed for a time; at sixteen, she fell in love with and married a boy named Morton Hoyt. (One of his sisters would become the poet Elinor Wylie and another, Nancy Hoyt, wrote several novels, of which at least one had as its central figure an actress drawn from Tallulah.) Eugenia's marriage to Hoyt was quickly annulled; she was to marry him on a couple of other occasions, but never for long. Will Bankhead had a bride to preoccupy him, and therefore it may have mattered less to him than formerly that his girls refused to acquire a conventional education and follow conventional ways. Eugenia had been able to win "A's" in every subject, including deportment, and surely Tallulah could have done the same, but there was something in her nature that rebelled against any formal organization and prompted her to do her worst inside its walls instead of her best. The girls had ricocheted from school to school and at every turn Tallulah—envious of Eugenia's slender good looks, of her skill in games, of her high grades and the admiration that accompanied them—would lash out in misery, a fat girl among enemies, and force a crisis that could be resolved only by her removal; again and again, she left behind a faculty trembling with relief at their last sight of her.

She was fifteen in 1917 and had reached her full height of five feet, three inches. People seeing her for the first time offstage were invariably astonished to discover how small she was. "I play tall parts," she used to say, but the truth was that her authority onstage made the characters she played seem bigger than they were and bigger, on some occasions, than the author intended. It was hard for Tallulah to play convincingly a slouching lower-middle-class housewife down on her luck. In Washington that year she was still overweight, but she was coming—was rushing pell-mell—into her beauty. It was all the more an occasion for rejoicing because it had been so long waited for and was nevertheless so unexpected. The pudgy girl in Jasper, who crammed herself with Cokes and candy and dreamed of becoming a famous movie star, was at the point of transformation. True, her nose was a trifle blunt, but the big, dark-blue eyes shone out of now unblemished milky skin and her hair hung down her back in a shower of gold. After her hair, her perfect, very white teeth were her greatest pride. She acquired the habit of washing her hair with a dry-cleaning fluid, Energine, in order to insure its brilliance, and the wonder was that she didn't brush her teeth with gunpowder for the same reason. Teeth were so important to her that she was eventually to use them as a means of judging character; on being introduced to someone, she would briskly force open the stranger's mouth and give it a thorough looking-over.

She had—and would always have—the loud laugh of her childhood. At fifteen, it was deep like her voice and sexy beyond her years. Nobody encountering her then would have credited her age, and when she was chosen as one of the twelve winners of a talent contest by mail sponsored by *Picture-Play* magazine, it was on the strength of a photograph of her in hat and furs that made her look twenty. The promised prize was a movie contract with a company in New York, at a salary of fifty dollars a week for nobody was sure how many weeks. The contest was a come-on, intended to build circulation for the magazine, but Tallulah desperately wanted the distinction of winning

"Who Is She?" a movie magazine asked. Tallulah knew and was quick to say.

something, as well as a chance to visit New York, and to its dismay the magazine found itself obliged to live up to the terms of the contract or face the public wrath of two members of Congress, both Bankheads. The magazine having promised to secure a contract for Tallulah, the next problem to be solved was how to pay for a chaperone for Tallulah; she could not be allowed to go to New York without one, and Will complained that the expense would be too great for him. According to Tallulah's autobiography it was at this point that her stern old grandfather intervened. "Stand back, Will," she reports him as saying. (The phrase may be Maney's. In Maney English, which bears a notable resemblance to W. C. Fields English, people are always standing back or being suspended, unhorsed, keel-hauled, or dirked. Maney's rule is vivid writing or none.) "Stand back, Will," said Captain John. "I'm underwriting this child. Let her go on the stage. She's not worth a damn for anything but acting."

Tallulah arrived in New York with her despised Aunt Louise as a chaperone. For a time, they rented a small apartment on West Forty-fifth Street and then moved to the Algonquin Hotel, on Forty-fourth Street. Presided over by an agreeable, easygoing man named Frank Case, the Algonquin was already celebrated as a gathering place for actors and writers, but it appears that Aunt Louise chose it as a suitable hotel for innocent Alabamans upon hearing that it was the favorite local residence of Commander Evangeline Booth of the Salvation Army. The Algonquin lobby, with its oak-paneled walls and scatteration of odds and ends of overstuffed couches and chairs, has always resembled the living room of some big, cozy, and not in the least stylish country house, and one sits drinking and chatting there in intimate proximity to one's neighbors—a couple happening to discuss San Francisco isn't unduly surprised when, a few minutes later, they overhear someone at the next table begin, "Speaking of San Francisco. . . ." Tallulah was enchanted to find herself in such a living room and among such godlike people. In the lobby or in one or another of the two dining rooms, to say nothing of the tiny hotel elevator, she could squeeze her way to within inches of Douglas Fairbanks, Laurette Taylor, the three Barrymores, and the two Talmadges. In *The Vicious Circle*, a book about the people who made up the so-called Algonquin Round Table, Margaret Case Harriman has described Tallulah's advent in a prose scarcely less purple than Maney's: "Tallulah was crowding seventeen when she arrived from Alabama, stage-struck, sultry-voiced, and brimming with a roseleaf beauty which she determinedly hid under the then-fashionable mask of white powder, blue eye-shadow, and bee-colored lipstick." Tallulah was, in fact, not quite sixteen, and whatever bee-colored lipstick may be, she must have been thought, wearing it, to be almost as great a prodigy in the art of making up as in the art of getting ahead. She was an aggressive child, with overwhelming zest and curiosity, and the people she cultivated at the Algonquin forgave her her many gaucheries because her obsession with the theater was so obviously genuine; she must have renewed in them the feeling, dimmed by time and experience, that their profession was not, after all, mere marzipan. Years later, Zoë Akins was to write a play based on the Tallulah of that era; it was called *Morning Glory*, and Tallulah's friend Katharine Hepburn played it to great effect in the movies.

In the background, the Washington Bankheads were constantly pulling strings in behalf of their lovely misfit. Will Bankhead had a connection in the office of the powerful, infamous Shubert Brothers, and through this connection Tallulah was given a walk-on role in a play called *The Squab Farm*. The *Times* described the play as "a garish travesty on life in the movies, all in bad taste," and a reviewer on the *World* wrote, "There are three or four young girls in the company who might better be back in the care of their mothers"—a rebuke not without irony for the motherless Tallulah. To make matters worse, it turned out that Daddy had pulled one string too many in behalf of his beloved Sugar; at his urging, a lengthy story was planted in one of the papers, praising Tallulah as a girl who had spurned wealth and debutante idleness in order to make a name for herself in the theater. The headline on the story was "SOCIETY GIRL GOES ON STAGE," and the rest of the company of *The Squab Farm* did not respond kindly to it. Indeed, they took care to snub her from that moment on, and if the play had not died a natural death after a brief run, Tallulah would have felt obliged to quit the cast.

Program for *The Squab Farm*. The Bijou, now a movie theater, will soon be rubble.

Within a week of the closing of *The Squab Farm*, Tallulah was offered, again through family influence, a role in a movie called *When Men Betray.* The movie was shot early in the summer of 1918, in New York, which was then still the movie-making capital of the country. When it was released, Tallulah received a couple of favorable reviews, including one from the *Tribune*: "Miss Tallulah Bankhead is new to the screen and she proves the truth of the theory that brains are better than experience." In the fall of 1918, Samuel Goldwyn signed her to appear in a movie, *Thirty-a-Week,* opposite Tom Moore, and in 1919 she got her first chance at a speaking role on stage. It was with the second company of Rachel Crothers' play *39 East,* and in it she played opposite another young Southern neophyte, Sidney Blackmer. Captain John came to town to see her perform and claimed afterwards that he hadn't recognized her until the curtain had been up for half an hour. One wonders why on earth not. Granted that she was caked with makeup and was doing her best to imitate Constance Binney, the star of the original company; nevertheless, how many girls did Captain John suppose had a voice like Tallulah's? Curious to think of the old soldier, born in 1842 and now a year away from death, crouched in the darkness of a Broadway theater and asking himself with pride and alarm which of the saucy flappers onstage was his granddaughter.

Tallulah and Blackmer had given only a few performances when, with the calling of the Actors' Equity strike of 1919—a strike that achieved the first substantial victory of actors over the hitherto all-powerful theater owners and managers—the show was closed, and Tallulah turned to carrying placards on Broadway (NO MORE PAY. JUST FAIR PLAY) and selling programs at actors' benefits. And to rubbing elbows with her betters, for with characteristic boldness she took advantage of this opportunity to meet as many prominent members of the profession as possible. At one benefit, when

Katharine Cornell, in her young beauty, photographed by James Abbe.

Ethel and Lionel Barrymore pledged donations of a thousand dollars apiece, Tallulah rushed forward—an adorable rosy Kewpie doll, bent on catching all eyes and winning all hearts—and pledged a hundred dollars she didn't have. Captain John was appealed to, and he sent her not only the hundred dollars but an evening dress as well. Plainly, Tallulah was as "spoiled rotten" as her mother had been and as determined to make a noise in the world. The strike became for her a useful social occasion by day, as parties had become useful social occasions for her by night. Aunt Louise, goaded past endurance—for Tallulah's tantrums were still a major weapon in her arsenal—had returned to Jasper in tears.

Tallulah was living alone in a twenty-one-dollar-a-week room at the Algonquin, where Frank Case promised her father he would keep an eye on her. (Privately, he complained that one could try to run Tallulah or one could try to run a hotel, but one couldn't do both.) Two well-established actresses, Estelle Winwood and Jobyna Howland, took charge of Tallulah and saw to it that she met the Barrymores and other celebrities who either lived at the Algonquin or regularly dined there. Tallulah would sit at their feet, making eyes at them and occasionally scrounging food from their tables, for she was receiving an allowance from home of fifty dollars a week and was nearly always broke and hungry. Miss Winwood and Miss Howland also saw to it that Tallulah got invited to the proper parties, and not alone for the refreshments.

Partygoing turned out to be what Tallulah did best. People noticed at once what excellent value she gave. She was so warm and full of promise and when she cared to (and at parties she cared to) she had perfect manners; moreover, her chatter, being candid and acute, proved unexpectedly amusing. She danced and uttered the curious moaning sound that was better than singing and threw back her head with its mass of pale gold hair and laughed aloud, childlike. She hugged her elders and made each of them feel that he was opening up to her, for the very first time, a garden of wonders, and sometimes it was so. She was afterwards to experiment with cocaine and other drugs and, later still, to depend on alcohol to carry her up onto a desperately sought-for plateau of near-frenzy, but between eighteen and twenty-two her abandon was a function of rude health and energy. She met everyone and everyone was valuable to her, as well as kind. Even Alexander Woollcott, then the drama critic of the *Times* and notorious both for his venomous eunuchoid tongue and his soppy mock-Dickensian prose style, treated her kindly. He would take her to opening nights—like many men who are unable to make love to women, he liked being seen in public places with, as he would say, a pretty creature on his arm—and it was between the acts of a play by Maeterlinck that

NEYSA MORAN McMEIN
57 WEST 57TH STREET
PHONE PLAZA 7686

April 11, 1922

Miss Tallulah Bankhead,
Hotel Algonquin,
New York City.

Dear Miss Bankhead:

As you probably know,
the Brown-Connelly-F.P.A.-Woollcott gang
is going to hold exercises behind closed
doors at the 49th Street Theatre on the
night of Sunday, April 30th. This will
be the No-Sirree.

You have been chosen
by acclamation as one of the nine girls
in the Ingenuisance - a musical number
for which rehearsal will be held at
studio 18,   5u West 57th Street, at
11:30 next Tuesday night.

Do you accept the
nomination, and will you be present at
the rehearsal?

Sincerely yours,

Neysa McMein

Inviting Tallulah to participate in *No, Sirree!*, a parody of *Chauve-Souris.*

Tallulah made the remark upon which her reputation as a wit was founded. "There is less here than meets the eye," she said, going up the aisle with Woollcott. He published her opinion in his *Times* review next morning, attributing it to "the beautiful young woman who accompanied me." He then made sure that she was given credit by name at the Algonquin Round Table, which numbered among its members at that time such sedulous and often-quoted wisecrackers as Franklin P. Adams, Dorothy Parker, Deems Taylor, Marc Connelly, Robert Benchley, Peggy Wood, Neysa McMein, George S. Kaufman, and Harold Ross. Tallulah denied that she ever said anything witty except by accident, but her champions have claimed for her at least a dozen well-known *mots,* mostly sexual and mostly unprintable. She was certainly funny if not witty and she was a frequent occasion of wit in others, especially in Benchley and Dorothy Parker. In their later years, Mrs. Parker and Tallulah constantly fought and made up, fought and made up; it was a kind of exercise for them— the only kind that did not interfere with their drinking.

One of the most important influences in Tallulah's life during this period was Frank Crowninshield, the editor of *Vanity Fair.* A brilliant, handsomely designed magazine, devoted to arts and letters and to people and places that Crowninshield considered amusing, *Vanity Fair* flourished until the Depression came; it went out of business in 1936. Crowninshield, a bachelor turning fifty when he met Tallulah, cultivated good-looking and intelligent girls, with whom, for his protection, he adopted the posture of an old uncle and born tease. Crownie, as he was called, was for long the president of the Coffee House Club, a snug, pleasantly down-at-the-heels-looking club on the second floor of a pair of small, ancient brownstone buildings on West Forty-fifth Street. The membership of the club consisted mostly of artists, writers, architects, and editors, and its attitude towards life was summed up in the preamble to the yearbook, which quoted rule six to the effect that there were no rules. Tallulah enjoyed being taken to the Coffee House by Crownie and she became a favorite there.

Everything that one reads about Alexander Woollcott (1887-1943) makes him seem a waspish, self-promoting little second-rater, but since he had many discerning friends the chances are that he possessed some eerie charm that has eluded history. Edna Ferber said of him that he was a New Jersey Nero who had mistaken his pinafore for a toga, and Howard Dietz gave an indirect critique of the quality of his writing by referring to him as Louisa M. Woollcott. Through some unfortunate glandular misadventure in youth, he grew up to be a fat, sexless pasha, and his persistent verbal abuse of friends may well have been based on a defensive need to strike the first blow. "Hello, repulsive" was a favorite greeting of his, and when he wished to dismiss someone after a pleasant enough encounter, he would say, "I find you are beginning to disgust me, puss." Wolcott Gibbs wrote a three-part Profile of Woollcott in *The New Yorker* that caused Woollcott great pain by telling the truth about him. He was a poor critic, an execrable actor, and a successful "personality" on radio, where he peddled with breezy unction pipe tobacco and breakfast food. He had the tastes of a provincial housewife; his idea of a great novel was James Hilton's *Lost Horizon,* and he called O'Neill's *Strange Interlude* an "*Abie's Irish Rose* of the pseudointelligentsia." He was kind to Tallulah when she first came to New York and often took her to opening nights in the course of his duties as drama critic of the *Times.* He was proud of her performance as Sabina in *The Skin of Our Teeth,* which he characteristically described as a "dauntless and heartening comedy [that] stands head and shoulders above anything ever written for our stage." Wilder was a friend, and friends were victims of his gross superlatives.

Frank Crowninshield, scion of an old Boston family, was born in Paris in 1872 and died in New York in 1947. From 1914 until 1935, he was Editor of *Vanity Fair,* a monthly magazine devoted to arts, letters, and other matters close to Crowninshield's heart, including golf and pretty girls, to whom he represented help and not danger. A typical issue of the magazine in the twenties would contain articles by Arthur Schnitzler, Louis Golding, Compton MacKenzie, V. Sackville-West, Corey Ford, Ferenc Molnar, Heywood Broun, John Dos Passos, Edmund Pearson, Deems Taylor, Bernard Darwin, and Frederick Packard; drawings by Covarrubias and Luks; and photographs by Steichen, Sheeler, and Muray. "Crownie," as he was universally called, was a founder of the Coffee House Club; among prominent members of the club in his day were Robert Benchley, William Adams Delano, Karl Vogel, Harrie T. Lindeberg, and George Chappell, who wrote under the name of Dr. Traprock. The photograph is of a portrait of Crownie by Gordon Stevenson; it hangs on a chimney breast of the Coffee House, presidingly. Crownie often took Tallulah to small dinner parties at the Coffee House; he also saw to it that she was asked to the big Park Avenue parties that would prove most useful to her in her career. Years later, Tallulah said of him that he had liked her for her "scorching eagerness to be somebody." He fostered ambition and was not surprised when, on occasion, the scorching went a trifle too far. That was the way of the world, and especially of his world, and he saw no better way for youth and beauty to be served and gifts made fruitful. Always a bachelor, he led a happy life, and he spent the last few days before his death sending cheerful Christmas messages to friends.

Crownie arranged for her to be invited to the fashionable parties given by Condé Nast, publisher of *Vanity Fair* and *Vogue.* At Crownie's own frequent parties, he would encourage Tallulah to run through her repertory of imitations, in the best of which she took off her idol, Ethel Barrymore. She had seen Miss Barrymore a score of times in the hit play *Déclassée,* by Zoë Akins, and was letter-perfect not only in the Barrymore role but in several of the other roles as well. One evening, Crownie asked her to entertain a considerable gathering with her Barrymore imitation, adding that Miss Barrymore was present and had requested it. Bravely, Tallulah did her turn, which delighted everyone except the subject of it. "But, my dear, you make me seem so fat," Miss Barrymore protested, and slapped Tallulah's face. That episode past, they became close friends. Once, paying a visit to London, Miss Barrymore settled her children in a hotel and went off to a party at Tallulah's tiny house in Farm Street. She intended to stay only a few minutes; instead, she spent the night, sharing Tallulah's bedroom, and then many nights.

Her years in London would be Tallulah's happiest. She was to discover this long afterwards, when her life could be looked back upon from a very late stage and, despite its seeming disorder of false starts and sudden stops, could be seen to have fallen into segments of time with boundaries unexpectedly precise. There were the nearly sixteen years of Jasper and all those schools entered and miserably departed from, the five years in New York, the eight in London, and then the thirty-odd years in which, no matter where her work required her to go for periods of weeks or months (Hollywood, Miami, Cape Cod, Texas, Vegas), New York remained her base—towards the end, the dark cave in which she crouched, with death often quite cheerfully in mind, an aging woman reluctant to go out, unwilling to exercise, unwilling to eat, pegging away at her Old Grand-Dad, and, though suffering from emphysema and forbidden to smoke, smoking her hundred and fifty Kents a day.

With Norman Trevor in *Footloose,* by Zoë Akins. It ran for four weeks.

She left New York for London in 1923, impatient and disappointed—at twenty-one!—with the progress of her theatrical career. She was a celebrity, a person constantly talked about and written about, a party girl of inexhaustible bonhomie (drinking little as yet and as yet, so she characteristically proclaimed to the world, a technical virgin, whatever she may have meant by "technical"), but as an actress she was still being described as a novice. Reviewing a play called *Footloose,* Burns Mantle said of her, "A most promising young ingenue …able to inject a telling realism into a most difficult role," and in *Nice People,* a vehicle that provided a small part for Katharine Cornell as well, Alexander Woollcott wrote of her that "there should be a special word of appreciation for the comely and competent Tallulah Bankhead, who luxuriates in a feline role." She left *Nice People* to star in *Everyday,* the play Miss Crothers wrote for her, and it proved a flop. She then played briefly in *Danger* and in *The Exciters,* which closed after a run of five weeks. Percy Hammond,

With Henry Hull in *Nice People.* She looks many pounds lighter here than in *Footloose.*

in the *Tribune,* said of her performance, "Few actresses can portray more convincingly than Miss Bankhead the difficult part of a pretty girl."

It was not enough. Success on so modest a scale irritated Tallulah. Once she had feared to compete and now she rejoiced in it; she must reach the topmost rung of the ladder without delay. She consulted the leading astrologist of the period, Evangeline Adams, who cast her horoscope and informed her that her future lay abroad. "Go," said Miss Adams, "if you have to swim." Miss Adams's clairvoyant abilities were confirmed when, shortly thereafter, Tallulah received a message from Charles B. Cochran. The most important impresario in London, Cochran had been paying his annual visit to New York in the fall of 1922 and had seen and admired Tallulah in *The Exciters.* He had been at Crownie's on the evening when Tallulah did her imitation of Miss Barrymore and received her painful reward. Cochran had tried in vain to purchase the English rights to a couple of Broadway hits—*Rain* and *Seventh Heaven*—in order to star Tallulah in one or another of them in London. He returned to London with a photograph of Tallulah by Ira Hill, which he showed to Sir Gerald du Maurier. He urged du Maurier to give the beautiful American girl a part in a play that du Maurier and Viola Tree had written, called *The Dancers.* Du Maurier having expressed an interest in Tallulah, Cochran dispatched a cablegram: POSSIBILITY ENGAGEMENT WITH GERALD DU MAURIER IN ABOUT EIGHT WEEKS   WRITING FULLY   CABLE IF FREE.

Sir Gerald du Maurier was one of the best-known theatrical figures of his time. He was an actor-manager, directing his plays and starring in them. *The Dancers* was his first attempt at authorship, and he and Miss Tree signed their joint handiwork with a pseudonym. The offhand, faintly mocking manner of acting that du Maurier perfected had a great vogue and can be studied at secondhand in the movies of Leslie Howard, who learned from him. To act with du Maurier was a fantastic opportunity for Tallulah; she cabled Cochran at once that she was free. In a few days, Cochran's promised letter arrived. Thirty years later, Tallulah was capable of reciting it without a single slip; because it provides such pleasant glimpses of both Cochran and Tallulah, it is worth quoting in full:

> My dear Tallulah,
>
> This is the position.
>
> Sir Gerald du Maurier is producing in about eight weeks' time a new play. The part-authoress tells me that there are two good women parts in it, one an American, the other an English girl. She tells me, and Sir Gerald confirms this, that the American is the better of the two parts. She is, I understand, somewhat of a siren and in one scene has to dance. She must be a lady, and altogether sounds like you. She is, in the play, supposed to be of surpassing beauty. I have told the part-authoress and Sir Gerald that I believe you are "the goods." They are quite excited about you and I think there is little doubt that if you care to take the risk of coming over you will be engaged. In any case your expenses will be paid.
>
> Now as to salary. You will get little more than half of what you had in New York, if, as I understand, your last salary was $500 a week. In favor of your coming I would say that the management is the best in London for comedy actresses. It is the ambition of every young actress to be with Sir Gerald. Moreover Sir Gerald is the best stage director in this country and Miss Gladys Cooper and several other actresses owe their present positions to his help.
>
> Against the proposition is the salary, the risk that Sir Gerald might think you too young, or in some other way not suitable for the part, or that you might not think the part good enough.
>
> I have put all the facts before you, as I know them, and feel that I can only leave it to you to make a decision. Think it over very carefully, ask the advice of your friends and cable me when you have come to a decision, please. I have no axe to grind other than my desire to see you properly launched here and to do a good turn to my friends, Sir Gerald and the part-authoress.
>
> With kindest regards to yourself, and all our mutual friends, believe me, yours sincerely,
>
> Charles B. Cochran.

At the time, Tallulah was a few weeks short of her twenty-first birthday. She telephoned her father in Washington and persuaded him to wire Cochran to the effect that Tallulah had his permission to make the commitment. A few days later, Cochran cabled again: TERRIBLY SORRY. DU MAURIERS PLANS CHANGED. Tallulah was desolate. The disappointment of being put aside unseen and untested was bad enough; what made matters worse was that she had spread word of her imminent debut abroad and would now be thought to have been snubbed by the great du Maurier. She consulted Estelle Winwood, who urged her to proceed undaunted to England on the grounds, not very flattering to an ambitious actress, that her hair was so beautiful that someone was sure to offer her a part in some something. Tallulah cabled Cochran: IM COMING ANYWAY. Cochran in his reply sounded as if he feared he had released a genie far bigger and more powerful than he had counted on. His cable vibrated with avuncular alarm: DONT COME   THERES A DEPRESSION HERE   ITS VERY BAD   THERES NOTHING GOING ON   ITS TOO MUCH OF A RISK I DONT WANT TO BE RESPONSIBLE FOR YOU TAKING THE CHANCE. Again with Miss Winwood's encouragement, Tallulah decided to ignore Cochran's sputterings. The problem was, as usual, one of money. She had none and she could not ask her father for any, since she had assured him that du Maurier would be paying her expenses. She turned to an old family friend, T. Coleman Du Pont, a financier famous for his pranks and generosity (he liked to startle friends with rubber snakes and exploding cigars; he built a concrete highway from one end of Delaware to the other and gave it to the state). Tallulah told Du Pont of the risky adventure she was determined to embark on and he arranged for her to be furnished with a letter of credit for a thousand dollars. She took ship on the *Majestic* and wired Cochran from mid-Atlantic, when it would be impossible for him to prevent her from coming. Cochran gallantly wired back: ILL MEET YOU AT PADDINGTON STATION.

And so he did. She had already made a reservation at the Ritz, that being the only hotel in London whose name she knew. Cochran took her to lunch next day and to a matinee of *Bulldog Drummond,* which du Maurier had just revived, with himself in the leading role. After the performance, they stopped by du Maurier's dressing room. Du Maurier was genuinely astonished and dismayed: "But didn't you get a cable telling you not to come?" Tallulah, falsely blank-faced: "What cable?" Du Maurier explained that he had engaged another actress and that she was already in rehearsal; Tallulah expressed cheerful regrets over the mix-up. Cochran presided in admiring silence over this performance and a couple days later arranged for Tallulah to meet du Maurier again. On the first occasion, she had worn a hat; on the second, at Cochran's insistence, she went

A portrait of du Maurier, painted by Augustus John and owned by Tallulah. Du Maurier was tricked into giving Tallulah her first role on the English stage, and that was fitting, because he was an incorrigible practical joker. He would fasten strings to cups and saucers in such a way that actors engaged in drinking tea in the course of a play would find the chinaware hopping uncontrollably about the table; once he arranged for water to fall—slowly, drop by drop, *à la Chinoise*—on an actor who was obliged by his part to remain seated in a certain place while delivering a very long soliloquy. He was a charming man and a difficult one. He was born in 1873, a son of the artist and writer George du Maurier, and he died in 1934, having been knighted in 1922. His daughter Daphne became a best-selling novelist. In a biography of her father, published a year after his death, she wrote: "It was a somewhat degraded and unattractive profession of which Gerald found he was the head in the early twenties, and nobody realized it more than himself. He belonged to the past and to the present—to the Victorians, the Edwardians, and to the post-war Georgians—and the very interbreeding of these qualities was enough to cause confusion and misunderstanding within him. He deplored the passing of tradition, of ceremony, of respect; yet he led the way to familiarity and easy-going tolerance with his careless 'darling,' his shrug of the shoulder, his desire to be liked by his fellows. He allowed anyone to call him by name, to drink his whiskey, and to borrow his money. . . . He complained of publicity and vulgarity, but he lunched at a restaurant every day of his life with a pretty woman, if he could find one, even if he took the unique measure of asking Mo [his wife] to ring up and make the appointment for him."

hatless. Du Maurier was suitably impressed by her extraordinary hair, and Tallulah was hired. (Having a new baby, the actress she replaced was content to remain at home and receive her full salary for the run of the play.)

The Dancers was a very silly play indeed and it was the making of Tallulah. She came on in a buckskin dress with a headdress of long white feathers and executed an Indian dance that owed much less to the Indians than to the Charleston and other dances she had learned in the course of many a nightclub visit to Harlem. She was a sensation in the play. Nothing as young and wild and beautiful had been seen in London and she became literally the talk of the town. Some years later, the critic and theater historian J. C. Trewin was to write of her debut: "Tallulah Bankhead . . . arrived at Wyndham's: a smouldering, pouting young woman with a voice like hot honey and milk, a face like an angry flower, eyes of violet-blue, and, at first, hair in a waving ash-blonde mane. (This was soon cut.) . . . The newcomer had some fierce little scenes that she acted with resolution and the magnetism that could all but draw her audiences upon the stage. The first-night house shouted for her (though it could not yet pronounce the name Tallulah). . . . The play could hardly have mattered less; but Tallulah Bankhead had acted herself into London, and for eight teeming years

Tallulah, by James Abbe. Over fifty years later, Abbe recalls the day of the sitting.

she was a West End cult, her followers ribboning out at the gallery doors thirty hours before any performance." A few years later, Arnold Bennett wrote with awe of the phenomenon of a Tallulah opening: "It begins on the previous afternoon. At 2 P.M., you see girls, girls, girls in seated queues at the pit and gallery doors of the Tallulah theatre. They are a mysterious lot, these stalwarts of the cult. Without being penurious, they do not come from Grosvenor Square, or even Dorset Square. They seem to belong to the . . . clerk class. But they cannot be clerks, typists, shop-assistants, *trottins:* for such people don't and can't take a day and a half off whenever their 'Tallulah' opens. What manner of girls are they, then? Only a statistical individual enquiry could answer the question. All one can say is that they are bright, youthful, challenging, proud of themselves and apparently happy. It is certain that they boast afterwards to their friends about the number of hours they waited for the thrill of beholding their idol, and that those who have waited the longest become heroines to their envious acquaintances."

Tallulah's following helped cause her fame and then itself became famous. It was the occasion for many news stories and editorials in newspapers and magazines, most of them deploring the existence of the cult without saying why it was deplorable. Its sexual connotations must have been what made people uneasy, but few editorial writers in the inhibited middle-class England of that day cared to come right out and say so. For Tallulah's following consisted almost entirely of girls, and this was odd—indeed, at first glance it was inexplicable. She was a classic vamp, alluring to men because of her manipulation of an intense femininity, yet she attracted few stage-door Johnnies;

instead, she would be greeted nightly by a host of stage-door Jennies, rapturously chanting "Tallulah! Tallulah!" These girls were very like the bobby-soxers who were one day to behave in a similar fashion towards Frank Sinatra. In their hundreds and thousands, the bobby-soxers offered themselves up in a sort of mass ecstatic sacrifice to Sinatra, and what they offered was obviously their bodies, for him to do with whatever he willed. In the case of Tallulah, the sexual offering was only implied, and most observers preferred to believe that what she represented to the girls pursuing her was something more general and therefore more easily able to be thought innocent—that she was for them the embodiment of flaming youth, of the newfound, postwar freedom to do and say and become whatever one pleased. The embodiment happened to be what the fifties would call a sex-kitten, with a husky, insinuating voice, a provocative laugh, heavy-lidded, inviting eyes, and a big red voluptuous mouth, whose reckless stream of words seemed to promise reckless deeds. Under the circumstances, it was downright wholesome that she projected a man's image of a woman as a sexually desirable object, not a woman's image of a woman. It was certainly the case, moreover, that Tallulah herself was not "one of those." She espoused no lofty separatist Lesbian principles. She did not think of men as very different from women. In her private life, there were plenty of men in love with Tallulah, and it appealed to her to go to bed with them; it never occurred to her when she was young that she would not someday marry and have children. There were also plenty of men in her private life who were homosexual and with whom she had good times. She was equally open to, and curious about, the attributes of both sexes, and it may have been this easy and uncritical open-ness that the Tallulah girls, prudes in their middle-class upbringing, joyfully responded to. There were, they perceived, promises in life, and Tallulah revealed them and magnified them. She did not withdraw from her following behind the conventional barriers of fame. She listened to the girls' distracted hullabaloo and recognized without dismay that it was love. And she loved them in return, with extraordinary civility and good nature. She sought to know as many of them as possible by name and she took an interest in their lives. One of them—Edie Smith—became her secretary and companion and remained close to her for thirty years; today, living in retirement in Chicago, she remembers that young Tallulah of nearly half a century ago as the incomparable novelty that trans-formed her life. As she was to say to many people in many places over the years, Tallulah would say to the girls crowding the dark theater alley after a show, "I love you all," and mean it.

Tallulah fell in comfortably with the tradition of bisexuality in the English theater—a state of affairs more common in the twenties there than in the United States, where the majority of people working in the theater were either strictly heterosexual or strictly homosexual and had a sort of Puritan distrust of the license implied in chancing both. A tradition of bisexuality existed also in the English upper classes, which Tallulah was soon invited to move among. One of the earliest and coarsest of her bawdy stories concerned an English lord and lady, to whose country house she had been asked for the weekend. Host and hostess proved equally eager to make a conquest of her, each in his/her way and concurrently, not consecutively. As one might expect, Tallulah was fascinated by the acrobatic ingenuities required to give simultaneous satisfaction to all. She was a quick study in sex, as she was in everything; it was a system of skills that she somehow hadn't to master but only reach out for and adopt at the moment that suited her best. In her autobiography, she spoke of being a "technical" virgin when she left New York for London. In middle age, she recounted privately that on arriving in New York from Washington she had been seduced by a celebrated American actress (still living in 1972), and it may have been because of the homosexual nature of this seduction that Tallulah used the—for her—curiously guarded word "technical." Also in middle age, she said that the last woman with whom she made love was another well-known American actress, also alive in 1972. She had been drawn to her, Tallulah said, "because she had the body of a boy." This rings true: Tallulah always preferred men's bodies to women's, and she imitated in respect to the carrying out of bodily functions a casualness much more commonly associated with men than with women. Nevertheless, Tallulah's reminiscences were notably unreliable when it came to specific names, dates, and places. She would say things to astonish and please the particular group in which she happened to find herself. Part of her fame had come from uttering shockers; like a good trouper, she did her best to live up to expectations. A young actress recalls meeting Tallulah in the sixties, when the actress was a teen-age apprentice at a summer theater on the Cape and Tallulah and her acting cohorts came tearing through on a week's engagement. In a fever of health-seeking, the little local company had sworn off alcohol, and when Tallulah turned up to rehearse the light cues, she found everyone drinking cranberry juice. "Oh, my Gawd, *cran*berry juice!" she cried out, in her most comic basso. Then she bent down and said to the young actress, "When I was sixteen, dahling, I had a shoebox full of cocaine." Well, yes and no. It was true that at sixteen she had been experimenting with cocaine and other drugs, and she may have kept cocaine in a shoebox in that little room at the Algonquin, but to claim that the shoebox was full was a characteristic Tallulahism.

In London during the long run of *The Dancers*—the longest run she was to enjoy until she played in *The Little Foxes*, in 1939—she renewed her passionate, difficult friendship with Napier Sturt, the third Lord Alington, whom she had met and fallen in love with and often quarreled with in New York. Alington was clever and prankish and calculatedly disreputable. In a set in which it was difficult to become conspicuous through selfishness, he achieved that feat with ease; no one could touch him in the art of failing friends and neglecting those who loved him and whom he professed to love. His charm must have been formidable; he was always forgiven. He was Tallulah's first encounter with a narcissism greater than her own. He taught her to raise her sights: to be bolder and more outrageous than she had yet dared to be. He was bisexual and tubercular, and Tallulah would gladly have married him, not least because she would have liked to be a "Lady." Alington had no intention of marrying until it was prudent, for family reasons, to have issue, ideally male. In 1928, he married an earl's daughter; they had but one child, Anna Sturt. Upon the outbreak of the Second World War, he enlisted in the RAF and was killed in action in September, 1940, at the age of forty-three; the title became extinct upon his death. The British *Who's Who* for 1940 volunteers nothing about Alington except his pedigree and the fact that he owned eighteen thousand acres. Since this information can only have come from him, one guesses that it amused him to claim so little a space in history with so large a space in land. Strangely, there is no mention of his death in Tallulah's autobiography. He died within a day or two of her father, and this joint loss of the two men she had loved most in the world must have been stunning. The omission is all the more notable because Tallulah had early taken an ardent pro-English stand in the war; it would have been an occasion for pride that her cheeky and mischievous former playmate, often close to death through disease, had died so unselfishly in a good cause. It is possible, however, that her silence springs from some remnant of bad feelings. Alington's wife having died in 1936, Tallulah went over to England the following year and attempted to reestablish a close relationship with him; she may even have sought to persuade him to make her Lady Alington. In vain: as was the case with so many of Tallulah's friends, marriage was not Alington's native country. Nor was it hers, though from time to time she was Alabama-belle enough to suppose it should be. Moreover, like any Southern woman of her time, she boasted of having received many more proposals of marriage than a strict tally would substantiate. No doubt hundreds of people made love to Tallulah and scores of people loved her, but as a marriage prospect she was, even in her youth and beauty, intimidating; a number of eligible men warily circled her and backed away, and the one man she came close to marrying in England—Count Anthony de Bosdari—was an attractive charlatan, who was counting on her celebrity to help him in certain speculative business enterprises. When she was married at last, it was to a man who would have been content without it. He was certainly miserable with it, poor John Emery, and he was grateful when, after a few years, the Tallulah reaping machine, having spun him round and round in its fearsome blades, cast him aside and let him mend.

7

By her own account, Tallulah behaved like a brat during the run of *The Dancers*. Since she appeared only in the first and fourth acts of the play, she would often recklessly go out to dinner with Alington and other friends during the second and third acts. She gave noisy parties in her dressing room before and after performances, she forced de Maurier to raise her salary from thirty pounds a week to fifty, and she exacted from him a two-week holiday, which she spent getting sunburned in Venice. She went there with, among others in a merry party, Sir Guy Francis Laking, a frail and lisping nineteen-year-old alcoholic, who took pleasure in constantly setting friend against friend. ("At one time," Tallulah said, "Lady Diana Manners and I were the only women in London who would speak to him.") Laking was to die a few years later, at twenty-six, and the newspaper headlines reported that his will included a charming bequest: "To my friend Tallulah Bankhead all my motor-cars." This was a double jest from beyond the grave. Tallulah had long since proved herself incapable of driving cars and Sir Guy had no cars. Tallulah was taken up in Venice by the Cole Porters and their fashionable, hard-playing set. This was her first visit to the Continent and the Porters must have enjoyed letting her see Venice through their eyes. It was a setting infinitely romantic but also comic; one had to keep both attributes steadfastly in mind. Here was Cole, his sad, crippled years far in the future, bounding up flight after flight of stairs in a *pensione* on the Grand Canal, in eager, unrewarded pursuit of an astonished Yale undergraduate; here was Linda calmly spreading her pleated skirt upon the Lido, turning those hot sands into a Louisville drawing room. Snapshots in the Porter albums show a plump, frowzy-looking girl, not at first glance Tallulah at all. In the snapshots one beholds the gravest of the misdeeds committed against du Maurier —Tallulah has cut off her long golden hair. She said years afterwards that du Maurier began to cry when he saw what she had done; if so, he may have been thinking of the effect her bob would have on the box office. Her hair *was* the attraction in London that Estelle Winwood in New York had predicted it would be. Impossible Tallulah! She was twenty-one and every inch a star.

With Cole Porter on her first visit to the Continent. She got sunstroke.

The difficulty was that after *The Dancers*, she had no play. Tallulah's lifelong fear of being passed by prompted her to accept a role in a melodrama called *Conchita*, important on two counts only. For the first time, she received billing above the name of the play:

TALLULAH BANKHEAD

IN

CONCHITA

Also for the first time, faced with an emergency in the theater, she did a ridiculous thing and thereby saved the situation. Her role in *Conchita* was that of a dark-skinned Cuban dancer; she wore a black wig over her golden bob and carried on her arm a tiny monkey. On opening night, the monkey panicked, grabbed Tallulah's wig, pulled it off, and darted to the footlights, whirling the wig above its head like a lariat. The audience started to titter, and Tallulah, for want of anything better to do, threw a cartwheel. The audience roared with laughter and approval. She had learned in childhood and again in school that when things go wrong the safest way out is to play the clown, and now she had done so, and it had worked. The success of her feat served her ill, because it proved the first of many; over the years, she was increasingly tempted to steal a laugh by no matter what discreditable means. More and more often, in moments of impatience or lost confidence, she would step out of character and silently destroy with antics the audience's will to believe in someone other than herself.

Conchita closed, and a comedy, *This Marriage*, in which she co-starred with Cathleen Nesbitt and Herbert Marshall, also quickly came and went. Poor as the play was, it provided the occasion for

39

Max Aitken, later to become Lord Beaverbrook, was born in Canada, in 1879. His father was a minister and so, according to the custom of the time and place, poor; Max took care that an opposite fate was his—he became very rich very young, through a series of shrewd business deals, and soon moved to England, where he went into politics, accumulated a newspaper-publishing empire, and was a celebrated London partygiver and partygoer. He affected, after the fact, to have accepted a title through absentmindedness, but the truth was that he enjoyed being a highly placed gadfly inside the Establishment. He and his friend Churchill moved in and out of government according to whether a crisis of sufficient importance tempted them to measure themselves against it; wars were up to their standard. Beaverbrook was a little man with a big head and a quick wit and he adored gossip. He said once, in respect to his incessant dining out, "It is an error to suppose that hours spent in pursuit of dissipation are entirely lost in the process of forming a character, or in laying the foundations of a career." He and Tallulah enjoyed each other's company, having the same convictions on how to form character. She wrote that she and her sister, Eugenia, spent an evening aboard the "Beaver's" yacht; he kept a full table of guests entertained until daybreak with his conversation. Beaverbrook had a country place, "Chertley Court," in Surrey; Tallulah liked to revel the night away there among companions as witty and tireless as she. Beaverbrook died at "Chertley," in 1964, at the age of eighty-five, a couple of weeks after a splendid birthday celebration at the Dorchester. He had always known when to go to a party and when to leave.

a long friendship with Miss Nesbitt (who, to Tallulah's delight, was nursing a baby backstage; the English theater was highly informal) and for a marked increase in her following. Louder and louder grew the cry from the gallery girls: "Tallulah, you're wonderful!" The name of a remote waterfall in the distant highlands of Georgia was becoming a commonplace of the London press. In any list of partygoers in the gossip and society columns, Tallulah was sure to be included and was almost sure to have said the one quotable if not memorable thing, as when she inquired of a peer staring blankly at her: "What's the matter, dahling? Don't you recognize me with my clothes on?" Those young partygoers were gaudy creatures, or they thought they were, and it pleased them to have their infinitesimal adventures in pubs and clubs and at masquerade balls and weekend parties recounted in print for the millions of people they would never need to know.

Tallulah appeared next in a mystery play called *The Creaking Chair*, with C. Aubrey Smith. The play itself creaked, and on opening night the author, summoned from the wings, was roundly booed. Overacted with shameless zest in order to provoke laughs, the play managed to run for

thirty weeks, and Mr. Smith, the actor-manager, persuaded Tallulah to let him put some of her weekly wages aside. The result was that when the play closed she was three hundred pounds to the good. She had never been solvent before. She felt for the first time the delicious sensation of possessing money not yet spoken for and waiting to be spent. There was enough of Jasper and old back-country Bankheads in her to make her doubt the reality of success unless it was capable of being measured in financial terms, but that was only a small part of her satisfaction. It would always be more important to her to make money than to have it. It was nearly as simple as this for her, that money was love, both in the getting of it and in the spending. The high salaries she demanded and received—in her time, the highest on Broadway, on the road, in radio, at Las Vegas—were a sign, visible to the whole world, of

In *Conchita,* her first starring role in London. She wore a black wig, very Spanish.

how worthy of admiration and love she was. She needed immense rewards for a reassurance that had little to do with getting rich, though she died rich—her estate, derived entirely from her earnings, amounted to almost two million dollars. When it came to money, she had a knack for being simultaneously prudent and abandoned. Though she could gamble away thousands of dollars in a casino without distress, the cash for the chips had to come from current income; she was a shrewd manager of her portfolio of gilt-edge stocks, and she would never sell a share or borrow a penny against her annuities in order to go back to the tables when her purse was empty. She would bet on anything—horses, the toss of a card, the match game, the color of a stranger's eyes—and she was a good loser, but with regard to investments she took care not to lose: she put her money into IBM and Eastman Kodak.

There are people who are extravagant but not generous; Tallulah was both. Giving for her was a means of reassurance as great as getting. She dispensed her money as she dispensed her favors, on precisely the same impulse and to gain the same ends. People came to think of her as a soft touch, and they sometimes took advantage of what they considered a weakness, but the weakness was, in fact, a form of strength; the giver remained in perfect control. Once in New York a young playwright down on his luck begged the loan of a couple hundred dollars. Knowing the sum was a trifle to Tallulah, he was astonished when she burst into tears. "*Don't* ask me for it, dahling," she said. "Ah, *please* don't ask me for it. You're the only person left who hasn't borrowed money from me." (It would be pleasant to report that the young man pulled himself together and went out and earned the two hundred by hard work. The truth is that he begged some more—he, too, by then in tears—and Tallulah gave him the money.) When she died and was discovered to have been a millionairess, many people grew angry with her, because she had deceived them by her constant talk of being poor. It was certainly an unbecoming fault, and the kindest thing one can say about it is that it sprang from a need in her that had little to do with money and still less to do with telling the truth.

Armed with her three hundred pounds, Tallulah hoped to put trashy plays behind her forever, but this was not to be the case: she blustered her way through trash to the very end, and for good reasons. Theater in the West End of London, as on Broadway, is a business whose primary purpose is profit and not the pursuit of excellence (though excellence is sometimes to be found there, and not by chance); ordinarily, more money can be made from new plays than from old ones, and it is of small concern to the producer that, in the nature of things, most of these new plays will be mediocre. Of the sixteen plays that Tallulah acted in during her eight years in London, all but two or three of them achieve mention in history solely because she appeared in them. There was a second—and sadder and more intractable—reason for her seeming commitment to plays of low quality. She had leapt into stardom without preparation, either in schools of acting or in one or another of the great stage companies with which the majority of her contemporaries in England would have served a long and onerous apprenticeship. Tallulah scorned teachers of acting and theories about acting; she pretended to believe that one simply got up and did what one had a talent for. This had been her only "method," and it was not for her to say that it had failed. The consequence was that she was always a star but only intermittently a superb actress. If there were many plays unworthy of Tallulah, there were also many plays that Tallulah was unworthy of—nearly the whole repertory of classic Greek, Elizabethan, Restoration, and eighteenth-century English drama was closed to her. With training in youth, what an actress she might have become in age! Instead, she devoted a long career to living beyond her professional means, pushing energy and intelligence to the limit and, when the pressure of panic mounted too high in her, exploding into farce and braggadocio.

In New York, a play called *Rain* was making a sensation, and its star, Jeanne Eagels, had decided against playing it in London. Taken from a short story by W. Somerset Maugham, the play depicted the corruption of a grimly upright clergyman by a saucy whore. Tallulah was determined to play the role of the whore, and she signed an agreement with Basil Dean, who had acquired the English rights to the play. The agreement was simple enough:

> I agree to play the part of Sadie Thompson at a salary of forty pounds a week. I note that the management is to commence the production of the play not later than 30th June, 1925. I agree that if Mr. Somerset Maugham should definitely disapprove of my engagement, I will cancel it and your company will not be under liability to me in respect to it.

There is something curious about the use of "definitely" in regard to Maugham's disapproval. Does it hint at some unease on Dean's part—some intimation, perhaps from Maugham himself, that he didn't expect Tallulah to prove equal to the role? In any event, as soon as *The Creaking Chair* closed, Tallulah took ship for America, in order to see and study Jeanne Eagels' performance as Sadie. Back in London, she started rehearsals. Somewhere in the darkened auditorium on the first day sat Maugham. Tallulah had mastered every line of the play and, quick study that she was, she had also mastered many of Jeanne Eagels' mannerisms. She gave what she considered an accomplished imitation of Jeanne Eagels, and at the end of the rehearsal was surprised when Maugham failed to offer congratulations. At the second rehearsal, he again avoided her, and she began to suspect that he disapproved of her and that his disapproval would indeed be definite. A couple of days later, with no preliminary word from Dean, she read in the newspapers that an actress named Olga Lindo had been given the role. Tallulah was furious, and her sense of having been publicly humiliated heightened her fury: everyone in London—everyone that mattered, that is—

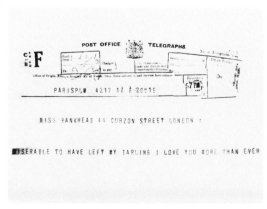

From an unidentified admirer. No matter what the occasion, the message is always welcome.

had known that she was rehearsing in the play and that to be Sadie meant more to her than anything else in the world. She stormed into Dean's office and learned that Maugham had complained that she lacked personality. As if a Bankhead could lack personality! Raging and sobbing, she went home and late that evening made the smallest possible attempt at suicide. She put on her Sadie

Thompson costume, wrote what she hoped would seem a heart-rending suicide note (the note read, "It ain't goin' to rain no moh," which was a line from a popular song of the day and wryly witty in this connection not alone because of the play but because London had been undergoing an unprecedented four weeks of continuous downpours). Then she swallowed some twenty aspirin.

A tense moment in *The Green Hat.* Tallulah is not only braless but waistless.

The next morning, she was awakened by the ringing of the telephone. Noël Coward was on the wire. He was faced with a critical emergency. An actress with a big part in his new play, *Fallen Angels*, had just dropped out. Would Tallulah be willing to take her place and, if so, would she be able to memorize the entire part in four days? Tallulah was feeling marvelous after her mock-heroic exploit of the night before—how ripping to find oneself alive and not dead!—and she told Coward, "Four days! Dahling, I can do it in four hours."

And perhaps she did: feats of that sort were for her the intellectual counterpart of her exuberant cartwheels and back-somersaults. The play was certainly able to open on schedule, with Edna Best and Tallulah as its stars. The critics admired their performances (James Agate wrote, "All praise to Miss Best, who overcame with complete triumph the handicap of natural modesty, and to Miss Bankhead, impersonating to the life a joyless creature whose spiritual home was the gutter") and denounced the play as obscene. This was good for it at the box office. A few days later, Maugham invited Tallulah to lunch, in the course of which he told her that her performance in *Fallen Angels* was the most brilliant comedy performance he had ever seen. She thanked him but remained

Dikran Kouyoumdjian was born in Roustchouk, Bulgaria, of Armenian parents, in 1895, lived for many years in England, and died in New York, in 1956. As a naturalized British subject, he changed his name to Michael Arlen. He was determined to become financially independent at an early age and his best-selling novel, *The Green Hat,* which he subsequently turned into a play, enabled him to attain that goal by the age of thirty. He was a handsome young outsider who longed to be an insider and readily became one; the Mayfair practices he chronicled sprang in part from fantasies about Mayfair that Mayfair was quick to adopt. Arlen married a princess, had a son and daughter, and led a life of extreme elegance. When his vogue passed, he behaved admirably, blaming neither himself nor the times and leaving unspoken whatever professional misery he may have felt. *The Green Hat* was a silly novel, but it was written with great verve and intelligence, and one forgave it sentence by sentence. Of the stage version, in which Tallulah created the role of Iris March, James Agate wrote scoldingly, "So far from having the moral force of *Ghosts* or *Damaged Goods,* this piece has no significance of any kind. It does not point out the folly of a pair of lovers who could have bought happiness at the cost of becoming invoice clerk and shorthand typist. It does not show that the net result of balancing a lust for self-sacrifice against unbridled appetite is that you will run full tilt into a tree." Despite this censure, the heroine, Iris March, "a young woman careening in canary-colored motor-cars between Deauville and Nice," became a favorite symbol of the twenties, one with Fitzgerald's Daisy and Hemingway's Brett.

unforgiving. *Rain* opened, and Agate slipped a comforting indirect compliment to Tallulah into his review: "As for Miss Olga Lindo, I think I must begin by saying that she faced her very difficult job with immense pluck. . . . I can think of half a dozen actresses who could have equalled Miss Lindo here, and one, at least, who could have surpassed her." Many years later, Tallulah in her autobiography was still brooding over the injustice of the treatment she had received from Maugham. She wrote, "Olga Lindo opened in *Rain*. It was an immediate failure." When the autobiography was brought out in England, Miss Lindo sued the publishers for libel and won her case on the strength of five untrue words: the play had not been an immediate failure, and the words were ordered omitted from all future editions.

In the fall, Tallulah opened in an adaptation of Michael Arlen's best-selling novel, *The Green Hat*. Her friend Katharine Cornell, who had been with her in the cast of *Nice People* a few years earlier, was playing in it at the same time in New York. Miss Cornell's version of the play became a hit; ever afterwards, when people thought of Iris March, that doomed, lovely girl ("I want the final ultimate decency"), they imagined her as Miss Cornell. In London, the critics dismissed the play as preposterous and unclean, though they liked Tallulah as Iris. In spite of its supposed raciness, the play did not enjoy a long run. Looking back over nearly fifty years, Miss Cornell thinks that she may have scored a greater success than Tallulah in *The Green Hat* because she herself was so unlike Iris March and Tallulah was so like her. "Tallulah had less to play against than I had," Miss Cornell has said. "Tallulah's life in those days was a series of extreme melodramas, and mine was not. I had to work my way into Iris; Tallulah was already there."

In *Scotch Mist*. If Tallulah wasn't undressing herself onstage, she was being undressed.

With Leslie Howard in *Her Cardboard Lover*. Howard's hair rarely looked so distrait.

Following *The Green Hat*, Tallulah played in *Scotch Mist*, by Sir Patrick Hastings, a King's Counsel far more distinguished as a barrister than he would ever be as a playwright. Agate concluded his acidulous review with the sentence: "Those skilful players, Messrs. Robert Horton and Edmond Breon, did wonders with two of the worst parts ever devised, and Miss Tallulah Bankhead greenhatted it to perfection." A few months later, in Sidney Howard's *They Knew What They Wanted*, Tallulah had the first satisfying role of her career. She demonstrated that there was more to her than being able to dance the Charleston and show off her sexy camiknickers. Agate was grateful: "Miss Bankhead made an instantaneous and a great success. . . . It would be ungenerous not to recognize that her performance in this piece is one of quite unusual merit." After *They Knew What They Wanted*—a title that the English critics for some reason vehemently disliked—came *The Gold Diggers, The Garden of Eden, Blackmail, Mud and Treacle*—now *there* is a title!—*Her Cardboard Lover, He's Mine, The Lady of the Camellias,* and *Let Us Be Gay*. The unimportance of most of these plays can be gauged by the amount of space the critics devoted not to comments on Tallulah's acting but on her clothes: appropriately, gold pajamas in *The Gold Diggers,* cream-and-chocolate pajamas in *Her Cardboard Lover,* a cast-aside wedding dress in *The Garden of Eden. The Lady of the Camellias* was what Tallulah called a "risky do," since her playing of Marguerite Gautier invited comparison with that of Bernhardt and Duse. She said of the play that it was less hallowed by time than weatherbeaten. Surprisingly, the critics found her interpretation of Marguerite too chaste, and their praise went mainly to the gorgeous costumes and well-upholstered sets.

Her bandbox of a house in posh Farm Street. Open plumbing openly arrived at.

As the twenties drew to an end, Tallulah passed from being merely famous to becoming an institution. Her opening nights caused much-deplored traffic jams in the comparatively carless London of that period. She was earning five hundred pounds a week and always spending more. During the run of *The Garden of Eden,* she made a movie, *His House in Order,* and for that too, her salary came to five hundred pounds a week—according to the newspapers, the highest salary ever paid to a movie star in England. The Farm Street house, decorated by Syrie Maugham, was a funnel through which poured an unceasing flood of Americans on their way to and from the Continent. Some were friends, some acquaintances, some brassy strangers. It scarcely mattered. Tallulah adored parties, her own and other people's. Her tastes were exceptionally catholic. Once at a large gathering she met a pale lanky young man, the scion of a noted New England family. He was an artist and a poet, and seating herself close beside him she told him with husky excitement that he was one of the most interesting men she had ever met. A few minutes later, he saw her seated beside a black musician at a piano, and as he passed them on the way to the bar he heard her saying with husky excitement to the musician that he was one of the most interesting men she had ever met. It was the same compliment, and in neither case was it untrue. She had a gift for admiring people; she was also insatiably gregarious. She liked being a celebrity and she liked pursuing other celebrities. Through her friend Lord Beaverbrook, she met Winston Churchill and Lloyd George. She was invited to have lunch at the House of Commons with the Prime Minister, Ramsey MacDonald; afterwards, he drove her to the theater for her matinee. Tallulah, the Prince of Wales, Bernard Shaw, and the jockey Steven Donoghue were said to be the four best-known names in the British Isles. She was painted by Augustus John and Ambrose McEvoy and sculpted by Frank Dobson. She was photo-

As Cleopatra in *Great Lovers of Romance.* Photo by Cecil Beaton.

graphed by Dorothy Wilding and Cecil Beaton, who wrote of her, in one of many high-flown passages: "Tallulah is a wicked archangel with her flowing ash-blonde hair and carven features. Her profile is perfectly Grecian, flow of line from forehead to nose like the head of a medallion. She is

A violent, happy man, John possessed a self-admiration that shines out of every self-portrait. He was a Victorian who saw himself as a romantic brigand. If a woman of his acquaintance seemed troubled in mind, he would suggest as a remedy that she should have a child by him; some did. He wrote in his autobiography that he came from a family of Welsh lawyers that, being weakened "apparently by repetition, seems to have exhausted itself, and in a final spasm brought forth a kind of recidivist, throwback, or survival of an imaginary golden age." This was not for him to say, but he said it. John knew everyone that mattered in the England of his day—he was born in 1878 and died in 1961—and painted most of them. It was wittily said of him that he was not a snob; he simply wished that everyone had a title. He made several drawings of Tallulah and painted her portrait in 1930. On being exhibited at the Royal Academy, it caused a sensation; Tallulah bought it from him for a thousand pounds, and it became her dearest possession. In fact, it was not a very good likeness. After Tallulah's death, the portrait was put up at auction at the Parke-Bernet Gallery, in New York. The National Portrait Gallery, in Washington, D.C., was eager to acquire it, but the bidding soon reached a sum too high for its budget. The portrait was knocked down to an anonymous bidder for nineteen thousand dollars. The bidder turned out to be John Hay Whitney. Unaware of the National Portrait Gallery's intentions, he had purchased the portrait in order to present it to the gallery, where it now hangs directly across the way from a portrait of Tallulah's friend Adlai Stevenson.

Medusa, very exotic, with a glorious skull, high pumice-stone cheek bones, and a broad brow, and she was equally interesting sculpturally when she was plump as she now is cadaverously thin. Her cheeks are huge acid-pink peonies. Her eyelashes are built out with hot liquid paint to look like burnt matches, and her sullen, discontented rosebud of a mouth is painted the brightest scarlet, and is as shiny as Tiptree's strawberry jam."

8 Tallulah left England in 1931. She was still in her twenties and more beautiful than ever—she had improved the Grecian profile that Beaton admired by having her rather blunt and fleshy nose narrowed and sharpened. She had had eight years of notoriety and intense and often foolish theater busyness. She could have remained in England for the rest of her life, but she was growing restless. She had used up the English experience and she hated to repeat herself. Edie Smith remembers how pleased Tallulah was by the prospect of undertaking a new life in New York. "Things were very quiet in England at that time," Edie has said. "The Depression was on. Besides, Miss B. had squeezed all the fun out of the twenties, and she saw that the thirties wouldn't be the same. When Paramount offered her a contract for five pictures, at fifty thousand dollars a picture, she jumped at the chance. In the past, she had always looked down on films, but not any more. She was bound and determined to do her best. That was the way she was. For as long as she was committed to something, oh, how she cared!"

Tallulah gave up her leasehold on the Farm Street house (by coincidence, forty years later the little house was again for rent, looking scarcely changed), packed up her pictures and clothes, and set sail on the *Aquitania*. The publicity department of Paramount Pictures was already at work creating a salable image of her. She was to be exploited as a symbol of unbridled sexual power over men, and for that purpose it was important to emphasize her foreignness. Traditionally, women movie stars who embodied sex—Pola Negri, Vilma Banky, Garbo, Dietrich, and the like—came from somewhere outside America, the implication being that standards of sexual conduct among foreigners were far looser than American standards. (It was characteristic that Theda Bara, the first actress to be called a vamp, should have played her man-hungry movie roles under that Byzantine-sounding name; she was born Theodosia Goodman.) In nineteenth-century America, as Henry Adams once ruefully pointed out, sex had become a species of crime, and in the first third of the twentieth century, thanks to the disguised, constantly pandered to prurience of moviegoing Americans, sex in movies was still a crime, punishable outside marriage by death, mutilation, poverty, and ostracism. American women movie stars were nearly always types of virgins: Mary Pickford, Lillian Gish, Janet Gaynor, and Jean Arthur. One felt about the roles that Katharine Hepburn played at the beginning of her career that such girls would make love only after marriage and then only with a certain fastidious reluctance, nostrils flaring. Carole Lombard and Jean Harlow were, in their day, revolutionary figures, and the comparative naughtiness of *It Happened One Night* was acceptable in part because the actress who played the heroine, Claudette Colbert, had a French name; everyone knew how the French felt about sex. Tallulah as an embodiment of carnal desire had to be made to seem exotic. Moviegoers were to get the impression that she had just emerged from some lewd temple of love in the dark heart of Middle Europe. A man would have to beware the least glance from those heavy-lidded bedroom eyes, the least brushing of that big red mouth, no longer expected to put one in mind of Tiptree strawberry jam. Press agents affected to catch hints in her husky voice not of Jasper but of Jaipur, not of sunny Alabama days but of patchouli-scented Arabian nights.

Sell her as a tireless young voluptuary; at the same time, get every possible inch of publicity out of the fact that she had had the good fortune to be born in God's country. Wanton though she had been and would be, she was a daughter of the Old South, with a father and uncle in Congress. Write nonsense about her on both counts, the more extravagant and contradictory the better; back of the nonsense was a serious commercial purpose. Millions of dollars were at stake. Despite the

When Tallulah was invited to come back to the States to make movies, the witless intention of the movie magnates was to turn her into a second Marlene Dietrich. With *Morocco, Dishonored,* and *Shanghai Express,* Dietrich was at the height of her first great movie success, and every studio was seeking to have a replica of her in residence. Despite the awkwardness for both of them implicit in Tallulah's being pitted against her, Dietrich went out of her way to welcome Tallulah to Hollywood and they became good friends. The campaign to turn Tallulah, a brilliant comedienne, into a sex goddess was a total failure, in part because, unlike Dietrich, she had no von Sternberg hovering over her and devising a suitable mask for her to wear. Dietrich went on living behind the mask and never mistook it for reality. Her warmth and intelligence made her a natural intimate of Hemingway and other writers and artists remote from the world of movies and nightclub engagements. Tallulah told her friend Al Morgan, "I first met Marlene in Hollywood, when she was a great and beautiful star and I was just starting to make pictures there, and she came over to my table in the commissary and said 'How do you do.' Years later, in Las Vegas, where we both did shows, she used to go around with no make-up on, her hair in curlers for the whole world to see, and then at night she was entirely transformed, all beauty and white chiffon! She told me always to wear chiffon and she was right. And one night there she was in this lovely white chiffon and it was hot and I was dying for something to eat and the kitchen was closed and Marlene went out and whipped up the most delicious scrambled eggs and tomatoes you ever tasted."

Depression, Paramount Pictures was enjoying an unprecedented momentary prosperity, thanks in large measure to Marlene Dietrich and the hit movies she was making under the direction of Josef von Sternberg. *Morocco* and *Dishonored* were already out and *Shanghai Express* and *Blonde Venus* were to be released the following year. Paramount was bent on turning Tallulah into a second Dietrich, and by the time the *Aquitania* docked, the ship's news reporters had been invited to believe they would meet a combination of Lilith, Salome, and Lucrezia Borgia. Nobody could have lived up to the claims made on behalf of Tallulah's beauty and sex appeal by the sedulous Paramount flaks, but Tallulah did well by not pretending to be a mindless engine of delight. She was neither a Tondeleyo nor a Sadie Thompson. She was a very good-looking girl with a first-rate mind, who talked well and at length—indeed, she had already the habit of outtalking everyone within earshot, but what she had to say was interesting, and for once the reporters did not have to make up suitable quotations. She was the real thing. She amused them and gave them good copy, and so they liked her. All her life, she was to enjoy an exceptionally favorable press. A. J. Liebling, who had a sharp eye for what was false in any public figure, described Tallulah on the occasion of her return from a later trip abroad:

> Miss Tallulah Bankhead arrived last night on the liner *Europa* with her two Pekes, Sally and Ann. She wore a blue dress with lumps on it by Schiaparelli, and was apparently transfixed by a long pin with a head like a polo mallet, but demonstrated, on request, that the pin merely passed through her belt, missing her body entirely.

Coming from Liebling, the interview amounted to a love letter. She was written about with affection by hundreds of reporters, male and female, from coast to coast. Tacked on a wall by a reporter's desk for years afterwards would be a curly glossy photograph, taken of Tallulah and him during the course of an interview in some hotel or other, when Tallulah had come through town on tour. Maybe, having kicked off her shoes, she would be sitting cross-legged on a couch, a cigarette in her gesturing hand, a tumbler of whiskey on the coffee table in front of her; and of course she would be talking. For some years, she was a fixture at Bleeck's Artist and Writers Club, a bar and restaurant adjacent to the *Herald Tribune* building in New York. She and Maney would meet there, roaring coarse greetings to each other down the length of the bar, and it appears that none of the other drinkers ever took offense, though it was a place that did not then look kindly upon women, even quiet ones.

Tallulah rented a suite at the Hotel Elysee, on East Fifty-fourth Street. It cost seven hundred and fifty dollars a month, a fantastically high price for those Depression days. Like the Algonquin, the Elysee after so many decades remains a familiar part of the New York scene. The lobby with its shiny bandbox-like furnishings and the little ground-floor Monkey Bar that Tallulah used to frequent are much as they were. The management of the Elysee was used to theatrical folk and their ways— the previous occupant of Tallulah's suite had been Ethel Barrymore—and the staff was grateful for

Tallulah's lavish tips. Her first movie was scheduled to be shot at the Paramount East studios in Astoria, just over the Queensborough Bridge from Manhattan. It was called *Tarnished Lady* and the screenplay was by Donald Ogden Stewart, who had made his name as a humorous writer but who found little to be humorous about in the dreary story on which his script was based. The director was George Cukor. By chance, Tallulah, Stewart, and Cukor were all making their first talkie, and they had reason to be uneasy. A studio limousine would pick up Tallulah and Edie early each morning and bring them back from the treeless wilderness of Astoria each night. Edie's duty on the set was to keep cranking the portable phonograph on which Tallulah liked to play, nonstop, records by Bing Crosby and Russ Columbo. After a prolonged advertising and promotion campaign, *Tarnished Lady* opened at the Rivoli Theatre in New York and was a flop. John Mosher in *The New Yorker* said:

> After the gossip about her brilliant London career and her noble Southern lineage, these being some of the items of the small-talk in the smarter speakeasies, she proves to be an ordinary young actress, gifted with no more good looks than are many women of the screen; and yet, more unfortunately for her prospects, suggesting mostly a feeble resemblance to more beautiful and able actresses, especially to Miss Dietrich. She fails in the end to establish any sort of identity of her own, at least as far as this first movie goes to show.

Tallulah had learned in London to face and survive the conventional humiliations of professional failure; part of the risk of going on a stage is that you may be driven off it at any moment by derisive laughter. The failure of *Tarnished Lady* was far more difficult to accept than, say, that of *Mud and Treacle,* and not alone because it was on so grand a scale and after so much paid for preliminary hubbub. Being novices, Cukor, Stewart, and Tallulah had proceeded by trial and error, and a large portion of the good they had achieved was left, she said afterwards, on the cutting-room floor. Still,

Irving Pichel reasoning with her in *The Cheat.* She ought to be more attentive.

reviewers were kind enough to her as an actress; what she found galling was that, thanks to the studio's insistence that the world was about to behold another Dietrich, she had been made to fail not in her own right but as an imitation of somebody else. If it was infuriating to a Bankhead to be told by the likes of a Maugham that she lacked personality, how much more infuriating it was to be touted as a second Marlene. Paramount had forced Tallulah into an impossible position in order to capitalize on the Dietrich vogue. She ought to have canceled her contract then and there, but, alas, the money proved irresistible. It was not a solace to her; it was only necessary. So many dresses to buy, so many parties to go to, so many parties to give! She had been paid five thousand dollars a week for her ten weeks' work on *Tarnished Lady*. Now, according to contract, she would be making two more movies in Astoria, on the same generous terms. She hoped that the studio, perceiving its error, would begin to call attention to her hitherto by no means unappreciated qualities ("Tallulah, you're wonderful!"); on the contrary, the movies she proceeded to make, the first called *My Sin* and the second *The Cheat*, were tailored to fit Dietrich's image instead of Tallulah's. Again, she was doomed to play an obligatory Dietrich cabaret scene. (One marvels at the cruelty of pitting Tallulah, who loved to sing but for whom singing took the form of warbling up and down in search of a key, against the confident alto purring of Marlene.) The pictures were directed by George Abbott, known then as now for his ability to put unpromising Broadway show-material into pleasing form. Abbott was an actor and playwright as well as a director, and a man of decorum. He and Tallulah were ideally unsuited to each other, and movies were not, in any event, his métier; *My Sin* and *The Cheat* fared no better with the reviewers and the public than had *Tarnished Lady*. Tallulah took some consolation from what Richard Watts, Jr., said about her in *My Sin*: "At least they have photographed the eminent Miss Bankhead properly. . . . It remains, nevertheless, another mean trick to play on a fine actress and a brilliant personage who is waiting for a part worthy of her. It is little short of magic to see England's favorite American star acting away resourcefully and honestly in a photoplay that is neither resourceful nor honest." The advertising for *My Sin* was as irritating to her as the script. She was especially incensed by a trailer shown at the Paramount Theatre, in Times Square:

COMING! COMING!
TALLULAH THE GLAMOROUS
TALLULAH THE MYSTERIOUS
TALLULAH THE WOMAN
WE GAVE YOU MARLENE DIETRICH
NOW WE GIVE YOU TALLULAH BANKHEAD

She protested to her Paramount producer, Walter Wanger, that she had made a name in the world long before Dietrich and that in London Dietrich was known as the second Tallulah. Wanger suggested making the last line of the trailer read: NOW WE GIVE YOU BACK TALLULAH BANKHEAD. The suggestion revealed more than it intended to, for to give something back is to reject it. Tallulah might have taken this hint; instead, she allowed herself to be persuaded that if she would go to Hollywood and make three more movies for Paramount, they would be of a quality certain to secure her a high place in the movie world. She would be enthroned between Garbo and Dietrich, where both Paramount and Tallulah ardently wished her to be. Her salary would again be five thousand dollars a week, with options leading to six thousand dollars a week and eventually to much more.

In the light of the economic conditions that prevailed throughout the world in 1932, the size of the salaries that Hollywood studios were then paying their stars is staggering. Tallulah at

George Abbott, who was eighty-five in 1972, has been an actor, a director, a playwright, a producer, and that exceptional thing, a stern man about town. In the world of the theater, where everyone employs affectionate diminutives on an extravagant scale, Abbott is addressed as Mr. Abbott. Tall, thin, bald, and magisterial, Abbott is a teetotaler and looks it; he is also an ardent dancer and golfer and doesn't look it. Abbott directed Tallulah in a couple of her early talkies—*My Sin* and *The Cheat*—and he did not find her casual ways winning. It would be hard to imagine two people with less in common, and their ways understandably crossed but twice. Tallulah referred to him afterwards, rather nervously, as "skilled." Abbott, who was born in Forestville, New York, and graduated from the University of Rochester, began his theater career at a comparatively advanced age, in 1913. He was first an actor; Richard Maney saw him play John Brown and complained of him in the role that he lacked the mettle of a martyr. Abbott and George S. Kaufman have been the two leading play-doctors of our time, usually taking care to direct the consequences of their doctoring. Their talent has been to improve the construction of a play and then direct it at a relentlessly fast pace. Abbott was the co-author and director of *Broadway, Coquette, Three Men on a Horse, On Your Toes, The Boys from Syracuse, Best Foot Forward, Where's Charley? The Pajama Game,* and *Damn Yankees,* and the director of such hits as *Boy Meets Girl, Brother Rat, Room Service, Pal Joey, On the Town, Call Me Madam, Flora the Red Menace,* and the original production of *A Funny Thing Happened on the Way to the Forum.*

thirty, almost unknown to the moviegoing public and with three unprofitable flops behind her, is offered five or six thousand dollars a week—why? Possibly because Hollywood was a money factory as well as a dream factory, and huge payments to actors, directors, writers, and producers had long been a commonplace there. Chaplin, Lloyd, Keaton, and Arbuckle thought nothing of making twenty or thirty thousand dollars a week in the nineteen-twenties, when income taxes were comparatively low and the purchasing power of the dollar comparatively high. In 1932, one could buy a car for a few hundred dollars and butter for a few pennies a pound; trained servants were to be had for ten or fifteen dollars a week; phone calls, shoe shines, and candy bars all cost a nickel; and many newspapers were three cents. Adjusted for cost of living and taxes, Tallulah's five thousand a week would be something like twenty thousand a week today. A remarkable sum for a proven failure! The classic Hollywood maxim, "You're only as good as your last picture," clearly did not apply to Tallulah. She had not planned on going to Hollywood, but between the temptation of the money and a heightened determination to make good, there was nowhere else to go. Never apologize, never explain: she had only to press on in order to get rich and become a great star.

As it turned out, the Hollywood period was so bewildering and unsatisfactory that Edie Smith was unable to recall afterwards how long it had lasted. It may have amounted to a year and a half, though it seemed longer. Tallulah rented a big house owned by William Haines, a former movie star who had become an able and successful decorator. She discovered that all the pretty Hattie Carnegie originals she had bought in New York to impress Hollywood with were just wrong for that purpose; everyone was wearing slacks, and one by one, in secret, Tallulah gave the originals away. Life in the movie colony was more informal and more hard-working than she had expected. For one thing, the Depression was at last beginning to have an effect there. For another, there was little to do that was interesting except work. When she was not at the studio, she swam, sunbathed, played bridge, and visited with old friends, among them Ethel Barrymore, Robert Benchley, George Cukor, and a brilliant and witty homosexual movie columnist named John S. Cohen, who once wrote to Tallulah and Edie, in the midst of a holiday abroad, "I waltzed my way through Germany and I was amazed at the rapidity and ease with which I followed." Tallulah met Marlene Dietrich at the studio commissary and they became good and lasting friends. From time to time, press agents and newspaper reporters tried to invent a quarrel between them, but the principals refused to cooperate. On a contrary tack, gossips tried to invent an affair between them, and once, as a gag, the principals appeared to cooperate. Some gold-dust makeup found in Dietrich's dressing room was distributed here and there between them, providing indisputable circumstantial evidence that the gossips were right. Tallulah and Marlene laughed like schoolgirls over their prank; they thought they were being very funny indeed.

Tallulah shared with millions of movie fans an unquenchable curiosity about Garbo. Now that they were living in the same city, Tallulah was eager to see her face to face. Her friends Bertold and Salka Viertel, being also friends of Garbo, arranged to have them both to dinner. Tallulah said afterwards that from sheer nerves she had shown off outrageously, but Garbo must have been amused; at any rate, she came to Tallulah's house for dinner with Edie and a couple of other close friends. Later in the evening, Ethel Barrymore joined them—she, too, for all her age and fame, had been abjectly eager to meet Garbo—and the group played charades and danced together to music provided by Tallulah's faithful wind-up phonograph. Garbo got tipsy, which was a rare event for her. The next day, Tallulah and Edie ruled that wherever Garbo had sat must be deemed sacred, and the sink at which she had washed her hands was proclaimed an altar. It would be hard to imagine two women more unalike than Tallulah and Garbo, and perhaps they got on well because of the gulf between them. Tallulah described one of Garbo's favorite companions, the elegant Mercedes de Acosta, as looking like "a mouse in a topcoat," but she took care not to make any wisecracks about Garbo. On at least one occasion, they played tennis together, and what a pity it is that no one made a home movie of the match. Garbo was as keen on exercise and fresh air and raw food as Tallulah was repelled by them. With her superabundant energy and quick reflexes, Tallulah ought to have been a superb athlete, as her father and Eugenia were, but she always preferred watching games to playing in them. She said once to Al Morgan, "I wish I could play something that doesn't take you too far away. Like with a golf course—you get out in the middle there, you can't get back." It is a Tallulahism well worth pondering on.

Tallulah made her three movies according to contract. They were better than the ones she had made in Astoria, which is not to say that they were very good but only that she was learning to accommodate her acting to the camera and that Paramount was learning to accommodate to her; gradually, the notion of a second Marlene was being abandoned by the front office. Her first Hollywood movie, *Thunder Below,* was a melodrama in which her body and soul were fiercely struggled over by Charles Bickford and Paul Lukas. ("One woman—desired, desiring—in a village of lonely men! Torn between passion and honor, lovers and husband! Below the Equator, where civilization's barriers swiftly burn away." So read the advertisements, and so went the plot.) In her next movie, *The Devil and the Deep,* she played the wife of Charles Laughton, the dotty captain of a U.S. Navy submarine. Among the crew were Gary Cooper and Cary Grant. It was Laughton's first role in an American movie, and he threw himself into it with appalling relish. The movie turns up regularly on television, very late at night; it is funny now, and it must have been pretty

Percy Hammond, who was born in 1873 and died in 1936, began his career as a drama critic in Chicago, which in his youth was an important theater town, second only to New York. According to Brooks Atkinson's account in *Broadway,* Hammond was lured East by an offer of twenty-five thousand dollars a year from the old New York *Tribune,* later the *Herald Tribune.* This fiscal seduction took place in 1920, when the dollar was worth a good deal more than it is today, so no wonder Hammond gave way; he may have been the highest paid drama critic of all time. Hammond had an attractive prose style and was almost without competition from his early colleagues—Alexander Woollcott, of the *Times,* wrote as if in melting fudge on a lace doily, and most of the rest of Hammond's circle were journeymen, hitting the keys of their typewriters hard and sometimes seemingly at random. Atkinson says of Hammond that he wrote his notices after the show in a cubicle off the composing room with a can of gin at his elbow; he quotes Hammond's dour witticism: "Never praise an actress because it will bite you." Still, he praised Tallulah often enough and had a certain amount of journalistic fun with her. It appears that on one occasion she took offense at his having implied that her theatrical opportunities derived from the political distinction of her family; in a subsequent review, Hammond referred to this family as consisting of Bob and Phil, who were, of course, LaFollettes and not Bankheads. On learning that Tallulah had been smoking a cigar in a theater, he said, "Doubtless that is her way of being inconspicuous."

funny then. For the last movie, Paramount, teetering on the brink of receivership, decided to lend Tallulah to MGM. There she made *Faithless,* with Robert Montgomery. It was a comedy and not a melodrama; instead of being torn between passion and honor, she was given a few mildly witty lines to utter, and she made the most of them. Montgomery has said he enjoyed working with her: "I got appendicitis just as the picture was starting. The studio offered to find her a new leading man, but she said she'd be glad to wait for me. That was nice of her, because I was a comparatively new boy." As *Faithless* was being shot, the Depression was deepening throughout the world and a wave of reform was sweeping Hollywood. The Hays Office was setting stricter standards for what could be seen and uttered on screen, and in the press there was much phony agitation over the private lives of some of the more prominent actors and actresses in Hollywood. *Faithless* was pruned of a few risqué lines and its plot garbled in the name of purity. Tallulah was drinking too much and was said to have had a couple of indiscreet sexual encounters with grips and other employees well below the permissible executive level. Her private life was becoming too public for the comfort of the studios. Paramount was prepared to keep her on without a raise and MGM was prepared to offer her a long-term contract, though at a figure much less than Paramount's, but both studios stipulated that henceforth her conduct would have to be above reproach. Tallulah reckoned that she had saved two hundred thousand dollars in the course of making her six movies. She did not find Hollywood attractive and she did not find movie-making attractive. She found it still less attractive to be lectured to on morality by the head of MGM, a sharklike and thoroughly immoral little tyrant named L. B. Mayer. She made up her mind to return her household to New York. She would go back on the stage, where she belonged. Her last interview with Mayer was highly satisfactory. He did not yet know that she had no intention of going to work for him. In his usual coarse and aggressive fashion, he was telling her that he had heard some very unpleasant things about the way she was behaving. She asked him to be more specific.

"Your sex life."

Again, he would have to be more specific.

"About women."

Still more specific.

The sour little face working with venom: "I hear you been hibernating with them."

Docilely, unsmiling, Tallulah said, "You mean ————?" She named the most important actress under contract at MGM. He blanched as she proceeded to tick off a few more MGM names. She was notoriously unable to keep secrets. MGM could be destroyed by her. He wished he had never said a word about her goddamn hibernating. She left him sweating behind his big round desk.

Tallulah and Edie came back to New York and moved into the Gotham Hotel, on Fifth Avenue and Fifty-fifth Street. It had been eleven years since Tallulah had acted on Broadway, and she felt even more uncontainably charged with energy and ambition now than she had felt in her teens, when, a chubby blond girl in the Algonquin lobby, she had stared with obsessed eyes at passing Barrymores and Talmadges. Having succeeded greatly in London and, in her judgment, having failed greatly in Hollywood, she needed at this moment to pick up the world and give it a good shaking. Scores of play scripts were raced through in search of a suitable vehicle, and at last, patience at an end, she settled for a drawing-room comedy called *Forsaking All Others,* which had once been optioned by her friend Hope Williams. The authors were a couple of former students at the Yale Drama School, Edward Barry Roberts and Frank Cavett, and their play concerned the tribulations of a jilted bride. Tallulah thought she could improve the play; she also thought she could find the necessary financial backing for it. The stock market was dropping daily, not to say hourly, and the country during the final weeks of the Hoover Administration was grinding towards a full stop. There were few angels to be found in the usual haunts of angels—indeed, the haunts themselves were hard to find, being in many cases shuttered, with the owners dead or moved away. Tallulah decided to back the

With Walter Pidgeon at the premiere of *Becky Sharp* at Radio City Music Hall.

play herself, with a portion of the two hundred thousand dollars she had saved from her movie-making. A friend consented to serve as the nominal producer, but it was Tallulah who made all the decisions: Hattie Carnegie to design her costumes, Donald Oenslager to design the sets, Harry Wagstaff Gribble to direct. And she chose the cast, which included Ilka Chase, Fred Keating, and Tallulah's then "official" young man, Anderson Lawlor.

It may be worth mentioning at this point that, since even when Tallulah was most in love she was never monogamous, there were many concurrent lovers, but one among them would be likely to have a recognized status. It was an aspect of Tallulah's respect for custom that she was reluctant to appear at social events without a male escort; she saw herself as a lady with perfect old-fashioned Southern manners and she expected, drunk or sober, to be treated like one. A gentleman of pleasing appearance and deportment must be beside her at all times to open doors, order food and drink, pay (with money given him beforehand) the bills presented in restaurants and bars, hail cabs, and see her safely home. In her youth, these companions were usually heterosexual or bisexual; as she grew older, they tended to be much younger than she and to be homosexual. Because so much of their time was devoted to waiting on her and picking up after her, Maney, with a characteristic Irish unease over irregular sexual relations, dubbed them her caddies. The word had, for Maney's peace of mind, connotations of healthy outdoors games-playing and not sex. Tallulah and the caddies themselves accepted the designation and used it cheerfully. The number of Tallulah's caddies came to be very large. Though many of them died surprisingly young, many more remain alive. Having loved her, they cherish her memory. They form a cult not in the least morbid, celebrating her life by continually recalling it. Often late at night, by long-distance telephone—Tallulah's time, Tallulah's method—they exchange their favorite Tallulahisms: how, having seen the movie version of *The Rose Tattoo,* she said to Tennessee Williams, "Dahling, they've gone and *ruined* that terrible play of yours." How, after a pre-Christmas lunch at a restaurant in the Village, she came out onto the street, dropped a fifty-dollar bill into the tambourine of a Salvation Army lassie, and said, "Don't bother to thank me! I know what a perfectly *ghastly* season it's been for you Spanish dancers." How, when a weekend guest at her country place had been awakened one morning by a servant bringing him a generous hooker of straight gin, Tallulah had called out from the adjoining bedroom, "Better drink it, dahling! I warn you there won't be another round served before breakfast."

After trying out in Boston, Providence, and Washington, D.C., where her father helped paper the house with eminences, *Forsaking All Others* reached New York in the care of its fourth director, Thomas Mitchell. Thanks to the frantic rewriting and redirecting it had undergone on the road, it had already a certain reputation as an embodiment of bedlam. The opening night, though it drew a fashionable audience, was not merry—it was March 1, 1933, the day on which every bank in the country had been shut down by Federal edict. Tallulah got excellent reviews. In *The New Yorker*, her friend Robert Benchley—of whom Tallulah once wrote that he was "as gay and thirsty a gentleman as ever I encountered"—said that she had given "a practically flawless performance," and in the *Times* Brooks

In which the props threaten to steal the scene. Tallulah in *Forsaking All Others.*

Atkinson was his usual equable self, mildly praising Tallulah and mildly damning the show: "This is Miss Bankhead's first appearance in this country since her canonization in England, so let's not be too peevish about her play." Because of the so-called bank holiday—curious euphemism for a financial catastrophe—the box office had to accept checks in place of cash, and the play, in that season of gloom, failed to catch on. Tallulah stubbornly kept it running for three and a half months and claimed afterwards that it had cost her a total of forty thousand dollars. The sum was probably

The relations between critics on the one hand and producers and theater-owners on the other being nearly always of an adversary nature, few critics live to see theaters named for them. Brooks Atkinson is an exception—he can march up and down outside the Brooks Atkinson Theatre on West Forty-seventh Street, taking satisfaction in being at once a man and a building. Now in retirement, Atkinson was the critic of his time who was universally respected; he wrote with a kind of dogged clarity, risking few flights of rhetoric and revealing few glimpses of personal emotion but taking care to be just to the intentions of production as well as to the not always very satisfactory results. Tallulah called him observant, knowing, gentle, quiet, and scholarly, and so he was and is. Born in Melrose, Massachusetts, in 1894, and a graduate of Harvard in the class of 1917, he was the drama critic of the *Times* from 1925 to 1942, took a leave of absence to serve as a correspondent in Chungking and Moscow during and just after the Second World War, and then returned to reviewing; in 1960, he was apotheosized into something known as critic-at-large, a position he held up to 1965. Atkinson has written several very diverse books. He is an ardent naturalist and when the fit is on him he appears to care as much for bobolinks as for Broadway. A student of Thoreau and Emerson, he lives in the country and watches the seasons change; this serene practice must be good for him, because he looks twenty years younger than his age. Of his old beat, he wrote recently, "On the street, Broadway is tawdry; in many corners, it is degenerate. On the stage, it is usually bright and occasionally inspired."

less; she always exaggerated her losses in order to seem poorer than she was.

Having demonstrated to New York reviewers and audiences that she was not simply an exotic personality, Tallulah was eager to find a play worthier of her than *Forsaking All Others,* and to that end she contracted to appear in Owen Davis's *Jezebel,* under the direction of Guthrie McClintic. Before beginning rehearsals, she spent a month in one of the cluster of pseudo-Spanish bungalows that made up the Garden of Allah Hotel, in Hollywood. (The hotel owed its peculiar name to the fact that it had been the residence of the movie star Alla Nazimova. When she turned the property into a hotel, she added an "h" to Alla.) In bungalows adjoining Tallulah's were Benchley and the composer Vincent Youmans. Tallulah and Benchley were lovers for a time; when he shied away into friendship, it was in part out of fear of her indiscreet tongue. She never kept a secret and she often made up secrets in order not to keep them. In most cases, her incorrigible journalistic particularity in respect to the who's, how's, and when's of her lovemaking did no harm, her companions being freebooters like herself. Benchley, however, was making a brave show of being in fact the respectable husband and father he always was at heart; he could afford Tallulah only as a drinking companion. On one occasion, they kept a party churning without interruption for thirty hours; it seemed to them that a number of extremely important topics remained on the agenda when their little discussion group was forcibly disbanded. It was during her stay at the Garden of Allah Hotel that she and Johnny Weissmuller, the swimming star and sometime movie Tarzan, climbed at five A.M. onto the diving board of the hotel swimming pool and plunged in full evening dress into the water. Tallulah sank to the bottom in her heavy, beaded dress, worked her way out of the dress, and clambered naked from the pool, shouting to sleepers in the nearby bungalows that if they wished to see her body, this was the moment. There were few takers. According to another version of the story, Tallulah did not know how to swim and Weissmuller had to fetch her up off the bottom of the pool, where she was already contentedly catching forty winks. In fact, swimming was the only form of exercise she enjoyed. She made it a practice to swim naked, and in later years her flagging body would prove an astonishment to people meeting her

A friend and favorite drinking companion of Tallulah's was the humorist, drama critic, and moviemaker, Robert Benchley. Born in Worcester, Massachusetts, in 1889, and a graduate of Harvard in the class of 1912, Benchley approached New York—and, for that matter, life itself—with a certain Yankee gingerliness, and it was quite a while before he discovered the pleasures of alcohol and wayward company. He maintained a family house in Scarsdale, a famously cluttered and undustable eyrie at the Royalton Hotel, in New York, and a summer place on Nantucket, where this picture of him was taken, as usual on the wing—bag in hand, book under arm—and, whether coming or going, looking extremely cheerful about it. For many years, he was the drama critic of *The New Yorker,* whose editors would await his copy with a practiced unease, sure that it would be delivered but not knowing when or from where. Like Tallulah, he kept long and unpredictable hours. She recalled his arriving once at her hotel very late at night, in the middle of a blizzard, dressed so peculiarly that her secretary, Edie Smith, thought he must be W. C. Fields. Benchley's opening remark was "I'm not hurt—I'm just tewibbly, tewibbly cold." He was one of the funniest writers of the century, and one has only to mention the titles of some of his books—*My Ten Years in a Quandary, After 1903, What?*—for people who remember them to begin to smile. He had an infectious laugh, which actors and especially playwrights would listen for on opening nights. His family adored him, and everyone who was not a member of his family ardently wished to be. He died at fifty-six, and all these years later his friends talk about him as if he were just about to turn up and make them feel especially good again.

for the first time at poolside. They would not know where to look, except away.

Tallulah had returned to New York and begun rehearsing *Jezebel* when she fell ill of a peritoneal infection that the doctors were slow to diagnose correctly. After many weeks in the hospital—Miriam Hopkins having by this time taken her place in *Jezebel*—she underwent a complicated series of abdominal operations, including a hysterectomy. When she left the hospital, she weighed less than eighty pounds. "Don't think this has taught me a lesson!" she told her doctors, as she tottered out the door. She spent Christmas with her father in Jasper, and in the spring of 1934 she and Edie took ship for England, where she set about restoring her health in characteristic fashion by incessant nightlong partygoing. She might have resumed her career on the London stage had she not received a transatlantic telephone call from John Hay Whitney. Tallulah was to say later of Whitney that he was one of the two great loves of her life—the other was Alington—and many of Tallulah's friends hold that she married John Emery only because she was unable to marry either Alington or Whitney. Poor Emery himself may have shared this opinion. She and Whitney had been seeing a good deal of each other, and he now wished her to return to New York and star in a play called *Dark Victory,* of which he was the chief backer. Tallulah was familiar with the play; she estimated that it had been rewritten at least twenty times and that an equal number of producers had held options on it. Still, if Jock believed in it, and, what was more important, believed in her starring in it. . . . Back she went and opened in *Dark Victory* in November, to a generally bad press. Benchley manifested his loyalty not only to Tallulah and his old friend Jock but also to one of the authors of the play—George Brewer, Jr., a convivial clubmate of Benchley's at the Coffee House. Fortunately for his readers, Benchley was funny as well as loyal. In *The New Yorker* he wrote: "There has always been a feeling among the admirers of Miss Bankhead that she should sometime play *Camille.* In *Dark Victory,* she makes a step towards this goal, without the unpleasantness of coughing. As a matter of fact, why should *Camille* be such a desideratum? She does very well with Judith Traherne, and in this day and age, *Dark Victory* is probably much better for her than the older, and more noisy, vehicle. In fact, she has a chance to show her mettle, and the

Since Tallulah was constitutionally incapable of discretion in respect to her own or anyone else's private life, people with a different view of how to conduct themselves took grave chances if they so much as consented to play bridge with her. Among the bravest of her friends was John Hay Whitney—"Jock" to his friends—who was soon known to the world as one of her two greatest loves, the other being Lord Alington. Whitney, a notably modest man, had the good sense not to be flustered by the fame she thrust upon him. He had, after all, lucky young fellow, other fames. At the time they met, he was one of the richest men in the world, as well as one of the most generous. Born in 1904, he attended Groton, Yale, and Oxford, and early fell in with his natural companions—not merely the plentiful rich, with whom he hunted and bred horses and played golf, but also the very witty, who are always in short supply. He and Benchley became close friends. Benchley wrote to his mother, "Jock Whitney is the finest young man I have ever met," and Whitney said of Benchley at his death, "He was the dearest man I have ever known." Whitney backed *Dark Victory*, which Tallulah starred in and which Benchley with his soft heart could not resist overpraising. Benchley was best man at Whitney's first marriage, to Elizabeth Altemus; Whitney subsequently married Betsy Cushing Roosevelt. (Osbert Sitwell said once, of social life in England, "Sooner or later, practically everybody marries a Guinness," and something like the same thing can be said in this country of both the Cushings *and* the Whitneys.) Whitney became the publisher of the *Herald Tribune,* though too late to keep it from dying. He has given tens of millions to Yale; in *Who's Who,* he lists among his clubs the secret society Scroll & Key.

sobs and sniffling which rock the Plymouth Theatre at the end of the last act ought to testify to her success. George Brewer, Jr., and Bertram Block have devised an exciting theatrical situation in the last six months of a girl who loves to live and has to die. They have written a first act which is clinical and intensely interesting, except possibly for a bit too much talk about the mountains, and they have handled the last minutes, which might so easily have been spoiled, with great delicacy and repression. In between, there are moments of static lag, when they were overtaken by writing. . . ."

With additional help from Whitney, an effort was made to keep *Dark Victory* running through the doldrums of the pre-Christmas season. At that critical moment, Tallulah again came down with a mysterious infection, thanks to which she lost her voice, and the play closed. (Afterwards, it became a hit movie, with Bette Davis as its star. Miss Davis also made a hit of *Jezebel* in its movie version.) A few weeks later, Tallulah opened in a revival of *Rain.* It was a chance to avenge herself on Maugham, ten years after his dismissal of her as Sadie Thompson in the early rehearsals of the London production. The reviews were unanimous in their praise of Tallulah. Benchley said, "As the harried prostitute who finds no balm in Gilead, Miss Tallulah Bankhead

Richard Watts, Jr., has been for many years the drama critic of the New York *Post.* Reluctantly, and without in the least looking or sounding the part, he has become the grand old man of the New York Critics Circle, whose nearly always confused discussions he observes with the skepticism of one who has been persuaded against his better judgment to visit the snake pit of an ill-kept zoo. The longer the discussions, the farther down his nose he allows his glasses to slip and the thicker the cloud of cigarette smoke behind which he takes refuge. Watts was born in Parkersburg, West Virginia, in 1898, and began his critical career as a reviewer of movies for the *Herald Tribune* from 1924 to 1936. He then moved sideways —or, as it was generally believed in those days, upwards—to the drama desk, where he served until 1942. He spent much of the Second World War in government service in Dublin and Chungking and has since kept a soft spot in his heart for the Irish and Chinese. A tall man with a shuffling gait, he lives on Fifth Avenue, reads innumerable detective stories, and appears to be consummately sedentary, but in the slack theatrical season he is transformed into an inveterate traveler; he defines "inveterate" as meaning that even if he doesn't want to go anywhere, he must, because his readers expect it of him. The accompanying photograph was taken by Jerome Zerbe, around 1939. Watts rarely looks this startled; his habitual mien is one of patient hopefulness. He and Walter Kerr wait on the curb outside the theater on an opening night, and if they are among the last to step inside it is not because they distrust the evening ahead but because they dislike being run down by first-nighters, many of whom are aggressive middle-aged businessmen with Coppertone tans and money in the show.

gives the performance of her career," and Howard Barnes reported in the *Herald Tribune* that she had brought first-nighters to their feet in the first notable acclamation of the season. "What is more significant perhaps to those who love the theater," Barnes wrote, in the engorged style of a newspaperman striving to express Big Thoughts, "is that Miss Bankhead emerges, without any lingering doubt, as an artist of full stature, mistress of an astonishingly wide range of roles and with a vivid power of recreating the emotional accompaniment of human experience. What she chooses to do from now on is not only a matter of vast excitement for her army of fans, but a matter of very real import for a theatrical season."

Tallulah and her friends had reason to assume that with *Rain* she would achieve her long-waited-for American success, but it was not to be. Broadway audiences have a tendency to think of revivals, if they are not of the classics, as secondhand goods, with the result that even when a revival is better than the original production it will often fail to enjoy a satisfactory run. *Rain* closed after a few weeks. Tallulah then unwisely consented to appear in a dismal work called *Something Gay*, which she flogged into a semblance of life and sustained against heavy odds for a couple of months. Her next play, *Reflected Glory*, was by the distinguished playwright, George Kelly, who also directed it. Opening in New York in September, 1936, it was adversely criticized by the reviewers, ran for sixteen weeks, and was taken on tour across the country until the following June. Tallulah rented a house that summer on the Connecticut shore. A performance of *Busman's Honeymoon*, a thriller by Dorothy L. Sayers, was being given one evening at the Westport Country Playhouse. The hero, Lord Peter Wimsey, was being played by John Emery. Tallulah, Edie, and Edward Barry Roberts, one of the authors of *Forsaking All Others*, were seated in a rustic box out front. Roberts, who had been spending a few days at Tallulah's house, has written a touching account of that evening and its sequel:

> When John Emery came on stage—a tall, blond, John Barrymore-like man—Tallulah sat up straight and said aloud, "Oh, God, he's divine!" Early in the action of the play, some draperies on the set happened to catch fire from the lighted kerosene lantern that was a key prop in the play. Emery put out the fire with his bare hands and made a short, graceful speech of reassurance, after which the play resumed. Tallulah was in ecstasies. I was sent backstage at the end of the first act to say, "Miss Bankhead is out front and will be back after the play." At the end of the second act, I was sent to say, "Tallulah is out front and will be back right after the play." At the end of the play, I was sent to say, "Cleopatra is out front and will be back immediately." By this time, John Emery and I were buddies, and he kept asking me, "What's she like? What's she like?"
>
> Cleopatra scarcely gave Emery time to change before she swept into his dressing room. They talked there for nearly an hour. She invited him to come to her place next day for the weekend and he said he'd be delighted. Then I had to draw him a map, showing him how to get to Tallulah's house on the Westport shore. Tallulah, Edie, and

I drove back to the house and seated ourselves in the enormous library. Edie got each of us a fifth of Scotch and Tallulah brought out a Bible and began to read aloud, mostly from the Book of John. "In my father's house there are many mansions . . . if it were not so, I would have told you," and the like of that. She read until dawn. As soon as she was in bed, I went upstairs, shaved and showered, packed my kit, and knocked on her bedroom door. When I came in and she saw the kit in my hand, she said, "Eddie, you always were tactful," and I said, "Yes, Tallulah, I know when I'm licked," and I blew her a kiss and went away. I learned later that Emery, having come for the weekend, spent six weeks there. Then they went down to Jasper and Tallulah got married in her father's house, like any proper Southern girl. I sent them a wire addressed to "Mr. and Mrs. John Emery, care of Tallulah Bankhead." I said in my message, "This is the best news I ever heard of," and I meant it.

When she and John came back to New York, they invited me up to the Gotham. Tallulah said, "Eddie, your wire was the only one that didn't say 'Who does what to whom,' or 'Darling, you've betrayed your sex,' or some such God-awful wisecrack." And I said to her, "Tallulah, you really love him, don't you?" And she stood on tiptoe and kissed John's cheek—he was at least a foot taller than she—and said, "Well, I married him, didn't I? I didn't marry the other five thousand."

10 At the time of their marriage, Tallulah was thirty-five and Emery thirty-two. He was a gentle, cultivated man, and most of the stories that are told about him and Tallulah and that are supposed to be funny end by seeming sad. Like the story of how, flustered upon meeting for the first time on the day of the wedding his prospective father-in-law, Speaker Will Bankhead, he said, "How do you do, Mr. Squeaker?" How, when a reporter asked Tallulah whether, having married Emery, she planned to retire, she replied, "If I wanted to retire, you idiot, would I marry an actor?" How Emery, playing with Tallulah and Conway Tearle in *Antony and Cleopatra,* was asked on opening night what he planned to do after the show and he replied, "I don't know, but I think I'm going up to Tallulah's." And how, when he overheard a man making an offensive remark about Tallulah in a bar, he knocked him down, and Tallulah on learning of the incident insisted upon being told what the man had said about her. When Emery repeated the insult—"Knocked him down! You should have killed him!" Tallulah exclaimed, and swung on him so hard she blackened one of his eyes.

Emery was a member of a family that been in the theater for six generations. His father, Edward Emery, was a well-known leading man with Minnie Maddern Fiske and Ethel Barrymore. For a time in his youth, while his parents were on tour, Emery was placed in the care of John Barrymore, and surely if one had combed the world one couldn't have hit upon a less appropriate guardian for an adolescent boy. Because Emery bore a striking resemblance to Barrymore, he was often rumored to be his illegitimate son, but because he bore an equally striking resemblance to Edward Emery, the rumor was a difficult one to keep in circulation. Emery grew up in the shadow of blazing figures and imprudently went so far as to marry a couple of them: Tallulah, who was his second wife, and Tamara Geva, who was his third. It is evident that he longed on occasion to blaze a little himself but lacked the necessary bravado; consenting to march behind others, he took revenge upon them by imitating them in their weaknesses instead of in their strengths. He was married four times and all four marriages ended in divorce. It was characteristic of him that even in death he was seen to be in someone else's shadow; when he died, in 1964, he and Tallulah had been divorced for twenty-three years, but the subhead on his obituary in the *Times* read in part "Tallulah Bankhead's Former Husband."

Emery was well trained in classical roles, and he would have been far better off acting with Tallulah's father than with Tallulah. (On the lawn of the Bankhead home in Jasper, immediately after the wedding ceremony, Emery and Speaker Will acted out a scene or two from *Julius Caesar*, with Emery playing the lean and hungry Cassius and Speaker Will playing the noble Mark Antony. The Speaker was getting what he would have called his "whack" at acting, and it wouldn't have been lost on Tallulah and Emery that he was also preempting the bigger and better role.) Tallulah had it in mind that Emery and she would become an acting team on the order of the Lunts, and the brave intention might have been fulfilled for a year or two, in a play or two—the Lunts, in 1972, have acted together for over fifty years—if Tallulah had not made the mistake of beginning their joint career with a lavish production of *Antony and Cleopatra*. All of the big guns were brought up: settings and costumes by Jo Mielziner, music by Virgil Thomson, adaptation of the Shakespearean text by Professor Strunk of Cornell. The play failed, and the blame was placed squarely on Tallulah. Nothing in her past had prepared her for the utterance of iambic pentameters, and if Conway Tearle, who played Antony, was accused by one critic of roaring like a bull of Bashan, it may have been to compensate for Tallulah, whom Benchley reproached for her tendency "to wax unintelligible in the

Souvenir of Genesee Depot. The one on the left is an illustrious cook.

clinches, a fault shared by several of her team-mates, all of which is too bad, considering the hard work that Shakespeare must have put in on his wording." The sharpest digs came from a couple of good friends of Tallulah's. Richard Watts, Jr., said she seemed "rather more a Serpent of the Sewanee than of the Nile," and John Mason Brown said not only that "Tallulah Bankhead barged down the Nile last night as Cleopatra—and sank," but also "As the serpent of the Nile she proves to be no more dangerous than a garter snake."

Her reviews were the harshest she had ever received, and it cannot have helped their marriage that Emery, accustomed as he was to playing Shakespeare, had been at least mildly praised for his Octavius Caesar. The play closed after five performances; they were

No one hearing the honeyed voice of John Mason Brown had any reason to doubt that he was born in the South. The place was Louisville, Kentucky, and the year was 1900. He graduated from Harvard in 1923 and drifted steadily downhill from teaching into drama criticism. During the Second World War, he served on the staff of Vice Admiral Alan G. Kirk and participated in the Sicily and Normandy landings. He served as a critic on several newspapers and magazines, and his reviews were gathered up from time to time in volumes characteristically entitled *Seeing Things, Seeing More Things,* and *Still Seeing Things.* He became one of the most popular lecturers in the country, especially before women audiences, he mesmerized them and caused them simultaneously to laugh at everything he said and believe everything he said. He was one of Tallulah's staunchest admirers. He wrote of her in *Private Lives* that she was "the only volcano ever dressed by Mainbocher." He teased her without mercy for her Cleopatra, in *Antony and Cleopatra,* and she forgave him. It turned out that Shakespeare's great heroine was a passion with him; only one actress ever satisfied him in the role: "To be wanton and witty, lustful and regal, mischievous and sublime, as the part demands that Cleopatra must be, is to ask for the impossible away from the printed page. Yet Miss Cornell succeeds in being all these things to an amazing degree. One has only to remember how Cleopatra suffered in Miss Bankhead's, Miss Cowl's, and Miss Marlowe's hands to realize the extent to which she is released in Miss Cornell's." Brown died in 1969; he remained young to the end, and none of his friends was ready to let him go.

not, it seemed, to emulate the Lunts. Unsavory newlyweds, they lounged about in the Gotham, drinking and glooming and discussing their lack of prospects and their imminent lack of money. Emery was habitually without it and Tallulah was habitually persuaded that she had less of it than she actually did. She taught Emery to make his breakfast as she did of Planter's Punches, for a reason consummately Tallulah-like in its cunning and medical inaccuracy: Planter's Punches were full of fruit, fruit was full of vitamins, therefore getting drunk on Planter's Punches would improve one's health. In the spring of 1938, she played in a revival of Maugham's *The Circle,* with Grace George. The play was well received. It was also the occasion for what has become a classic specimen of theatrical blooper. Many years later, Tallulah described the episode in a taped interview with Al Morgan. Tallulah in spate: "It was opening night in New York, and there was a line in Maugham's dialogue about Mary Anderson, who had been a great beauty in England many years before, but because this was a revival, and in America, at that, we decided to make it Maxine Elliott, who had been a very, very great American beauty indeed, and in the scene in which a man was turning over the pages of a photograph album with me, he was supposed to say, 'Ah, Maxine Elliott, her beauty took your breath away,' and instead on opening night the poor actor said, 'Ah, Maxine Elliott, her breath took her beauty away,' and there was an instant of the most terrible silence, and then Grace George nearly fell off the sofa laughing, and at that moment I was supposed to say, with a perfectly straight face, of course, 'Oh, Lady Kitty,' but I couldn't bring out a thing, and the audience started laughing, and they laughed and they laughed, stopping for a while to try and get hold of themselves, as *we* were trying to get hold of *our*selves, and then starting up again, and it's a wonder we're all not still there, still laughing!"

During the summer, Tallulah and Emery toured in a play called *I Am Different,* freely adapted from the Hungarian by Zoë Akins and memorable only for having provoked another classic blooper. Glenn Anders and Tallulah were chatting backstage, just before it was time for him to go on. His cue was the sound of a gun being fired, upon which he was supposed to rush from the wings and cry "I heard a shot!" glance down at a body on the floor, examine it, and say, "It's only a flesh wound."

Anders was listening so intently to Tallulah that he was a second or two late in responding to his cue. Embarrassed, he hurled himself onto the stage and shouted, "I hear a flesh wound." Then he bent over the prostrate victim, examined him, and said, "It's only a shot." Tallulah's laughter boomed out of the wings and filled the whole theater.

In 1939, Tallulah opened in what was to be the finest role of her career—that of the venomous Regina Giddens, in *The Little Foxes*. For once, she had a role that was worthy of her and of which she was able to prove worthy. Much of the credit for her good fortune goes to Lillian Hellman, who wrote the play, and to Herman Shumlin, who directed it. Shumlin forced Tallulah, not against her will but against her usual wilfulness, to enter the role and remain without self inside it; he would not permit her to improvise responses from one moment to the next behind the surface of her always so

 easily attained mastery of the lines. He imposed on her a discipline of obedience, emotional and intellectual. It galled her, but she must have sensed that it would be the making of her, and so it proved. The play was universally acclaimed. Tallulah was in glory. Moreover, since by the terms of her contract she was to receive ten percent of the weekly gross of the play, her delusions of poverty were temporarily allayed. *The Little Foxes* played four hundred and eight performances in New York, then went on tour. By that time, Tallulah had quarreled violently over political matters with Miss Hellman and Shumlin and was no longer on speaking terms with them. Today, Miss Hellman will say of Tallulah only that she was a bore. She applied the same epithet to Tallulah thirty-odd years ago, at the height of their ill-feeling. Tallulah thereupon indignantly accused Miss Hellman of plagiarism, arguing that she, Tallulah, had called Miss Hellman a bore before Miss Hellman had called Tallulah a bore. With Tallulah, it was not often possible to reach a very high level of debate.

Eugenia Rawls was engaged to understudy the role of Alexandra Giddens, the seventeen-year-old daughter of Regina Giddens. After several weeks, she took over the role, replacing Florence Williams. She first encountered Tallulah backstage, while Tallulah was waiting to make her entrance as Regina, erect and beautiful in dark red dress, red picture hat, and red umbrella held like a rapier in her gloved hand.

"Who are you?"

"Eugenia Rawls, the new understudy."

"You look enough like me to be my own child."

True and prophetic: Tallulah came to treat Miss Rawls like a daughter, provided a wedding reception when Miss Rawls married Donald Seawell, stood up for their daughter and son when they were christened, remembered the Seawell children handsomely in her will, and asked Seawell to serve as the executor of her estate. More and more as she grew older, she would share with the Seawells the consolations of a domesticity that, though she attempted it on two or three occasions, she could never sustain for long. She had been a tyrant from birth, ruling by tantrums and sudden bouts of love, and the last thing a tyrant is fit for is to rule a household. Tallulah had chosen for herself a life that was sure to have painful passages; she could arrange, at a high cost in money and a sometimes higher cost in self-respect, never to be alone, but she could not arrange never to be lonely. In Frost's phrase, home is "something you somehow haven't to deserve," and for Tallulah in time of need the Seawells' home was, all simply and contentedly, what she hadn't to deserve.

By this time, relations between Tallulah and John Emery were at a point of détente. They had had hard times together and a few good times, and now there was scarcely any reason for them to remain married except that it might distress Speaker Will for them to be divorced. He had been so relieved to have Tallulah settle down, or seem to—to be a Mrs. Somebody at last! Besides, it was Sister who made a practice of continually getting married and divorced; Tallulah had no wish to rival her in that. Sad enough for poor Daddy that his daughters led scandalous lives; sadder still if both those lives were incoherent as well as scandalous. There was also the fact that Daddy was being spoken of as a possible candidate for the Vice-Presidency under FDR. His children owed it to him to put on, if only for the time being, a certain respectability. Emery and she would be very civilized. They would accommodate.

The first tour of *The Little Foxes* began in Washington, D.C., in February, 1940, with Speaker Will out front in a state of fatherly exaltation. Making life comfortable for Tallulah on the road was Rose Riley, a handsome, quick-witted woman, who nominally served as Tallulah's maid but who was also, like Edie, a close friend and companion. (Many years later, Rose ended by refusing any

longer to accept Tallulah's reckless abuse of a personal relation. She would not see her; instead, she would be her friend at a distance, speaking to her daily on the telephone and keeping Tallulah's account books in perfect order from a snug, well-out-of-Tallulah's-way apartment in the Bronx.) The play moved in triumph to Philadelphia, Boston, Toronto, Detroit, and Chicago. After the show one evening in Toronto, on the April day when Germany invaded Denmark and Norway, Tallulah's dressing room was full of young kilted officers of the Princess Pat Regiment. Tallulah ordered supper

With her friend, the noted jeweler and man-about-town, the Duke di Verdura.

for all, Rose Riley opened the trunk that accompanied Tallulah everywhere as a portable bar and started handing round drinks, and the officers and the cast sat on the floor and sang "The Road to the Isles" and "Sixpence" and "Bless Them All."

There were many theater people in Chicago that May. Tallulah introduced her "daughter" Eugenia to Noël Coward, Katharine Hepburn, Clifton Webb, Irene Castle, Joseph Cotten, Van Heflin, Shirley Booth, Gower Champion, and Ina Claire; Eugenia felt that the theater was living up to expectations. On May 29, when the British were obliged to evacuate Dunkirk, Tallulah vowed that she would not take another drink until they had returned to the mainland. She claimed afterwards that she had faltered from the vow only once or twice, and then for grave medical reasons.

In 1933, Katharine Hepburn won an Oscar for her performance in *Morning Glory*, a movie taken from Zoë Akins' play of the same name. The exotic photograph on the left, taken of Miss Hepburn in her *Morning Glory* glory, does not convey that she was a no-nonsense outdoor girl with reddish hair and freckles, who played a wizard game of golf and could outrun and outswim almost any man of her age. She was born in Hartford, Connecticut, in 1909. The Hepburns were dazzling outsiders in that exceptionally inward-looking community—free spirits, as much gossiped about and, in general, as much admired as another outsider, Mark Twain, had been a couple of generations earlier. Miss Akins based the leading character in *Morning Glory* on Tallulah as she remembered seeing her in her first importunate Algonquin days, pursuing and beguiling her elders and betters. This was the time when, at fashionable parties, Tallulah was doing her impersonation of Ethel Barrymore, not altogether to Miss Barrymore's pleasure; a few years later, young actresses were starting their careers with impersonations of Tallulah. Miss Hepburn, who was to win other Oscars for her roles in *Guess Who's Coming to Dinner* and *The Lion in Winter*, was a lifelong friend of Tallulah's, despite a notable difference in their characters. Miss Hepburn being all disciplined intelligence must have been appalled at Tallulah's spendthrift expenditure of energy and talent, but she remained her champion to the end.

The Little Foxes company returned to New York early in June, and Tallulah and Eugenia Rawls began rehearsing *The Second Mrs. Tanqueray*, with which Tallulah would be undertaking for the first time a round of summer theaters. The experiment turned out to be not only extremely profitable but refreshing as well. The little company, with Tallulah as the lady of the title, the distinguished British actor Colin Keith-Johnston as Tanqueray, and Eugenia as his daughter, opened in Maplewood, New Jersey, to excellent notices (even in Maplewood, a good notice pleases). Despite the grim news from abroad, the summer passed like a long, happy dream. They were driven from theater to theater in their own bus; like true strolling players, they could stop wherever they pleased, to picnic or swim or take a nap in a pasture.

Keith-Johnston liked to recite poetry as well as compose it; it became a summer for reciting and composing poems. Tallulah said that she could never utter the words "Edna St. Vincent Millay" without adding "Boom! Boom!"; so from that time forth neither could anyone else. Riding through the steepled green and white New England villages, they took turns reciting Housman's "Because I liked you better than suits a man to say" and "In summertime on Bredon" and—Tallulah's favorite —"I did not lose my heart in summer's even, When roses to the moonrise burst apart." The bus windows were open to catch the breeze, and Tallulah would stretch out along a seat with her head in Eugenia's lap and her bare legs sticking out through the window, and they would all be singing. Once, somewhere in the Berkshires, they stopped at a wayside cafe for Cokes. An old man who was sitting across the way came slowly up to Tallulah and said, "Aren't you Edna St. Vincent Millay?" Tallulah was startled, perhaps in part because the old man had failed to add "Boom! Boom!" She said to him tenderly, "No, but I am somebody *very* famous. I'll write my name on a slip of paper and after I'm gone you must open it and see. Meanwhile, my friend here, Colin Keith-Johnston, will recite a poem for you. Colin, this man is thirsting for poetry. Recite for him!" As if reciting a poem to an elderly stranger in a cafe on a summer afternoon were the most ordinary matter in the world, Keith-Johnston recited with great feeling Swinburne's "At a Month's End." As they boarded the bus, the old man came out of the cafe with the piece of paper in his hand and waved to them and called out, in a quavering voice, "Thank you, Ella Wheeler Wilcox!" It had not been a cruel joke to play on him; he had wanted Tallulah to be somebody famous, and for his sake she had wanted to be somebody whose fame was known to him.

The summer tour of *The Second Mrs. Tanqueray* ended on the last day of August, and Tallulah and Eugenia Rawls immediately started rehearsing for the national tour of *The Little Foxes*. The play was booked to travel some twenty-five thousand miles, zigzagging from coast to coast over an intricate cat's cradle of rail lines that have long since given up passenger service; in the course of the long journey, the company would be called on to play the astonishing total of eighty-seven consecutive one-night stands. The play opened in Princeton, on Saturday, September 14. Shortly before curtain-time, Tallulah received a message from Washington: Speaker Will was dying and she must come at once. The house was sold out and people were beginning to take their seats; Tallulah decided to play. After the performance, she was driven to Princeton Junction, where it had been arranged for a Washington express train to stop for her. By the time she reached the hospital in Washington, Speaker Will was dead. A state funeral was held for him in the capitol on the following Monday, after which, with the help of a police escort, Tallulah was driven to Hershey in time for her performance. As so often happens in the presence of death, the lines of the play took on new meanings. At one point, Regina says to Alexandra, "Tell your Papa that I want him to come home again, that I love him very much," and at another, "You've had a bad shock today. I know that. And you loved Papa, but you must have expected this to come someday. You knew how sick he was." Tallulah spoke the lines without flinching.

The tour was as successful as it was strenuous. Bradford, Youngstown, Akron, Wheeling, Zanesville, Dayton, and Cleveland, where Bette Davis was out front; it was rumored that she would be playing Regina in the movie version, instead of Tallulah. Fort Wayne and St. Louis, where John Emery, on tour with Gertrude Lawrence in *Skylark*, joined Tallulah and Eugenia Rawls for drinks and a movie. Decatur, Danville, Champaign, Peoria, South Bend, Joliet, and Milwaukee. In Milwaukee, some ladies in the audience started screaming "Fire! Fire!" Stepping out of her character as Regina but in Regina's sharpest voice, Tallulah hissed, "Ladies! This is ridiculous. Go back to your seats. There is no fire." She did not learn until after the show that it had indeed been an imaginary whiff of smoke that had led the ladies to panic. The ladies had gone back to their seats; the show had gone on. In Madison, a blizzard was raging, and Tallulah was told that no trains would be able to leave the city that night. Tallulah: "Put on your biggest snow-plow. If necessary, my company and I will push!" The train took off on schedule. Reaching St. Paul, they found it snowbound. Only thirteen people were in the auditorium where *The Little Foxes* was to play. Tallulah: "If they could get here, we can play!" Cedar Rapids, Davenport, Des Moines, Sioux City, Omaha, Kansas City, Wichita, Colorado Springs. Tallulah charged Eugenia with waking her in time to catch a glimpse of Pike's Peak. Having been waked, she stared at it for a moment, said, "All right," and went back to sleep. Denver, Salt Lake City, Butte, Helena, Missoula, Spokane, Seattle. Eugenia fell ill, and Tallulah sent for a doctor. Doctor: "Miss Rawls, when was your last period?" Eugenia: "Butte,

Montana." Tallulah never forgot that; twenty years later, she was still telling the story. The illness was diagnosed as exhaustion, and Tallulah set about nursing Eugenia back to health. She was invited to share Tallulah's suite at the hotel in Tacoma. Tallulah had opened her bedroom windows wide before going to bed; next day, snow lay in drifts over the carpeted floor. Tallulah called room service and ordered breakfast, then added: "And please send someone to shovel the snow." In San Francisco, Eugenia and Donald Seawell announced their engagement backstage, and on Christmas Eve Tallulah gave them an engagement party. In Hollywood, there were celebrities for the young folk to meet and be awed by. At one party in Tallulah's honor, Eugenia and Donald noted Marlene Dietrich, Gary Cooper, Cary Grant, Joan Crawford, and a dozen lesser stars. John Barrymore arrived in a cutaway and striped trousers, looking old and wasted but still handsome of profile and mocking in manner. After he had taken a few drinks, his speech became an unbroken stream of obscenities, and the room fell awkwardly silent. Tallulah—of all people, Tallulah!—undertook to save the situation. She patted Barrymore's arm affectionately and said, "Now, John, dahling! We've all heard those words. Kit Cornell used them on the radio last week."

The Little Foxes company made its way slowly back across the country and ended the tour in Philadelphia, on April 5, 1941. Eugenia and Donald were married that morning, with Tallulah acting as their matron of honor and presiding over their wedding breakfast. (She had protested vehemently beforehand that she could not afford to have fresh asparagus served along with the champagne and chicken à la king; it turned out that there was fresh asparagus.) "A beautiful service," she said to the vicar who had married the Seawells. "Was that the Henry the Eighth version of the Bible you used?" "I believe it was the King James, Miss Bankhead," the vicar replied. The last performance of *The Little Foxes* was given that evening. The orchestra played "Auld Lang Syne" and the company joined hands and sang along with the audience. They had been on the road for many months, in all weathers and under the pressure of an intolerable schedule, and Tallulah had not missed a single performance.

11

That summer, Tallulah spent six weeks in Reno, securing a divorce from Emery on the usual grounds of mental cruelty and, as a sort of reward for the carrying out of this unpleasant task, purchasing from a local circus a lion cub that she named Winston Churchill. (She kept Winston for several months, until his bites grew sizable and actionable, and then gave him to the Bronx Zoo. For as long as she had him around the house, he served as a useful straight man for Tallulah one-liners. During the course of a bridge game or dinner party, if Winston started chewing away on the leg of a table or guest, Tallulah would protest dramatically, "My God! Hasn't *any*one fed the *lion?*") In the fall, she unwisely consented to appear in a new play by Clifford Odets, called *Clash by Night.* Her fellow stars were Lee J. Cobb and Joseph Schildkraut, and the producer was Billy Rose. A tiny, ugly man,

Winston Churchill as a cub. The photo is by the novelist Carl Van Vechten.

with an ego that nothing could satisfy for long, Rose would one day die extremely rich and reviled by all, including members of his own family. In late 1941, having made a fortune running a water circus at the World's Fair of 1939, he was bent upon making his name as a producer of high-class plays on Broadway. It was certain that Tallulah and Rose would clash by day and by night, and they did, with a zest that showed them at their worst. Maney was Tallulah's press agent and friend; he was also Rose's press agent, if not friend, and was the inventor of Rose's repellent but conspicuous public image. Maney abused him in anonymous newspaper hand-outs as "the Mad Mahout," "the Bantam Barnum," "the Basement Belasco," and "the deflated midget," and Rose was grateful to pay Maney for these insults, because what mattered to him was seeing his name in print. At first glance, it seems strange that Maney did not take care to prevent a collision between two of his most prominent clients. Perhaps, though, he foresaw the collision and welcomed it, as leading to more free publicity than either they or the play deserved. Maney may even have composed on his own office typewriter the invective that the two adversaries rancorously exchanged. Tallulah called Rose "a filthy little bully," and Billy replied by asking, "How can you bully Niagara Falls?" The play deserved the bad press that it received. Wolcott Gibbs, in *The New Yorker,* called it the saddest disappointment of the season and added, "In view of the discouraging nature of the script, the acting is probably as good as can be expected, although Miss Bankhead herself certainly seems a little miscast. She is an actress of considerable range, but as the wife of a Polish laborer on Staten Island she persistently reminded me far more of a Southern belle out slumming."

A year later, Tallulah was playing Sabina in Thornton Wilder's *The Skin of Our Teeth,* along with Fredric March, Florence Eldridge, Florence Reed, E. G. Marshall, and Montgomery Clift. Sabina was to be her greatest role after Regina Giddens. According to Gibbs, she gave "what may be the most brilliant and is certainly the most versatile performance of her career," and the other reviewers were in agreement with him. When *Variety* took its annual poll of New York critics that spring, she won their vote as the best actress of the year. Trouble accompanied success—by this time,

Clifford Odets (1906-1963) found his voice as a playwright in the left-wing "protest" theater of the thirties, with *Waiting for Lefty* and *Awake and Sing.* He was later thought to have betrayed his talent by selling out to Hollywood. In fact, his talent was of a small order and he was at least as fruitful in the exercise of it in movies as he would have been on Broadway. *Clash by Night,* which Tallulah played in with Lee J. Cobb and Joseph Schildkraut, was an old-fashioned melodrama, and she was ill-advised to undertake it; all the more so because the producer was that self-aggrandizing popinjay Billy Rose (1899-1966), who spent his days in a constant, vain pursuit of prestige. Richard Maney said of him that he knew less about the drama than he did about the migrations of the Arctic tern. Towards the end of his life, Rose became known as the largest individual stockholder in American Tel & Tel; that was better than nothing. He hired many press agents, including Maney, to get his name in the papers, and by an irony it was often in the papers after his death, at no cost to him. Members of his family bickered vituperatively over the disposition not only of his fortune but also of his body, which remained for months on a shelf in a mortuary waiting to be buried.

she would scarcely have recognized success without it—and backstage at *The Skin of Our Teeth* tempers were as vexed as they had been at *The Little Foxes*. Tallulah quarreled with the director, Elia Kazan, and with the producer, Michael Myerberg, who appears to have raised a knack for disagreeableness into a principle: he held that the more miserable actors were made to feel, the better the work they did. He treated Tallulah so harshly that for the first time in her life some of her fellow-actors expressed sympathy for her. She developed ulcers and was often in severe pain and yet managed to give over two hundred consecutive performances. As soon as her contract was up, she quit the show.

Her greatest satisfaction in this period came from a country place she had bought in Bedford Village, New York, slightly over an hour and a half's drive from town. The property consisted of an ample white brick house and some seventeen acres of rolling fields and woods. Tallulah named the property "Windows," in honor of the remarkable number of windows the house possessed, planted thousands of daffodils and other flowers, multiplied the number of her pets, and built a swimming pool that ended by costing more than the house. There were five fireplaces at "Windows," and she liked to keep a fire blazing in one or another of them, especially in her bedroom. Fires to her were "Sunset," back in Jasper, and Farm Street, in London, warmth that had little to do with heat or cold. Soon, she found herself running what amounted to an everlasting house party on a scale that was often both lavish and skimpy, since servants came and went, guests came and went, Tallulah herself came and went, and one never knew from one moment to the next how much food and drink would be available. Potluck at "Windows" was no metaphor; meals ranged from *cordon bleu* to cornflakes. Tallulah was never at ease before a stove. Someone had told her once that if a vegetable grew above ground it should be fried, and if it grew below ground it should be boiled. That was all very well, provided one knew certain things—for example, whether a potato grew above ground or below. Tallulah did not and was obliged to omit potatoes from her menus. One day, attempting to make an omelet, she dropped an egg on the floor. "Oh, God!" she exclaimed in horror. "I've killed it!"

Tallulah's unfailing and, on occasion, insistent hospitality struck many people as a sign of her being not generous but selfish. The truth was less simple than that. If her generosity sprang in part from certain desperate and unfulfillable personal needs, it sprang also from a tradition, common enough in the South and unknown to most of her Northern friends, of keeping open house as a pleasant social obligation. "Southern hospitality" is a cliché because it is a fact, like Yankee dourness. Tallulah would have remembered that in Jasper, though "Sunset" might be packed from cellar to attic with people, room could always be found for one or two more guests—distant relatives down on their luck, a near-stranger on his way through town and in want of a night's lodging. Moreover, every Southern family had its favorite story about someone who, invited to spend a week, had remained for a year, or five years, or a lifetime. In the plantation country from which the Bankheads came, slaves had lightened the burden of dispensing this exceptional hospitality. Tallulah had been raised among vestiges of the old dispensation: as a bride, her Great-grandmother McAuley, who lived on at "Sunset" until Tallulah was thirteen, had brought with her into Alabama long before the

Civil War half a dozen of her own slaves, and some of the help at "Sunset" were descended from them. Hospitality requires planning and discipline; Aunt Louise had always kept a firm grip on household affairs at "Sunset," and when the number of guests in the dining room increased, so did the number of help in the kitchen. At "Windows," discipline was unheard of; nobody was formally in charge of the household, and when the number of guests in the dining room increased, such help as there was would be likely to move in from the kitchen to join them.

As for vegetables, "just chives for the vichyssoise and mint for the juleps."

Throughout much of this period, Tallulah's immediate "family" consisted of Edie Smith, Rose Riley, Dola Cavendish—a wealthy, unmarried Canadian woman, who chain-smoked and drank neat gin and followed Tallulah about like a bigger than ordinary pet—and the incumbent caddy, whoever he might be. Estelle Winwood, protector in the Algonquin days and staunchest of all her friends, spent upwards of two years at "Windows." It was important that the entourage be big enough to guarantee four for bridge; ideally, it would also be diverse enough in its habits, as between "night" people and "day" people, so Tallulah could be kept company all round the clock. The ordinary problems of country living—shopping, meeting trains, and the like—were in the hands of a stalwart and resourceful chauffeur, Robert Williams. A couple from North Carolina, Lillian and Sylvester Oglesby, came to preside over the kitchen. The Canadian artist Charles Redfern was visiting "Windows" on the day that Tallulah was interviewing Sylvester in regard to the job, and he subsequently wrote a letter to Tallulah from abroad; in it, his mimicry of her is to the life: "I picture you every day at 'Windows' and often wonder how Sylvester the butler worked out. That interview I'll never forget. It began with his asking what the hours would be, and your reply (and this is considerably shortened) was, 'Well, darling, I live a very quiet life in the country and I can't say it's any different from any other country place, except that people do come and go and never get up early so that part of the day, darling, isn't difficult. What are you drinking, bourbon? Dinner is different, naturally we do sit down unless of course the Giants are playing and no one can move if there's a game on but it never lasts forever and we're never more than six for dinner because you see my table is oval and won't seat any more unless of course we have a buffet which is generally on Sunday and then any number of people can eat which, of course, they never do if it's hot because the pool is cooler d'you know, darling, and if supper is cold it doesn't matter anyway and I have a bird that says who are you and laughs just like me and Gaylord my parakeet who drinks champagne, don't you, darling, and I like a hot bath in the morning around three in the afternoon and breakfast on a tray, does your wife know how to make vichyssoise?' "

Tallulah starred in three movies during the nineteen-forties. The first, *Stage Door Canteen*, was a stitched-together "here comes everybody" sort of picture, which Tallulah and many other prominent actors and actresses—among them, the Lunts, Ina Claire, Judith Anderson, Cornelia Otis Skinner, Ethel Waters, Katharine Hepburn, Gertrude Lawrence, Jane Cowl, Gypsy Rose Lee, and Paul Muni—made as a contribution to the so-called war effort. The Second World War was raging, and Tallulah was characteristically eager to do her share in achieving victory. In imagination, she saw herself standing beside Churchill and Roosevelt, and in fact she often did stand beside Mrs. Roosevelt, with whom she helped raise funds for the United Services Organization. This was a time of continual personal appearances not only at service canteens but also at Army and Navy bases and in hospitals, where she visited wounded soldiers and found that her gift for raillery and foul language helped bring her into close touch with GI's. The second movie was *Lifeboat*, directed by Alfred Hitchcock. Tallulah and Hitchcock had long admired each other; she trusted his skill above that of anyone else in Hollywood and she was grateful for the seventy-five-thousand-dollar stipend he offered her. During the course of shooting *Lifeboat*, she twice came down with pneumonia, and no wonder: the setting was supposed to be an open boat somewhere at sea, but the movie was made in a Hollywood studio, with process shots that provided a grim ocean background and with tons of real water sloshing about in the tank that held the boat. From time to time, the characters in the boat were given a realistic drenching; Tallulah soaking wet in a mink coat sat chilled and yet burning under the studio lights, and she ended the picture with a temperature of one hundred and four. It was the most interesting performance of her movie career and it won for her the New York Film Critics Award as the best actress of the year. It also led to her making a movie called *A Royal Scandal*, of which Ernst Lubitsch was the producer and Otto Preminger the director. A farce about Catherine the Great, the movie received mixed reviews and was a failure at the box office. According to Tallulah, Lubitsch called her Catherine the greatest comedy performance he had ever seen on film. That was a consolation, and so was the one hundred and twenty-five thousand dollars she was paid to make the picture.

In 1945, Tallulah returned to Broadway in Philip Barry's *Foolish Notion*. The cast included Donald Cook, Aubrey Mather, Mildred Dunnock, and Henry Hull, with whom Tallulah had acted in *Lifeboat* and, twenty-four years earlier, in *Everyday*. Barry ought to have been the ideal playwright

Frank Sullivan, who has been writing funny pieces for *The New Yorker* for over forty years, and the late Sherman Billingsley, proprietor of the Stork Club, in a picture taken around 1940. During the thirties and forties, the Stork, as it was always called, was the most important nightclub in New York; to be barred from it was, for members of the cafe society of that period, like death. The building that the Stork Club occupied, on East Fifty-third Street, just off Fifth Avenue, was pulled down long ago and Paley Park, with its waterfall and dappled trees, stands in its place. Tallulah and Sullivan were often drinking companions at the Stork. In the well-known poem of Christmas greetings that Sullivan writes every year for *The New Yorker* and that many prominent New Yorkers have hungered all their lives to be mentioned in, he saluted Tallulah three times. In 1948 (an election year), he wrote:

And myrrh and mink and plenty of moola
For that sterling Democrat Tallulah.

In 1952, when she was making a hit on the radio show called "The Big Show," he wrote:

And a holiday hoot from me to you,
My radioactive friend Tallu!

Finally, in 1962, enchanted with the rhyming possibilities of the names, he wrote:

Hail to the Congo's Cyrille Adoula;
Ahoy to our rowdy pal Tallulah.

for Tallulah. They had minds similar in acuteness and irony; above all, they possessed style and they liked to move about among stylish people. "Windows" was a Barry setting; Edie, Dola, Robert Williams, and Sylvester Oglesby were Barry characters. Tallulah's "I've had six juleps and I'm not even sober" is a line worthy of Barry, and so is her "We've just been reminiscing about the future." It turned out on the road that Barry was unable to master some of the difficulties inherent in the plot of *Foolish Notion*. Nevertheless, the play was well received by out-of-town reviewers. Elinor Hughes, in the Boston *Herald*, wrote of Barry, "He has written a witty and engaging fable about a group of amusing people facing a situation one way in their minds and another way in actuality. . . . The audience had a wonderful time." In an interview with Miss Hughes, Tallulah took a more skeptical view: "No play that's really good is ever easy, even after it's been running a long time, and we're pretty new to this one. Barry is working continually on that last scene, which is quite a problem. . . . I'm glad that audiences here like it—I just hope they don't expect too much of us in New York."

Whether too much was expected or not, the play was a critical failure and a mildly popular success. Gibbs began his review, "In *Foolish Notion*, Philip Barry has what must have looked like a fine idea for a play, the services of Tallulah Bankhead, and a very handsome production by the

With Henry Hull and Donald Cook in *Foolish Notion*. Note the Cook moue.

Theatre Guild. He has, in fact, just about everything except that continuity of mood necessary to transmit an author's emotions to the spectators." For Tallulah, Gibbs had his usual praise: "Miss Bankhead gives another example of her rare accomplishments as an actress. . . . I'm afraid that she isn't quite enough to save Mr. Barry's play from its fundamental shapelessness, but I can't think of anybody who could have made a better try at it." The play gave a hundred and four performances at the Martin Beck, and Tallulah subsequently took it on tour.

Finding no suitable play to hand, Tallulah turned next to a revival of *Private Lives*. It was then generally believed among producers that Coward's comedy—first seen in New York in 1931, with Gertrude Lawrence and Coward playing the leads—was too dated to risk bringing back to Broadway. Tallulah took it on tour, with Donald Cook as her leading man, drinking companion, and, for a time, lover. The tour was an unexpected financial if not aesthetic triumph. After a few months, Tallulah gave it up to play the sad queen-heroine of Jean Cocteau's *The Eagle Has Two Heads*, produced and directed by her friend John C. Wilson. Out of town, her leading man was a young actor named Marlon Brando, who had yet to make his name in the world. It appears that Brando did not much enjoy his role as the queen's lover and assassin. Maney writes with indignation about this early Brando in his autobiography, *Fanfare*, and the passage is worth quoting at length as a specimen of the cranky Maney prose style:

I first encountered this fakir [Brando] when John C. Wilson engaged him to shoot Tallulah Bankhead in *The Eagle Has Two Heads*. In this Cocteau charade Miss Bank-

Wolcott Gibbs, who was born in 1902 and died in 1958, spent almost all of his professional career on the staff of *The New Yorker*. He worked behind the scenes as an editor, quickly and coolly ("This manuscript," he would say, "will cut like butter"), and for years he contributed anonymously to the Notes and Comment section of "The Talk of the Town." He also wrote Profiles, short stories, verse, and a number of hilarious parodies of Hemingway, Aldous Huxley, Maxwell Anderson, and other prominent literary figures of the day. He succeeded Benchley as drama critic of the magazine, and after a certain preliminary unease about dealing with Shakespeare—he wrote of a production of *Hamlet* that it was a good thing to take the children to on a rainy afternoon—he became a superb judge of plays and acting. He liked musical comedies and was always easy on them. Tallulah was a favorite of his among actresses; he was a shy man and often a panic-stricken one, and he admired Tallulah for the courage with which she sailed, head high, through terrible plays. She wrote in her autobiography that she once tried to repay him for his many tributes to her by visiting him when he lay bedridden at Lenox Hill Hospital. "Eager to divert him, I put on a one-woman show designed to kill or cure," she wrote. "The nurses swore it was the most exciting vaudeville ever seen on the floor." A modest compliment; the likelihood is that she was far from sober and that Gibbs was mortified—there was nothing he enjoyed less than being made to feel conspicuous. Gibbs spent his summers on Fire Island, where he liked to lie on the beach with a shaker of ice-cold martinis buried up to its neck in the sand. He died there, cigarette in hand, reading a newly arrived advance copy of one of his books—not the worst death in the world for a writer.

head was Queen of a Graustarkian country. On the curtain's rise she was mourning her mate, victim of an assassin's bullet fifteen years earlier. Into her chamber burst Stanislas (that's Brando), a loutish revolutionary hell-bent on doing her in. In a thirty-minute monologue, the Queen undertook to dissuade the hothead. Come to slay, Stanislas remained to love. But the Queen brushed off his advances. Crazed by her taunts, Stanislas shot the Queen, then drained a lethal cup.

The conduct of Mr. Brando on our arrival in Wilmington, where the conundrum was trying out, was off-beat. The company manager invited Brando to share his cab to the Du Pont Hotel. Marlon declined. He needed a cab to himself. He was going to ride about for an hour, practicing on his African drums.

Throughout the rehearsals, Wilson had interpreted Marlon's trancelike conduct as a manifestation of genius. He hesitated to correct him lest he upset his mood. That night Wilson's mood was addled while watching Brando during Tallulah's soliloquy.

He squirmed. He picked his nose. He adjusted his fly. He leered at the audience. He cased the furniture. He fixed his gaze on an offstage property man instead of his opponent. But these didos were nothing compared with his surprise finish. On cue he plugged the Queen and watched her pitch headlong down the stairway. Then, in defiance of Cocteau, Wilson, and Equity's Board of Governors, he refused to die. Instead he staggered about the stage, seeking a likely spot for his final throe.

The audience was in convulsions. Spread-eagled on the stairway, head down, Miss Bankhead was having a few convulsions of her own. Why wouldn't this misbegotten clown cash in his chips? Marlon had been mooning about for a full minute on the apron when suddenly he collapsed as if spiked by an invisible ray. The curtain came down with the audience in hysterics. If Tallulah could have gotten her hands on a gun, the coroner would have had a customer then and there.

Brando was dropped during the run in Boston, evidently to his relief, and his place taken by Helmut Dantine. Tallulah's opening speech in the play is said to be the longest soliloquy ever written. According to Maney, it took her thirty minutes to deliver it in Wilmington. In Boston, it was clocked at twenty-two minutes, and on its opening in New York it was down to seventeen minutes. To hold an audience with an uninterrupted speech of that length, and at the very start of the play, was a remarkable feat of acting; not content with this, Tallulah added a scarcely less remarkable feat of acrobatics. At the moment the Queen was shot, she was standing at the top of a long flight of stairs, and John Lardner was prompted in his review of the play to speak of her performance in sporting terms: "Miss Bankhead spared herself nothing on opening night at the Plymouth. In a plunge that I would hesitate to make with football pads on, she toppled headfirst, majestically and in a pure line, down several stairs. She was fresh as a daisy, however, for her curtain calls, which were up to the standards of the Bankhead public." Donald Oenslager, who designed the set, recalls the gesture as characteristically brave and extreme. "I took care to put a lot of padding under the carpet on those stairs," he has said, "but who except Tallulah would have taken such chances, and not once but night after night?"

Twenty-nine nights in all, for *The Eagle Has Two Heads* found few admirers, and Tallulah returned to what amounted by then to the homely comfort and unprecedented financial rewards of *Private Lives*. It was as if the world were eager to have her go on playing Amanda Prynne forever; no matter how she distorted the role through boredom or irritation or some passing impulse of

mockery, as far as her audiences were concerned the play belonged not to Coward but to her, and she could do whatever she pleased with it. At forty-five, she was far too old for the part; nobody seemed to notice. She could play Amanda at fifty, at sixty, at seventy. Her little company opened in Chicago, anticipating a moderate run; it played to full houses for seven months. By the time the tour ended, on the West Coast, a year and a half had gone by and the company had grossed well over a million dollars; Tallulah herself had been making something like five thousand dollars a week, and try as she would she could no longer speak convincingly of being poor. She brought the play to Broadway in October, 1948, and it is plain that she had the reviewers stumped; they didn't approve of what she had done to the play, and yet they found her irresistible. Gibbs wrote, "As a man who had considered *Private Lives* a polite comedy and a good one, I was a bit disconcerted at first to find that its star was under the impression that it was vaudeville and that the best way to play it was to give what looked like a rather damaging impersonation of herself, perhaps as Sabina in *The Skin of Our Teeth*. Nevertheless, her performance grew on me, and by the time she was roaring her way through the second act, I was helplessly fascinated, though not, I'm afraid, in precisely the way intended by Mr. Coward, who has seldom taken a worse beating. On the whole, I'm inclined to think that Miss Lawrence was a better—or, anyway, a more rational —Amanda but that Miss Bankhead is a funnier one, and also, in a sense, an acute critic of the author's talent, which she clearly demonstrated to be very delicately balanced on the edge of absurdity.''

A decidedly tacky view of *Private Lives*. Even the fruit has begun to look its age.

Private Lives ran for seven months in New York. In the course of the run, there were several pleasing indications of the increased breadth and height of Tallulah's fame. In October, during the presidential election campaign, she introduced President Truman to a nationwide audience from her dressing room in the Plymouth Theatre. The address was sponsored by the International Ladies Garment Workers Union, and Tallulah—no doubt with Maney's covert assistance—offered a stinging critique of the Republican candidate, Governor Dewey. The critique began, of course, on a personal note: "There were Alabama Bankheads in one or another of the houses of Congress for sixty consecutive years. My father was Speaker of the House for four years, served with that body for twenty-five. My grandfather, John, sat in the Senate for thirteen years. My Uncle John spent twelve years of his life in the Upper House. They all died in harness. I would be outraging their memories, I would be faithless to Alabama, did I not vote for Harry S. Truman. Yes, I'm for Harry Truman, the human being. By the same token, I'm against Thomas E. Dewey, the mechanical man." Ten days later, Truman was giving a campaign speech at Madison Square Garden. Tallulah was invited to say a few words after the President had finished his address. She spoke for three minutes, and the President and an audience of twenty thousand people gave her a big hand. Truman was expected to lose the election, and Tallulah was always vehemently for the underdog. When Truman won, he remembered to send Tallulah a pair of tickets to the inaugural ceremonies.

It was also a proof of fame, though scarcely on the same level with becoming the valiant political comrade-in-arms of a President, when a singing commercial dared to take advantage of her name, and Tallulah sued Procter and Gamble, NBC, CBS, and Benton and Bowles for a million dollars. The commercial celebrated the supposed virtues of a shampoo called Prell:

> I'm Tallulah, the tube of Prell,
> And I've got a little something to tell.
> Your hair can be radiant, oh, so easy.
> All you've got to do is take me home and squeeze me.
>
> I'm Tallulah, the tube of Prell,
> And I'll make your hair look swell,
> I'll shine, it'll glow so radiantly,
> For radiant hair, get a hold of me—
> Tallulah, the tube of Prell Shampoo.

It was a far from admirable sample of the singing-commercial-maker's art—Tallulah, with her love of Housman and elegant rhymes, might well have taken offense at the rhyming of "easy" and "squeeze me"—but even if the commercial had had a certain charm, Tallulah would have felt humiliated by it; she took seriously the value of both of her names, and the suit was no prank. "This is not a publicity stunt," she told a reporter. "For two months, I tried to settle the matter out of court. I have never allowed my name to be attached to anything, from soap to spinach. Suddenly I find it attached to this damn shampoo. I didn't like my name when I was young, but I do now, and I consider it highly objectionable of Prell to try and profit from it in this way. When I was in school, everyone else was always named Virginia. I came to New York and met Ethel Barrymore and she urged me to change my name to something simple, like Mary. My God, *Mary*! Of course it turned out that she hated the name Ethel. By that time, I wouldn't have changed my name for anything, though I did think of shortening it, so it wouldn't be too long for the electric lights on theater marquees. I hadn't even got my first part, baby, and already I was worrying about those electric lights!"

Tallulah settled the suit out of court. The jingle was silenced and she collected five thousand dollars in damages.

12

She had gained, or it seemed that she had gained, a sort of equilibrium. She drank and shouted and quarreled and took lovers who, in comparison with her own increasing age, looked to the world's eyes ever younger and less fitting, and the lovers themselves would escape into other relationships after affairs with Tallulah that were of shorter and shorter duration, but she had become that long-dreamed-of and struggled-for thing, a somebody universally recognized simply because she existed. The price had been high but no higher than what everybody else had been obliged to pay—it would have been too high only if she had failed. It was demonstrably the case that tens of thousands of people throughout the country considered her a sight worth traveling many miles to see. She could earn a torrential income as an actress, and it appeared that she could earn an even larger income from merely being herself. She had emerged as a public figure suitable for magnification by all the media,

A "Big Show" broadcast—Ginger Rogers, Tallu, Lucienne Boyer, Margaret Truman.

as they were then starting to be called—newspapers, magazines, radio, TV, the lecture circuit. It was tempting to avoid the labor of getting up a part, of becoming a gratuitous other; tempting to remove oneself from the arduousness of the actor's life, where one was always at the mercy of other people's failing to do their jobs (a playwright hemorrhaging as he tries in panic to revise the last act, a designer building his sets a few inches too large for the out-of-town stages, a director falling in love with the juvenile lead). Tallulah had been encouraged to turn *Private Lives* into a

76

Richard Maney (1892-1968) was a plump, dusty-haired, self-educated Irish Catholic from Chinook, Montana, who became the most successful theatrical press agent of his time. His specialties were a prose so ornate that pigeons could have nested in it and a willingness, drunk or sober, to treat his clients with surly contempt. He said of one of the plays he publicized that it flew shut like a door, and when a neophyte producer asked him what would be proper to wear on opening night—black tie or white?—Maney suggested a track suit. Like W. C. Fields, he had a genius for making innocent words sound obscene; his friend Wolcott Gibbs called him the master of the disinfected epithet. Once, on a night out in Harlem, Maney and his taxi driver got lost; Maney stumbled out of the cab and addressed a passerby. "Tell me, my wily Corsican—" he began, with his usual snarl. The passerby flattened him. Maney represented Tallulah for a quarter of a century. They drank together and insulted each other and remained devoted friends. Maney ghostwrote Tallulah's autobiography; on his death, she wrote a brief, touching obituary for the *Times*, remembering his blue eyes

circus, but she wondered if it would not be more honorable—and far less bother—to stop twisting roles out of shape and exploit oneself in one's own person. She had the two ways to choose between, one of them prudent and the other reckless, and for a time she hung fire, hoping that the decision would be made for her by somebody else.

In 1950, NBC radio was attempting to counteract the first substantial financial inroads of television by putting on the most lavish radio show in history—a Sunday evening extravaganza, running from six to seven-thirty and called, with what amounted under the circumstances to modesty, "The Big Show." The budget for the show was reputed to be fifty thousand dollars a week. Tallulah was invited to serve as mistress of ceremonies, at a salary of five thousand dollars a week, and she accepted. During rehearsals of the show, she felt so terrified that she assumed, as she had often done before, a mask of not caring; she mumbled her lines and made bad jokes and ignored instructions and badgered the producers of the show with trivial, despairing inquiries. The stars of the opening show were Jimmy Durante, Fred Allen, Portland Hoffa, Danny Thomas, Ethel Merman, Russell Nype, Paul Lukas, Mindy Carson, Jose Ferrer, and Frankie Laine. A forty-four-piece orchestra and a choral group of sixteen were under the direction of Meredith Willson, who also provided a theme song—"May the Good Lord Bless and Keep You." The writers of the "material" for the show were among the best in the trade (Goodman Ace, Selma Diamond, Frank Wilson, Mort Green, and George Foster), and the producer-director was Dee Engelbach. The first show succeeded beyond anyone's expectations. The reviews were all raves. John Crosby wrote, "The opening program of 'The Big Show,' presided over and more or less blanketed by that extraordinarily vibrant lady known as Tallu, was one of the fastest and funniest ninety minutes in my memory," and *Variety*, in its clotted shorthand, said of Tallulah, "Miss Bankhead's give-and-take in her overall conferenciering, her froggy vocalistics, her crossfire with La Merman in a distaff Hope-Crosby routine, and her bantering with the Schnoz, added up to one of the show's surprises. Stacked up against the best in radio talent, it's a tribute to Tallu that she pulled into the stretch maintaining the same fast clip. . . . NBC can take a bow for perpetuating bigtime radio. They don't come any bigger than this one and it rates Nielsen's best."

"The Big Show" became, for a time, the most-talked-about entertainment in the country. Something like thirty million people were reputed to listen to it every week. Among the celebrities with whom Tallulah bantered and displayed her froggy vocalistics were Groucho Marx,

Dr. Ralph Bunche, Gary Cooper, Bob Hope, Gloria Swanson, Marlene Dietrich, Louis Armstrong, Edith Piaf, Jan Peerce, and Lauritz Melchior. Her old friend Ethel Barrymore appeared, first reciting a poem by John Masefield and then briskly pitching into what had become the show's formula of exchanged insults, in this case with Tallulah serving as Miss Barrymore's willing victim. A transcription of a portion of their dialogue gives a fair impression of the show as a whole:

TALLULAH (following the poem): Bravo! Bravo! Ethel, dahling, I'm at a loss for words.

ETHEL: I've been wondering when you'd run out. [Laughter] And for goodness' sake, Tallulah, pull up your stockings!

TALLULAH: Oh, Ethel, please! Don't talk like that! I'm grown up now. I'm not the fourteen-year-old child you knew when I first came to Broadway.

ETHEL: I always remember you as that fourteen-year-old child. No other living actress can make that statement. [Laughter]

TALLULAH [with throaty laugh]: Now, Ethel, dahling, I'm trying to maintain some dignity here. After all, I am in charge of the biggest show in radio!

ETHEL: This mishmash is the greatest show in radio? [Laughter]

TALLULAH: Well, it's the only . . . half an hour . . . hour and a half, I mean. Excuse me, Bing! [she laughs] . . . hour and a half program on the air. Every Sunday I appear on this show for one hour and thirty minutes from start to finish!

ETHEL: You've changed, Tallulah. I never knew you to finish anything in an hour and thirty minutes, unless poss—possibly a man or two. [Laughter] What exactly do you do here, aside from smirking at your friends in the audience and violating every cardinal principle of theater deportment?

TALLULAH: Well, Ethel, this is not the theater you brought me up in, dahling. There is no barrier here between the audience and the performer, y'see?

ETHEL: Ho! You always lived dangerously. [Laughter]

The show ran for the better part of two years, before succumbing to TV, high costs, and its own rigidities. Among the hazards of self-exploitation is an inevitable loss of freshness. A man grows over-familiar with his faults when they become the goods he traffics in; quickly he discovers how to display them to the best advantage. The more unconfessable they would be under ordinary circumstances, the better they will please. The audience grows jaded before it is sated; defects of character lightly enough touched on at first must be more and more recklessly gouged out and disclosed as the difficulty of arousing shock and pleasure increases. The self-exploiter perceives that he must daily become more drunken, lustful, narcissistic, miserly, and foul-mouthed than he actually is. Soon, having no new faults to confess, he is on his knees begging the audience to laugh at him for faults he doesn't possess. The burden of inventing vices becomes a welcome necessity;

Her godson, Brockman Seawell, in
A Midsummer Night's Dream.

perhaps it will help him score a hit. In the end, there is no abasement that a performer is not willing to risk and no abasement low enough to satisfy his audience.

The disagreeable fate of the self-exploiter faced Tallulah from the moment she undertook to star in "The Big Show." It was a fate that had been awaiting her from the cradle, and she knew it. She had always feared that some day she would be weak enough to strike that hard bargain with the devil of fame; by ill luck it happened that the rewards of self-exploitation became greater in the nineteen-fifties and -sixties than they had ever been, and by further ill luck, the increased rewards coincided with Tallulah's slow march into late middle age and the loss of beauty and a diminished strength. Having taken the wrong turn towards a profitable self-mockery, she was intelligent enough to see her plight and try to regain lost ground. In 1954, she returned to Broadway in *Dear Charles,* of which Walter Kerr wrote, *"Dear Charles,* the new showpiece at the Morosco, has had something less than a checkered career in this country. Written quite a few years ago by an American, it failed. Rewritten into French, retranslated into English, and reopened on the road here last season, it failed. The moral for this morning seems to be: if at first you don't succeed, try Tallulah." John Chapman in the *News* said, "Miss Bankhead is a thoroughly expert comedienne; she and Bert Lahr are the two best muggers in show business, and she wears prettier clothes." Robert Coleman wrote of her in the *Mirror* that she acted "with devastating authority. Her performance reminds one of a Heifetz or a Horowitz bestowing his genius on a pop trifle. We can only regret that our Tallulah didn't return to us in something more worthy of her talents." The regret expressed by Coleman was a familiar one; reviewers had begun to utter it when Tallulah was twenty and appearing in her second or third play. *Dear Charles* was indeed a trifle, and without her it would have been nothing. She carried it in New York for a hundred and fifty-four performances. A couple of seasons later, her friend Jean Dalrymple, of the City Center, in New York, persuaded her to undertake a revival of Tennessee Williams' *A Streetcar Named Desire.* Here was a real play, of the sort that she claimed to be always looking for in vain. There were many reasons for her to play in *Streetcar* before she grew too old to seem a credible Blanche DuBois; one of them was that Williams had written the play with her in mind—in the course of setting it down, he said once, he heard her voice speaking every line that he put into Blanche's mouth. Irene Selznick, who had presided over the original production of *Streetcar,* in 1947, had argued that Tallulah was too strong to play the wavering, moonstruck, vulnerable Blanche, and the role had gone to Jessica Tandy.

It was arranged that Tallulah would play in *Streetcar* at the Coconut Grove Playhouse, in Miami, for four weeks, then play in it at the City Center for a limited engagement of two weeks. She worked exceptionally hard during rehearsals, and they were not made easier by Williams' presence. It had been expected of them that they would become close friends because they had so much in common; on the contrary, because they had so much in common they became rivals for the

Tennessee Williams was born Thomas Lanier Williams, in 1911. His preoccupation with the South early embraced Tallulah, and it is possible that his adoption of a romantic new first name was prompted in part by the attractive strangeness of hers. He has said that she was in his thoughts when he was writing *Battle of Angels, A Streetcar Named Desire* and, later, when he was writing *Sweet Bird of Youth* and *The Milk Train Doesn't Stop Here Anymore*. The real Tallulah was scarcely more like the Williams characters she helped inspire than the real South was like the South of Williams' imagination; he was brought up in Missouri, but he brought himself up in a Deep South that existed largely in his mind, as a domain Gothic in its contours, cannibalistic in its appetites. Williams saw Tallulah as a doomed creature, violent and forlorn, and she was not like that. It was characteristic of her—and a proof of how little she had in common with Williams' image of her—that she was eager to play his miserable heroines, not caring a straw that the public would be sure to identify her with them. Williams said of Tallulah that she was the strongest of all the hurt people he had known.

attention and affection of others. People were given to understand that they must choose between the two curiously named Southerners. One took sides as if in a border dispute, though the country being quarreled over existed only in the imaginations of the protagonists and no one, perhaps not even they, knew where any of the boundaries lay. In many respects, Tallulah's relationship with Williams resembled her relationship with Sister. Their likeness to each other, instead of drawing them together, set them just far enough apart to make it certain that when they moved they chafed each other; sooner or later, they would draw blood. Tallulah was in desperate need of reassurance in her playing of Blanche, and nobody ought to have been able to give her that reassurance better than the creator of the role; instead, at night in the big house that had been lent to her for the month and in which she was living with her usual army of actors, friends, and hangers-on, they would sit flicking each other with maudlin cruelties about their sexual natures and the nature of their talents and fame.

On opening night, Tallulah did her best to dissemble her celebrity inside the troubled presence of Blanche, but an audience sprinkled with worshipful young men refused to accept what amounted for them to an abdication; they had come to see the Tallulah of Vegas nightclubs and rowdy summer stock, the Tallulah of the stunning wisecrack (Earl Wilson: "Have you ever been mistaken for a man on the telephone?" Tallulah: "No, have you?"), and the Tallulah of the innumerable caddies, and they would not be fobbed off with accomplished acting. Alert savages, they waited to interrupt with laughter and applause the heavy emphases and mannerisms that were now as natural to her as breathing. The play did not exist for this coterie, and neither did her valiant embodiment of Blanche. After the last curtain-call, Tallulah, crushed and bewildered, pleaded to know what she had done wrong. For the rest of the engagement, she labored to eliminate from her interpretation of the role every applaudable glimpse of her familiar self. The labor was in vain—on opening night in New York, the mindless interruptions of Miami were repeated. In *The New Yorker*, Gibbs hints at strange conduct but refrains from identifying the culprits. One of the handicaps she has faced and been unable to overcome in the role, he says, is her "reputation for unusual vivacity in private life. On opening night, sustained and imbecile laughter greeted every line that could conceivably be taken as a reference to the star's career outside the theater. While this had no visible effect on her composure, which is, of course, a legend of our era, it relentlessly destroyed, time after time, whatever mood she was struggling to create. There is, I suppose, no cure for this kind of vulgarity and stupidity in an audience, except possibly the brisk employment of a machine gun. I would have been delighted, and not especially surprised, if Miss Bankhead had had recourse to just that."

The group that prompted murderous thoughts in Gibbs, a man whose only known violence consisted of jingling change in his trouser pockets, was but a portion of a large cult of young male Tallulah followers. The cult, which surprisingly continues to gain in number (though to become less young: Tallulah herself would have been seventy this year), was an extension of her system of caddies. Many of these satellite caddies had met Tallulah in person once or twice, or had been introduced to her over the long-distance telephone by an intermediate caddy. A complex network of Tallulah communicants stretched from coast to coast; some of them were disk jockeys and announcers in radio and TV stations, and one or another of them could be counted on to provide companionship for Tallulah by telephone at any hour of the night or day. They gossiped with her and jollied her and helped make the grimmer reaches of her increasing insomnia bearable. They cherished her malapropisms ("Don't talk to me! I've got laryngitis!") and made them the common coin of their conversations about her. They were her champions and they were proud to render her many humble services. They collected newspaper and magazine interviews with her and they became authorities on her notices: Brooks Atkinson had said this of her, Elliot Norton had said that. Because her success mattered to them, they took care to be modest and attentive members of her audience; they were "family," silently urging the house to hush itself as the curtain went up and, if a neighbor threatened to cough, pressing a mint on him. There would be time enough later backstage in the smoky clutter of her dressing room, with Rose Riley manning the trunk-bar, to express their admiration. They were far from being mere descendants in the male line of the shrieking gallery girls of her London days; they were her friends. But the small, noisy portion of the cult had different needs and different intentions. When they interrupted her performances with campy clamor, it was obvious that they were malicious as well as approving. If they worshipped Tallulah, they also despised her. A reviewer for *Cue* said of their behavior at *Streetcar* that they had come hoping to see a travesty of the play, and "despite Miss Bankhead's sturdy refusal to commit one, they applauded, as though by their actions they could call one into being." They had demands to make on her and little enough to give back. For them she was an ideal scapegoat—the renegade and image-breaker and chance-taker who was at first to be

Eugenia Bankhead, that indefatigable partygoer, at a gay occasion in 1969.

made much of and then punished in their behalf. They would egg her on and wait to see the first blood fall. What they required of her was that she be brave enough to lead them in their mockery of the world and then be brave enough to die because she was a woman.

81

13 By now, she had sold "Windows." Much as she loved it, the difficulty of maintaining it became too much for her. It wasn't a question of money—despite her habitual protestations of poverty, the stock market was making her a millionaire—but of incompetence. She could no more run a house than she could drive a car. Trained servants were unable to accommodate themselves to the spiraling topsy-turviness of Tallulah's domestic ways; either they quit, or they forgot their training and were no longer servants. Tallulah "dahling'd" them and had them constantly with her at table and beside the pool. A reporter who had been invited to lunch at "Windows" was mildly surprised when the cook came in along with the dessert, pulled up a chair, sat down beside him, and poured him and herself a sizable shot of brandy. "Very smooth," said the cook, rolling the brandy under her tongue.

The theory was that Tallulah would simplify her life. Moving in from the country, she purchased a handsome four-story townhouse on East Sixty-second Street, in Manhattan. The house had a small, sunny garden and even more fireplaces than "Windows," and its location was convenient as well as fashionable. Tallulah affected to be astonished that one had only to walk around a block to encounter food shops, restaurants, art galleries, plumbers' shops, movie theaters. Not that she ever walked if she could ride. She liked taxis in part because she liked taxi drivers. The moment they heard her giving them directions, they would turn with a grin: "Oh, my God! Tallulah!" "The Big Show" had made her voice known everywhere in the country, and she enjoyed this continuously renewed harvest of recognition. When strangers would stop on the street to speak with her, she had to repress an urge to give them a tip, and this was not because she felt patronizing towards them but because she felt grateful. She also repressed an urge to ask advice of them. More and more as she grew older, she missed what, when she was young, she had scorned the presence of—somebody stronger than she, who would give her good advice and make her follow it. Daddy had been weak, and so had Alington, and Emery, and "the other five thousand." She could not count on her caddies to recommend a course of action that, even if it were right, might prove repugnant to her; they would not have been caddies if she could have. Only her grandfather, Captain John, had been stronger than she, but being old he had doted on her and she had got from him whatever toy she begged for. Once very late at night in the house on East Sixty-second Street, she was drinking with a new acquaintance, a TV producer. She pleaded with him to tell her what she should undertake next. Under the inspiration of drink, he proposed that she star in an opera that, because everyone knew she could not sing, would be composed entirely in recitative. Tallulah leapt at the idea. It was the very thing she had been longing to do. She could see the whole thing so clearly! At four o'clock in the morning, she made a strenuous if vain effort to ring up Gian-Carlo Menotti and order him to set to work.

What was she to do with her career? Was there no one who could tell her, by day and cold sober, what was to become of her? She agreed to star in a review called *The Ziegfeld Follies*, which was budgeted at the then formidable sum of half a million dollars and was intended to recapture the beauty and extravagance of the original Follies. The revue closed out of town, to universally bad reviews; for Tallulah, it was a strenuous and exhausting failure. Some of the skits from the revue were salvaged and turned into a show, *Welcome, Darlings,* suitable, it was thought, for summer stock. To patrons of summer theaters, it scarcely mattered how ramshackle a vehicle Tallulah appeared in—from their point of view, a poor show might be better than a good one, since there would be sure to be more of Tallulah in it, gallantly offering herself in place of amusing lines and situations. She came to Broadway in a play adapted from a novel, *The Europeans,* by Henry James. The play was called *Eugenia,* after the leading character; the name held ambiguous echoes of Tallulah's mother, her sister, her friend Eugenia Rawls. Kerr began his review of the play with a sentence that made it unnecessary to read any of the sentences that followed it: "There can be no question whatever that Miss Tallulah Bankhead is an irresistible force, but in *Eugenia* she has flatly, finally, and irrevocably met an immovable object." It was not, as they say wryly on Broadway, a "selling" review, and *Eugenia* survived for but twelve performances. Next, she went on tour in *Crazy October*, a so-called black comedy by James Leo Herlihy. The intention was to bring the play to Broadway after testing it in the provinces, but the provinces disliked it, and the play closed in San Francisco. As usual, Tallulah emerged from the ordeal with praise: the *Variety* stringer in New Haven wrote, "This is a weirdie . . . a questionable bet for Broadway . . . the actress [Tallulah] does okay with what she has," and Paine Knickerbocker, a reviewer in San Francisco, wrote, "Tallulah could be funny on a pogo stick . . . but *Crazy October* is too much even for her." Time passed, innumerable play scripts were sifted through and rejected, and she was again on Broadway in *Midgie Purvis*, a comedy by Mary Chase. She was pleased to be in the hands of old friends; the play was being directed by Burgess Meredith and produced by Robert Whitehead and Roger L. Stevens, and they were determined to secure a rousing success for her. Miss Chase's plays are nearly always flung together in a helter-skelter fashion, and on the road there was much frantic rewriting of *Midgie Purvis*. The New York reviewers were delighted with Tallulah and less delighted with the play. Years later, Whitehead said of Tallulah, as Schildkraut had done, "I could have killed her. She was a character. She *had* character." *Midgie Purvis* ran for three weeks and sadly petered out.

Tallulah claimed to have been offered the lead in Tennessee Williams' *Sweet Bird of Youth* and to have turned it down in part because she found its language shocking. Her own language was never a standard she wished other people to repair to, especially onstage; there, her preference was for elegance in speech, costume, and settings. More and more often, she would be asked to depict a decayed or lost elegance, a decayed or lost beauty, and now and then she would be counted on to accept—with a forgiving smile and the waited-for salacious wisecrack—the fact that the ruinous figure in a play or movie or nightclub skit was based on herself embalmed in time, an already historic cautionary figure. Frank Crowninshield had written of her in *Vanity Fair*, when she was twenty-two, that she had become a legend in her own time, and with what a vengeance the friendly puff had come true! Tallulah read the script of Tennessee Williams' *The Milk Train Doesn't Stop Here Anymore*, which had been sent to her without his knowledge. Its heroine was Flora Goforth, an aging Southern has-been of an actress, groggy from drugs and alcohol and sexual excess; the play concerned her relationship with a young gigolo whom she nicknamed "The Angel of Death." Williams has written concerning the play that if it manages to achieve, even partially, its artistic intention, "you will find it possible to pity this female clown even while her absurd pretensions and her panicky last effort to hide from her final destruction make you laugh at her." It was characteristic of Williams that he did not hesitate to draw a Flora that the public would be sure to identify with Tallulah and it was characteristic of Tallulah that she did not shrink from seeing herself so cruelly caricatured. Eugenia and Don Seawell were with her the evening she finished reading the script, and she said to them, "Tennessee has written a play that's absolutely right for me—in fact, he has written it for me and I am going to call him right now and tell him I want to play it." She put in a call to Williams, in Key West, and repeated what she had said to the Seawells, who then heard her say, "Well, dahling, that's all right, and I *do* understand if you've promised it to someone else, but you *did* write it for me, and I just want you to know that if anything happens, I want to play it, and I *will* someday."

The play opened on Broadway, with Hermione Baddeley as Flora Goforth, and was unfavorably received. A year later, Williams offered it to Tallulah in a revised version. After rehearsals marked by repeated lacerating quarrels between Tallulah and Tony Richardson, the play passed a miserable Christmas week of trying out in Baltimore and opened in New York, at the Brooks Atkinson Theatre, on January 1, 1964. It was again unfavorably received. One reviewer said only, "Miss Bankhead was hoarse and unhappy." That six-word review may have been the shortest she ever received. David Merrick, the producer of *The Milk Train Doesn't Stop Here Anymore,* mercifully closed the play after five performances. It was Tallulah's last appearance on Broadway.

Again she had moved. The East Sixty-second Street house as she grew older proved almost as heavy a burden as "Windows" had been, and she had bought in its place a cooperative apartment high up in a building near the river on East Fifty-seventh Street. There were doormen to help her

Walter Kerr was the drama critic of the New York *Herald Tribune* from 1951 to 1966, and upon the extinction of that newspaper he went to the *Times,* where he wrote daily reviews for a time and then retreated to a weekly column in the labyrinth of the Sunday edition. Unlike most of his local colleagues, Kerr has been intimately associated with the theater as a teacher, writer, and director. With his wife, Jean Kerr, he wrote the books of a couple of musicals; the photograph shows the Kerrs trying out a show on the road. For most playwrights, this is a time of frantic rewrite, but the Kerrs are looking characteristically self-possessed. Kerr is the author of a number of books about the theater. A good-looking, stocky, soft-spoken man, he was born in Evanston, Illinois, in 1913. His practice in reviewing a play is to take copious notes throughout the performance; crouched in the dark and scribbling away, he has prompted his wife to wonder whether he may be said to have ever "seen" a play in the conventional sense. Kerr has always written with affection of Tallulah. Concerning her efforts to salvage a chestnut of her late years called *Dear Charles,* Kerr said that at a certain desperate point in the play "we are getting Bankhead in comfortable beige, Bankhead in dazzling red, Bankhead in sequins, Bankhead with flowers, Bankhead on a staircase, Bankhead enveloped in smoke. I'd say that every single Bankheadism worked. . . . I'd say that the play was appalling for this day and age, but that it is difficult to remain honestly appalled while you are rapt in admiration. A blithe spirit with a rusty voice is at work here. Hail to her."

in and out of cabs and elevator men to see that she reached the right door on the right floor. And there were no stairs to climb, which was helpful now that she had difficulty breathing. The doctors had diagnosed emphysema and had forbidden her to smoke, of course in vain. She had been chain-smoking morning, noon, and night for over fifty years; too late to give it up simply because it was killing her. There is scarcely an informal picture of her in existence that does not show her smoking, and even in some of the more formal pictures, including a movie still of her in sumptuous full fig as Catherine the Great of Russia, a cigarette may be noticed burning in one hand. Sick as she was, she would light up and puff and choke on upwards of a hundred and fifty cigarettes a day. In former times, she had smoked only her beloved English Craven

In *Die! Die! My Darling!* she was made to look even ghastlier than she felt.

A's. Nowadays, she was smoking, and thoroughly disliking, those detestable !#!$&! filtered Kents.

The East Fifty-seventh Street apartment was a safe base from which to set forth at intervals, always with increasing reluctance, on certain silly but profitable tasks. There was a horror movie to be shot in England (released here under the title of *Die! Die! My Darling!*), for a fee of fifty thousand dollars; a couple of appearances on the TV show "Batman," for a fee of twenty thousand dollars; and innumerable other appearances on TV comedy and talk shows, the least uncomfortable of them being those of her old friend Merv Griffin, who, when she begged for a glass of water, saw that she was handed a kindly, necessary glass of gin. No matter how unworthy of her, these tasks served to keep her occupied until the day when something "absolutely right" would come along.

14 Horrible to grow old. Horrible to grow ugly. And far more horrible for Tallulah than for most people, because unlike most people she had used youth and beauty, coupled with remarkable energy, as the sources of an unprecedented gift for pleasing people. It is hard to take in this astonishing fact about her: that at fifteen and sixteen, with none of the performing skills of the prodigy and, indeed, with almost no schooling, she succeeded in captivating a large portion of the most intelligent and talented people in New York; and at twenty-two and twenty-three she would be doing the same in London. She was also, as it soon turned out, not unlike her admirers in talent and intelligence, but she early placed these attributes at the mercy of what she had found would suffice; she linked them together and risked them together, and when some went, all had to go.

Tallulah never troubled to school her superior mind—she would often refer, and no doubt correctly, to her sister, Eugenia, as the intellectual of the family. Instead, she lived by her untutored wits and on sheer brass. She read incessantly and at random, and her memory was a grab bag of facts accurate, inaccurate, and made up on the spur of the moment, in the exigencies of debate; the latter she regarded thereafter as true because they passed the test of her remembering them. She fancied herself as a student of medicine, and whenever she felt cornered on some discussion of obscure diseases she would fall back on the authority of her friend Dr. Craig, of the Mayo Clinic, to prove her point. Dr. Craig was an invaluable ally, and it was not altogether a defect in his character from her point of view that he did not exist—the range of his knowledge, so convenient for her, was all the greater for his never having had to specialize, like ordinary mortals. She spent much of her life

In rehearsal for *Midgie Purvis,* a play in which Tallulah slid down banisters.

in the care of doctors and it gratified her to say that she was known in the profession as "the doctors' dilemma." "My symptoms are always much more mysterious than other people's symptoms are," she said. "I can run a fever of a hundred and six over the merest trifle. I am never just sick, I am drastically sick." When one considers the lifetime of insults that she dealt her body in the form of drugs, alcohol, overwork, and overplay, it is obvious that she must have had an exceedingly strong constitution; even as late as *Midgie Purvis,* she was able to ride swings and slide agilely down banisters on the stage of the Martin Beck. At the same time, she had a knack for breaking bones and setting herself afire. Caddies would look in on the sleeping Tallulah from time to time to make sure that neither she nor any of her shaggy, combustible pets was ablaze.

Horrible to grow old, but if one has been beautiful, how much more horrible to grow ugly. When Al Morgan was interviewing Tallulah in 1961, he pressed her hard on why she, who had once been a tireless party girl, no longer went out very often. She fenced with him to no avail, and at last: "What the public wants—they want glamour. That's why I don't go out. I don't dare. I think they're disappointed in me. One day someone was taking me to lunch and a matinee, so I tried to look my best. I mean, knowing I would be out in public and be recognized and all. And at the theater, during the intermission, I went up the aisle with my head held high, so as not to show my double chins, if I had them, and then in the crowd at the back of the theater I overheard a woman who must have seen me in some show or other say to a friend, 'How do they make her up to look so good?'" She hated to have her body decay. She observed the process closely and did what she could not only to resist the process but also to reverse it. She had her breasts operated on, with excellent results, and she may have had a facelift or two (caddies speak of seeing tiny scars). Like any woman, she remained proudest of her legs because they had changed least. She was small-boned and had tiny feet and she made a habit of sitting cross-legged on sofas and beds to show them off.

There was no denying the terrible changes that befell her face. Every year, she would draw with lipstick a bigger and bigger smear of red over the outline of her natural mouth, as if, like a circus clown, by exaggerating a single feature she would make sure that all the others were ignored. She let her hair go gray; when photographed or on TV, it looked almost as blond as it had looked in her twenties. As for her hands, there was nothing to be done about them; they had always looked older than they should have. She said, "It takes me ten minutes to do my nails, two hours to do my face."

And to strangers on the street who asked her if she was Tallulah Bankhead she said, "What's left of her." When she was invited to Truman Capote's masked ball at the Plaza, in 1966, she spent days preparing for it. She was grateful that masks were to be worn; she got herself up to look like some bizarre but not unbeautiful bird of prey, and she was pleased by the number of people who came up to her table and spoke to her. She had had the curious notion that perhaps nobody would approach her, nobody speak. The party girl had lost her nerve.

With her goddaughter, Brook Seawell. Tallulah was proud of having tiny feet.

A fortunate thing happened at the Capote ball. Among the guests was an acquaintance of Tallalah's named Jesse Levy. She invited him, along with a few other people, to stop off for a drink at her apartment after the ball. Levy spent the night, or the little that was left of it, at East Fifty-seventh Street. Shortly thereafter, Tallulah proposed that he become her paid steward-secretary-escort, and Levy accepted the proposal. He was good to her and good for her. Seeing that it was too late for making changes, he helped her through each day as it came. He played the piano for her and, when necessary, cooked for her and measured out her pills and drinks and got her safely in and out of bed. When her will was read, it turned out that Levy had been left the piano, ten thousand dollars outright, and a quarter of the residuary estate. Tallulah always loved giving presents, and it must have pleased her to think of the lovely presents she would be giving Levy. Soon.

For she cannot have failed to know that she was growing weak. Each of us, it is said, begins to die when his organism becomes too puzzled to go on, and Tallulah's bewilderment was of long standing and past cure. She said in an interview that she was not afraid of dying. She had, she

Easter, 1968. Tallulah had been painted by John thirty-eight years earlier.

confessed, no very profound ideas on the subject. She quoted from *Hamlet*, which is to say she quoted from Daddy. No doubt he had recited "To be or not to be" many times to her and Sister back home in Jasper, teetering, more than a little tipsy, at the foot of their cots in the summer dark, on the sleeping porch at "Sunset." Looking back, she was struck by the fact that she had been a child for so short a while. She had tried to relive as much of childhood as possible through her godchildren, Brook and Brockman Seawell. (They too would be getting lovely presents: half of her estate.) Luckily, they were beautiful children—"The only kind to have," she said. "I wouldn't have had any other kind myself." When Brockman was being christened at the Little Church Around the

Corner, she held him in her arms and as he burst out crying she said, "I'd cry, too! Think of all the lovely sins we've just renounced in his name!" She presided over their growing up and saw to it that they were enrolled in a reputable acting school (she who didn't believe that acting could be taught!) and in proper hat and white gloves attended their opening nights, which were afternoons.

At six, Brock made his debut as Puck in *A Midsummer Night's Dream*, and Tallulah went backstage afterwards to congratulate him. He held up his arms to her and she said, "Brock, do you love me?" Brock said, "To infinity." Tallulah hesitated a moment. That was not the answer she had got from Daddy on the last day she ever saw him. She had hoped that his "Why talk about circumferences?" had meant that his love was boundless, but why had he not answered, like Brock. "To infinity"? Why had an ambiguity been the best he could manage? And in the form of a question, at that? Tallulah said crisply to Brock, "Dahling, get out of that costume and let's go home and have a drink."

During the summer of 1968, Tallulah and Jesse paid a long visit to Sister at her house in Rock Hall, on the Eastern Shore. In December, having caught flu and then pneumonia, Tallulah would die after a few days' illness in New York and be brought back to Rock Hall for burial. In the course of that long visit, for pain and pleasure and because they could not help themselves, the sisters went over and over the old ground of their Jasper childhood. The rivalry between them had lasted more than sixty years and was as keen as ever, but to no purpose. They were old ladies, each with the heart of a child hammering away inside her at the injustice of her lot. How hard they had struggled to make a noise in the world and how little it came to! They remembered their Great-grandmother McAuley's maxim, "Fools' names are like their faces, often seen in public places." They had taken good care not to listen to her. They had played in the big yard at "Sunset" and waited for Daddy to come home and tell them funny stories. Once he had brought home to dinner with him a stranger who had a couple of fingers missing from one hand. The girls asked their father afterwards the reason for the mutilated hand, and he answered at once, with a straight face, "A steamboat ran over it." They remembered England and their friends there, mostly dead by now, and Tallulah told one of her favorite stories about the tall and eccentric Lady Viola Tree. "Lady Tree was at one of those charity bazaars that actors are always doing over there," Tallulah said. "When she got up to entertain, she was wearing a long lace dress caught up with safety pins, a large flowered garden-party hat, and walking brogues on her feet, and she began by saying to the audience, 'Now, I want you all to think of me as a rather splendid old London cabdriver.'"

Lady Tree had been the co-author, with Sir Gerald du Maurier, of the play that Tallulah had made her London debut in. That seemed a thousand years ago. Tallulah's motto, borrowed from those London days, had been "Press on!" Now, disobeying her principle, she looked back and she saw that something was gaining on her, and it did not matter. There were still things to be laughed about: things that it made you feel good to remember, even if they did not make you happy. She would go on getting up for as long as she could and then she would stop getting up. That would be Jesse's problem. She had said once, "Naturally, one wants to be a star." She wondered now about that strange word, "naturally." A girl who was capable of saying that was capable of anything.

Tallulah's mother, Adelaide Eugenia Sledge, photographed as a child in the eighteen-eighties. At the time, the Sledges were richer and grander than the Bankheads. They bred celebrated fighting cocks, known with some wit as Sledge Hammers. Later, sadly, the Sledges grew poor and less grand.

A well house on the Bankhead plantation, in Moscow, Alabama, where Tallulah's grandfather was born. The picture was taken just over a hundred years ago, and the occasion for it is likely to have been the heavy snowfall, which is rare in those parts.

A Bankhead field hand, photographed around 1900. He had been born a slave on the Bankhead place in the eighteen-twenties. A number of black Bankheads in and around Detroit trace their ancestry back to Moscow. Once, while on tour, Tallulah visited the Detroit Bankheads and was delighted to discover that they were tall and handsome, "like all the rest of the family."

Tallulah's grandfather, John Hollis Bankhead, as a Confederate officer in the War Between the States. "Captain John" was the last Confederate veteran in the United States Senate, and he made the distinction pay off handsomely in government funds for Alabama. He was known as the Father of Federal Good Roads—so claims a little-read sundial in Washington, D.C.

Tallulah's father, William Brockman Bankhead, was a big man on campus at the University of Alabama and a graduate of the Georgetown Law School. At the time of this picture, he was soon to marry Adelaide Eugenia, whom he intemperately wooed and won on the eve of her marriage to another man.

Adelaide Eugenia. To her contemporary, the critic Stark Young, she was "a creature out of The Arabian Nights." *She attended Salem College, where she learned Greek dances and how to faint at will during flirtations. Nobody who saw her ever got over her beauty. She married Will Bankhead, had two daughters, Eugenia and Tallulah, and was dead of blood poisoning at twenty-one.*

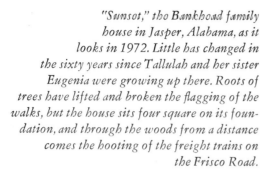

"Sunset," the Bankhead family house in Jasper, Alabama, as it looks in 1972. Little has changed in the sixty years since Tallulah and her sister Eugenia were growing up there. Roots of trees have lifted and broken the flagging of the walks, but the house sits four square on its foundation, and through the woods from a distance comes the hooting of the freight trains on the Frisco Road.

From infancy, Tallulah regarded the taking of baths as a social activity. In adult life, her bathroom was as public—and often nearly as crowded— as Grand Central Station.

Tallulah at four, looking, not for the last time, rather Churchillian. She was later to buy a lion cub and name it after Winston Churchill, who was moderately gratified.

And at eight. Her grandmother, the first Tallulah, had been a Brockman, and the Brockmans tended to be short and plump, like bollards. Throughout her life, Tallulah was always either overweight or underweight and therefore either starving or gorging. At this period, her father called her Dutch, partly because she was fat and partly because of her Dutch-boy haircut.

Eugenia and Tallulah—each called the other Sister—hamming it up on a sleeping porch at "Sunset." Plainly, they had been seeing too many "dar–ing" movies and reading too many trashy movie magazines. Their father and mother had both been gifted amateur actors, and it was beginning to dawn on the family that there was nothing else in the world that Tallulah would ever be fit to do. This was precisely what she wanted the family to think. She was a classic "dropout" long before the word had been invented.

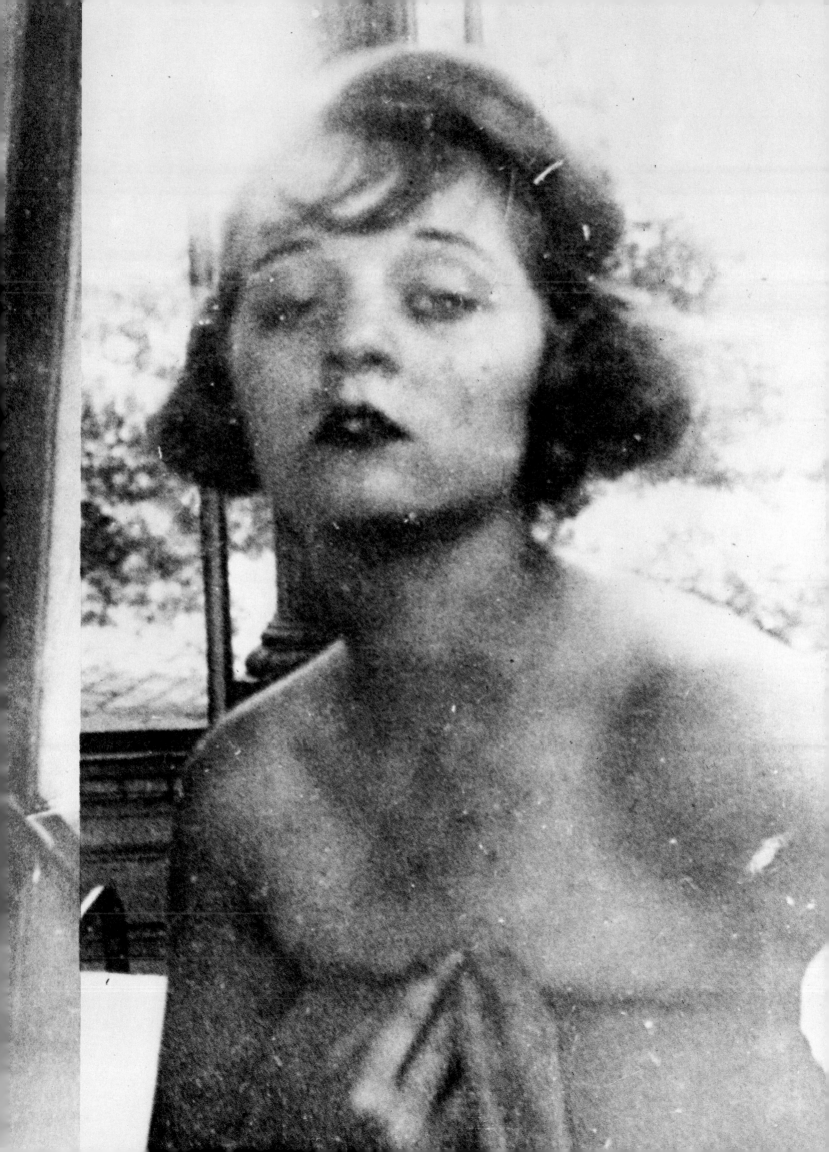

Tallulah at fourteen making a successful attempt to seem a jaded woman of the world. A year later, she won a so-called Screen Opportunity Contest conducted by Picture-Play *magazine and set out for New York to make movies.*

The apartment house in Washington, D.C., where "Captain John" and his wife lived on the top floor with Tallulah; Will Bankhead and his second wife and Eugenia lived on the floor below. The girls' stepmother wisely had little to do with the girls except offer them gingerly praise.

The Bankheads, father and son, on Capitol Hill. There were Bankheads in Congress for sixty years, and they all died in office of old age, according to Southern tradition.

HOTEL ALGONQUIN

59-65 West 44th St., New York

The Club Block of New York

HOTEL ALGONQUIN
NEW YORK

*My Darling Little Mamma,
Thank you so
much for your sweet
letter and the "love-
gift." Forgive me for
not answering sooner but
we have been rehearsing
night and day and
have been so busy
that this is really
the first chance I have*

With the exception of prices and air conditioning, little has changed at the Hotel Algonquin since Tallulah lived there in 1918, in a small, unpretentious hall bedroom with bath for which she paid twenty-one dollars a week. The façade now has a somewhat different marquee, and the oak-paneled lobby has wall-to-wall carpeting instead of Oriental rugs on a mosaic tile floor, but otherwise the management has left well enough alone: the great carved grandfather's clock still strikes the hour with a sustained force that sets seiche waves in motion on the surfaces of nearby martinis, and in the elevator one still encounters, just as Tallulah did, the celebrated actors, writers, and directors of the time—Julie Christie, Peter Ustinov, Thornton Wilder, Jeanne Moreau, Warren Beatty, Peter O'Toole, Günter Grass, Dustin Hoffman, Ella Fitzgerald, John Updike, Vanessa Redgrave, François Truffaut, Alan Bates, and the like.

When Frank Case died, his heirs sold the hotel to Ben Bodne, who is generally in residence, with his brown Rolls at the curb out front, in all its reassuring glossy amplitude. (It is one of the least important aspects of Mr. Bodne's career that he once played semi-pro baseball in Tallulah's hometown.) Mrs. Bodne makes an ideal wife for the proprietor of a theatrical hotel: she claims that she has never seen a play she didn't like. Obviously, she often disagrees with critics, but she is nice to them. One evening, a critic found himself dressed in a dinner jacket but unaccountably lacking a black tie; Mrs. Bodne dashed upstairs and brought down one of Mr. Bodne's. The Critics Circle meets several times a year at the Algonquin, in something known as the Stratford Suite. They regard one another with justifiable suspicion and vote, according to a system too complicated to remember for long, on the "best" plays and musicals.

The Algonquin Round Table, in the authoritative drawing (with five Nina's) by Al Hirschfeld. In real life, the group can rarely have boasted so many big guns at a single sitting. Among those present on this delightful imaginary occasion are, precariously from left to right, the Lunts, Dorothy Parker, Robert Benchley, Robert E. Sherwood, Frank Crowninshield, Alexander Woollcott, Heywood Broun, George S. Kaufman, Marc Connelly, Frank Case, Edna Ferber, and F.P.A. (Franklin Pierce Adams).

The Squab Farm *was
Tallulah's first play. She
walked on and walked off,
and no harm done. One
sees from this picture how
beautiful she was and how
original and perverse; the
photographer had obviously
urged everyone to face
forward, and Tallulah has
chosen to turn sideways.
She had been frequenting
Barrymores at the Algon-
quin, and John Barrymore
had admired her profile to
the point of asking his
sister, "Ethel, did Father
ever play Alabama?"*

105

Another of Tallulah's 1918 movies, Thirty-a-Week, *produced by Samuel Goldwyn and starring Tom Moore, natty here in cap and puttees. A phenomenon of those days was the way actors came in sibling clusters instead of one by one. Early movie stars included Tom and Owen Moore, Constance and Norma Talmadge, Charlie and Sid Chaplin, Mary and Jack Pickford, and Dorothy and Lillian Gish. Tallulah's sister, Eugenia, tried her hand at acting in England, got good reviews, and rushed impetuously on to something else. To contemporary eyes, the Packard touring car in* Thirty-a-Week *is almost as delectable as the fashionable little creature peering over its hood. It is worth noting that in 1918 cars needed no bumpers; there was little to hit except an occasional pedestrian or tree.*

A fellow-beginner with Tallulah in the cast of Nice People, *in 1921, was Katharine Cornell. They were to be friends ever after, though it would be difficult to imagine two people more different in their professional and personal lives.*

Tallulah in a movie called The Trap. *At this time, she was playing bit parts in so-called daring movies, the most daring thing about them being in almost every case their titles—*When Men Betray, The Virtuous Vamp, *and the like. Movies could be made in a couple of weeks, in Fort Lee, Long Island City, or even in midtown Manhattan, often in studios that had been converted from livery stables or breweries. (One sniffed to guess which.) Tallulah looked down on acting in movies compared with acting in plays. Some of her movie jobs took only a sunny morning or so, and she quickly forgot them. In* The Trap, *her mouth is visible in its natural outline for perhaps the last time.*

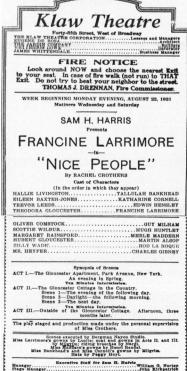

To judge by the verandah setting, Ethel Barrymore in an implausible wig and with a couple of beauty patches is attending a costume ball and has been asked to step outside for a moment to have her picture taken. From the point of view of displaying her beauty, it was not a good idea. The palms and the voluptuous wicker chair photograph better than she does.

John Barrymore striking a virile John Barrymore pose aboard his sloop. (The loincloth has obviously been airbrushed in.) Barrymore was the consummate matinee idol of the day, but his Hamlet was a serious and successful attempt to embody a great role. The play caused a sensation on Broadway and enjoyed a substantial run.

Three portraits by James Abbe, one of the most gifted theatrical photographers of the period. At the age of eighty-eight, living in retirement in California, he has enjoyed, in 1972, the sensation of being "discovered" and made famous by photographers seventy years his junior. Abbe talked many of his subjects into undressing in the course of sitting for him; one of the most charming consequences of this understandable practice is his study of the silent movie star Bessie Love pensively warming herself before a stove.

The lady in Restoration dress is Estelle Winwood, who championed Tallulah from her earliest days at the Algonquin. Until recently, Miss Winwood, whose birthdate is unknown but who is almost certainly older than Abbe, has remained active in movies. She made her debut on the stage in England, in the nineties, and was an established star in New York in the early twenties. She and Tallulah acted many times together through the years, and by the terms of Tallulah's always very specific and stringent contracts, Miss Winwood was the only person who was allowed to share billing of equal size with her.

The girl in ruffles is, of course, Helen Hayes, who was not given to undressing. Tallulah envied her because she had got her start on the stage at the age of six and was already playing with Weber & Fields at eight.

An Abbe study of Tallulah. Oddly enough, she appears not to have undressed for him, or at least not entirely.

A party at the Coffee House Club, in honor of the English actress Marie Tempest. Tallulah is at the extreme right in the front row, smoking as usual; she averaged a hundred and fifty cigarettes a day for over fifty years. Beside her sits Ina Claire. To the left of Miss Tempest is Laura Hope Crews and directly behind her is Lenore Ulric. At the far left in the second row is Carlotta Monterey, who eventually married Eugene O'Neill.

SUPPER TO
MISS MARIE TEMPEST
COFFEE HOUSE CLUB
SEP. 7, 1922.

A letter from Lawrence Langner, of the Theatre Guild. Langner's secretary, like so many people in the opening days of January, misdated the letter by a year.

The letter of credit from an old family friend, T. Coleman Du Pont, that made possible Tallulah's risky assault upon England. It took her several years to pay back the money. Mr. Du Pont was a famously generous multimillionaire, but he appears to have believed that it did the young good to learn to pay their way, and Tallulah certainly learned.

The portrait of Tallulah by Ira A. Hill that the impresario Charles B. Cochran carried with him from New York to London, in order to persuade Sir Gerald du Maurier to hire Tallulah. The portrait was on display for many years in a vitrine affixed to the building on Fifth Avenue that housed Hill's studio. Prolonged exposure to light caused the picture to fade almost to the point of obliteration. Tallulah took it and wrote on it, in recollection of her first, much-touted witticism (spoken to Woollcott after the opening of a play of Maeterlinck's): "There is less here than meets the eye."

January 5th, 1922.

My dear Basil Dean:-

This letter will introduce to you one of our most talented and important young American actresses, Miss Tallulah Bankhead, who has gone to England under contract with Mr. Cochran. She is a serious young actress, not at all satisfied with playing so-called "type parts", and I have told her that you are the most serious and important producer in London. Miss Bankhead has made good over here, has a remarkable stage personality, and I think she will make a triumphant success in England. With kind personal regards, I remain,

Sincerely,

Basil Dean, Esq.,
c/o Rean Dean
St. Martin's Theatre
London, England.

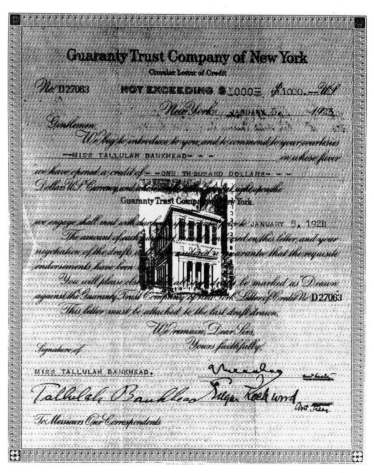

Progressing

Anton Dolin writes to me about his Sylphides ballet: "Sorry about spelling Slyphides wrong. I ought to know the correct spelling, though I did the same thing when I sent the Coliseum the bill matter."

Well, Dolin's progressing, and in due course he will get it right, but these things take time, and it hasn't happened yet.

Tallulah as a Ballet Dancer

"I saw Tallulah's show last night," he goes on; "what a marvellous performance, and what a pity, with all her vitality, that she wasn't a dancer!

"She could have gone through any modern ballet and not even been out of breath at the end."

WYNDHAM'S THEATRE.
CHARING CROSS ROAD. W.C.2.

Thursday Evening, February 15th, 1923, at 8.15

THE DANCERS

By HUBERT PARSONS

Characters in the order of their appearance:

ACT I.

Tony	GERALD du MAURIER	A Settler	J. PHILLIPS-ROBERTS
Billy (his Somali Servant)	H. W. FURNISS	Another Settler	GUY FLETCHER
Maxine	TALLULAH BANKHEAD	An Entertainer	FRANK ESMOND
Mack (a Film Producer)	NIGEL BRUCE	Buke	ERNEST BUCALOSSI
Mrs. Mack (his Wife)	NOEL BARKER	John Carruthers	BASIL S. FOSTER
Nat	WARD McALLISTER	Hon. Charlie Paxton	EDWIN UNDERHILL
Wal	LYN PERRING	Station Agent	WILLIAM G. FAY
Nellie	JULIETTE COMPTON		

SCENE—Tony's Bar. Western Canada. Winter

ACT II.

Mrs. Mayne	LILIAN BRAITHWAITE	Evan Carruthers	JACK HOBBS
Miss Pringle (her Typist)	UNA VENNING	Una Lowry	AUDRY CARTEN
James Fothering (a Solicitor)	NORMAN FORBES		

SCENE—A Room in Mrs. Mayne's Flat in Hyde Park Place

ACT III.

Una Lowry	AUDRY CARTEN	Billy	H. W. FURNISS
Day (her Maid)	DORIS COOPER	The Earl of Chievely	GERALD du MAURIER
Mrs. Mayne	LILIAN BRAITHWAITE	French Waiter	DINO GALVANI
James Fothering	NORMAN FORBES		

SCENE—A Room at the Savoy Hotel

ACT IV.

John Carruthers	BASIL S. FOSTER	French Stage Manager	DINO GALVANI
Evan Carruthers	JACK HOBBS	The Duke of Winfield	A. SCOTT-GATTY
Jeanne (Tawara's dresser)	JOAN PEREIRA	The Earl of Chievely	GERALD du MAURIER
Tawara	TALLULAH BANKHEAD		

SCENE—A Dressing Room in the Theatre de Luxe. Paris

Miss Braithwaite's Gowns and Miss Bankhead's Fur Coat by BERMEL.
Miss Carten's Wedding Gown by OSPOVAT. Character Costumes by L. & H. NATHAN.

MATINEES WEDNESDAY AND SATURDAY AT 2.30.

MUSIC.

ERNEST BUCALOSSI'S STRING SEXTETTE will play the following:—

1. PRELUDE—"THE DANCERS" ... ... Ernest Bucalossi
2. INTERMEZZO—"FLEURETTE D'AMOUR" ... ... Percy E. Fletcher
3. SELECTION—"VERONIQUE" ... ... Messager
4. ENTR'ACTE—"MANON LESCAUT" ... ... Puccini
5. MELODIE ... ... N. Connu
6. AIRS from "LA BOHEME" ... ... Puccini

The proud father and one of Tallulah's rare letters to him. She disliked writing and receiving letters, and at her death hundreds of unopened letters were found among her effects.

A characteristically offhand and delightful letter from Sir Gerald, which Tallulah no doubt solicited. She wanted Daddy to know how important she had become. Sir Gerald wrote, "Dear Mr. Bankhead: A very charming and beautiful young lady who brags about being your daughter has made a great success at my theatre—deservedly—and everybody is very fond of her—rightly—even the King and Queen of England. Thank you for allowing her to come here. She is most welcome. Yours very truly, Gerald du Maurier."

Tallulah in The Dancers. A critic wrote of her that she was a "smouldering, pouting young woman with a voice like hot honey and milk, a face like an angry flower." Descriptions of this sort do no harm at the box office.

William Somerset Maugham, in a portrait painted by Sir Gerald Kelly. Maugham wrote twenty-one novels, thirty plays, and a hundred and twenty short stories, one of which was adapted into the play Rain. He boasted that he wrote for money, and he made millions. He tried marriage once and fatherhood once, and he found both experiences distasteful. He was a catty young man and a cattier old one, and a publisher once said of him, "Willie's been true to himself—he's always had a bad word for everybody." Maugham enjoyed bridge and traveling and his splendid villa at Cap Ferrat, and for decades he spoke of himself tiresomely as a very old party. He was accurate at last, dying at ninety-one.

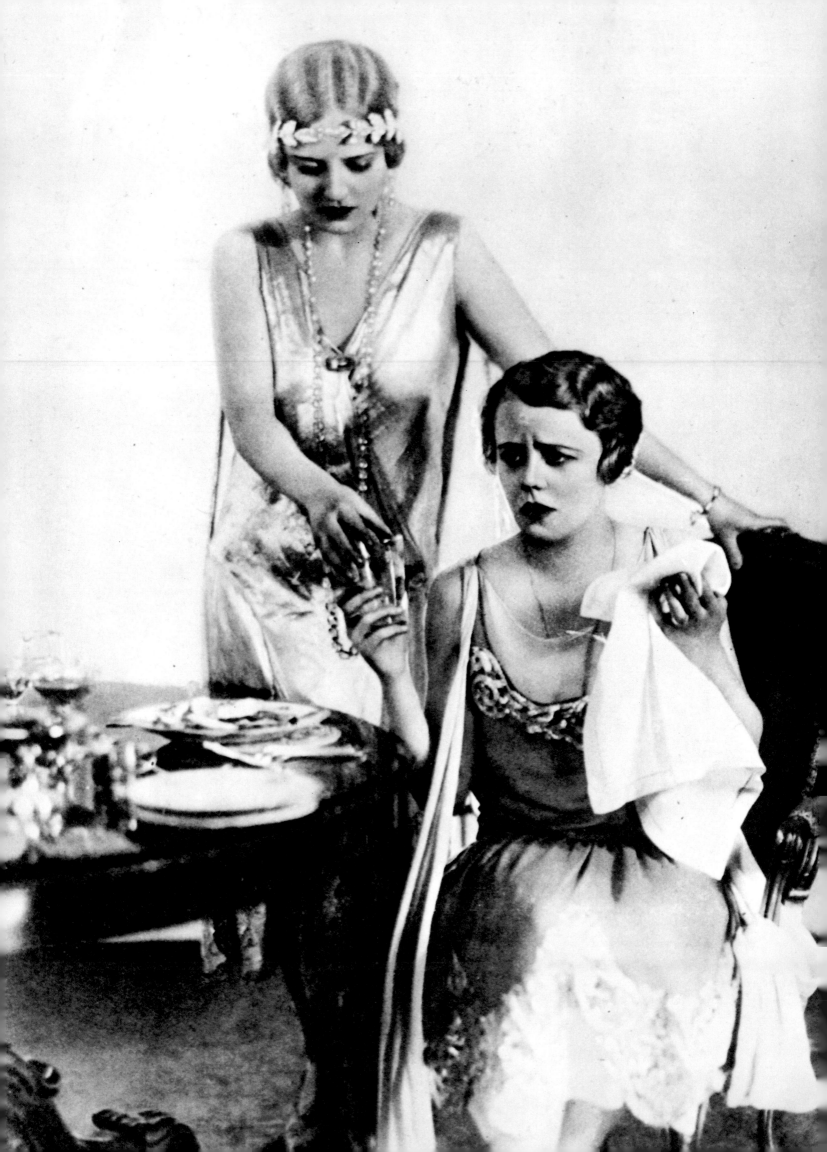

Noël Coward and Lilian Braithwaite in his play The Vortex. *This was an ambitious work in which Coward sought to establish that he was more than a writer of flippant one-liners.*

Tallulah and Edna Best in a scene from Noël Coward's Fallen Angels *(1925). This was the part that Tallulah got up in four days, having been dismissed by Somerset Maugham during the early rehearsals of* Rain. *The English critic James Agate wrote of* Fallen Angels *that it "glitters with the phosphorescence of decay . . . shows not a nasty mind but a juvenile preoccupation with nasty things." The photograph records what appears to have been considered a fairly racy, if not phosphorescent, moment in the play; on the road to hell, Tallulah asks, "Will you have some more champagne?" and Edna Best says, "No, thank you." Then Tallulah says, "Oh, come on, do—" and Miss Best replies, "Well, tidge it up!"*

"The London success of Tom Douglas and Tallulah Bankhead (she was playing, that night, in The Creaking Chair*) was a phenomenon of the two-faced Twenties. The American accent was unknown and these had particularly attractive ones, with a timbre steeped as deep in sex as the human voice can go without drowning: both were born fondlings, beings of such allure that with no seeming effort it overflowed normal domains, and each ruled with authority a shadowy hinterland. The girl, twenty-two, husky-musky and with a face like an exquisite poisoned flower, was empowered not only to make strong husbands in the stalls moisten their lips behind a program, but to cause girls hanging from the gallery to writhe and intone her first name in a voodoo incantation. She radiated like a lazy Catherine wheel."—*George, *an autobiography by Emlyn Williams (1961)*

A magazine spread that purported to show Tallulah frolicking about her country place. In fact, she had no country place; the pictures were taken at "Chertley Court," in Surrey, which belonged to her friend Lord Beaverbrook. He gave marvelous parties there, at which Tallulah could dance all night and talk all night and dash back to London next day, a few minutes before the first-act curtain was due to rise.

"THIS MARRIAGE," AT THE COMEDY.

Cathleen Nesbitt in This Marriage. *Miss Nesbitt added a pleasant domestic note to this production by bringing her baby to the theater and nursing it backstage between the acts.*

Tallulah and Herbert Marshall in This Marriage. *The critic James Agate, who nearly always had a soft spot in his heart for Tallulah, wrote, "The success of this {play} must be attributed largely to the actress, who would however have made it easier for me to swallow the false heroics if she had not swallowed quite so many of her words. The producer should ask Miss Bankhead to give value and meaning to syllables, and not to run three or four of them into one." The criticism amounts to a compliment, since most Southern girls have a tendency to turn one syllable into three or four. Tallulah was acquiring the accent of Mayfair.*

Picking flowers: Miss Tallulah Bankhead.

Studying the sundial: Miss Tallulah Bankhead.

th her pet terrier: Miss Tallulah Bankhead.

Reflections: Miss Tallulah Bankhead & her sister Jean.

th her sister Jean: Miss Tallulah Bankhead.

Rolling the lawn: Miss Tallulah Bankhead.

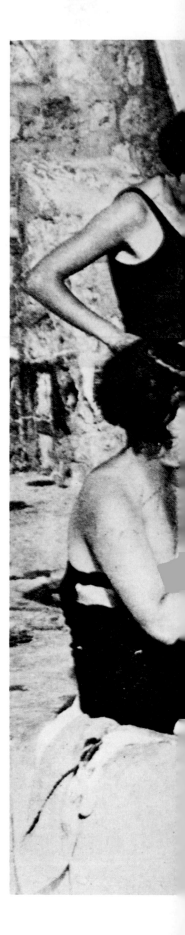

Katharine Cornell in The Green Hat, *in New York.
Based on Michael Arlen's best-selling novel, the play
was a far bigger hit in New York than it was in London.*

Tallulah in The Green Hat. *The play was considered
shocking and preposterous. Agate wrote of the
world it portrayed that it was "over-nourished,
over-dressed, over-laundered, and over-sexed. . . .
There can be no objection to showing sensuality
for what it is. . . . It is the attempt to gild sensuality
with the trumperies of sham generosity which is
objectionable. Also I take it that Mr. Arlen's
metamorphosis is wrong in fact. Lady into fox
may be thinkable; vixen into goose is absurd."
Nevertheless, Tallulah and her "husky charm"
were, as usual, much praised.*

*On the Riviera with some fashionable friends:
the Marchioness of Milford Haven and Mrs. Reginald
Vanderbilt are the seated figures lighting up; the other two
are unidentified. On this brief holiday, Tallulah renewed her
friendship with an old Montgomery, Alabama, classmate
of her sister, Eugenia—Zelda Sayre Fitzgerald. "I was there
in the South of France," she said years later, "when Zelda,
poor darling, went off her head. She had gone into a flower
shop and suddenly for her all the flowers had faces." Then,
with her usual extreme reasonableness, Tallulah added,
"Of course, some flowers, such as pansies, do have faces."*

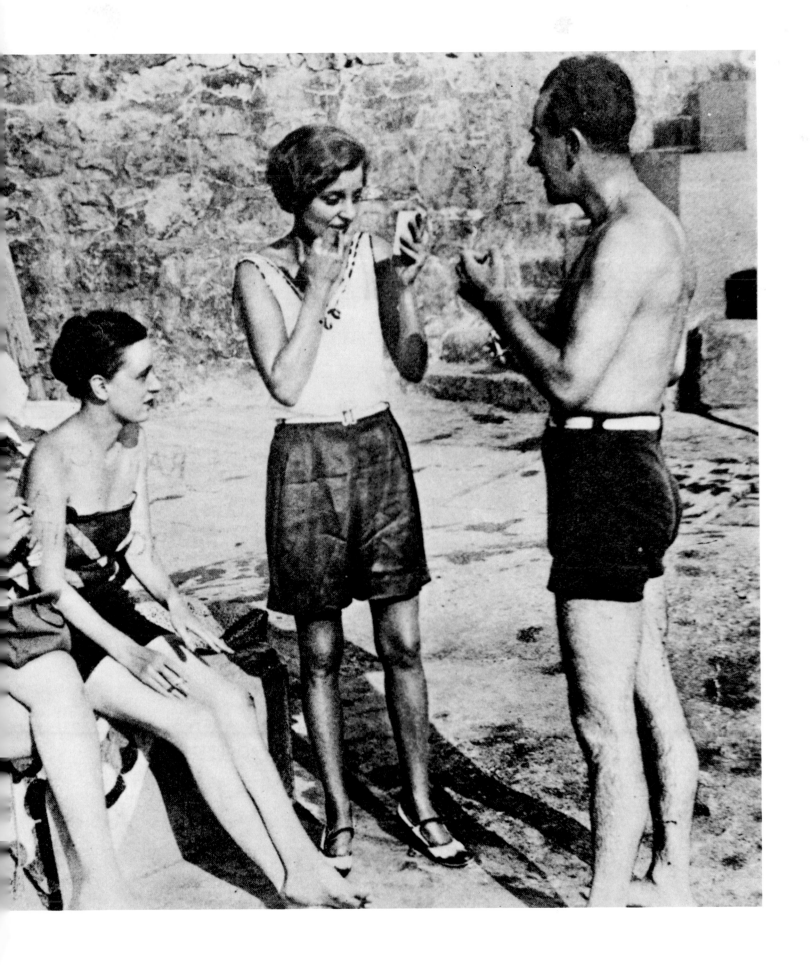

The *Sketch*

No. 1740 — Vol. CXXXIV.   WEDNESDAY, JUNE 2, 1926.   ONE SHILLING.

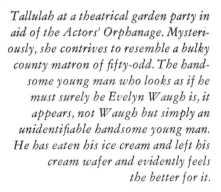

"I WAS WAITING OUTSIDE HIS TURKISH BATH"—THREE MODERN YOUNG WOMEN

THE WOMAN WHO DRIVES MEN MAD — MISS TALLULAH BANKHEAD AS MARY DENVERS

Tallulah at a theatrical garden party in aid of the Actors' Orphanage. Mysteriously, she contrives to resemble a bulky county matron of fifty-odd. The handsome young man who looks as if he must surely be Evelyn Waugh is, it appears, not Waugh but simply an unidentifiable handsome young man. He has eaten his ice cream and left his cream wafer and evidently feels the better for it.

Tallulah in They Knew What They Wanted, *by Sidney Howard. It was the first play of merit that Tallulah ever appeared in, and the critics, if not her public, were delighted that she was no longer merely "an actress whose successive incarnations had connoted a fallen angel, a green hat, and a Scotch mist."*

Four glimpses of a play called Scotch Mist, *by Sir Patrick Hastings, K.C., which was hailed with what amounted to enthusiasm as one of the worst plays ever written.*

125

Tallulah in The Gold Diggers, *and a newspaper account of Captain MacEachan's party. A magazine called* Eve *published an account of another merry occasion: "Fame's favourite, Mr. Beverly Nichols, gave a party in his very charming little house the other night, and the tiny room seemed to be filled with a mob of 'stars' and 'stuntists.' Miss Tallulah Bankhead was there, a successful gold-digger in black, 'Willie' Somerset Maugham and his wife, 'Syrie'; Mr. Noël Coward and Mr. Jack Wilson, Mr. Oliver Messel, who did his latest recitation, 'Bouncey Bally,' Mrs. Garland, Miss Todd, Mrs. Richard Guinness, Miss Angela du Maurier, and P. G. Wodehouse's daughter; and added to that a flood of talented youths who did imitations of each other and played the piano without ceasing."*

ANOTHER GROUP AT CAPTAIN NEIL MacEACHAN'S PARTY

e more of the bright young people at this venturesome party, Mr. Richard Wyndham, Mr. C. Howard (sitting on left), the Hon.
hen Tennant, Mrs. Sitwell, Miss Inez Holden, Mr. Harold Acton, Miss Tallulah Bankhead, Miss Elizabeth Ponsonby, and
Cecil Beaton. Miss Tallulah Bankhead was Jean Borotra, Miss Elizabeth Ponsonby Miss Iris Tree, Mr. Stephen Tennant Queen
Marie of Roumania, Mr. Dick Wyndham Dcbson the sculptor, Mrs. Sacheverell Sitwell his model

Tallulah acquired a reputation in London as an actress who was always taking off her clothes onstage. She denied that this was so, not out of the conventional modesty of the time but out of professional pride; there was more to her as an actress than the removal of a pretty wardrobe. Still, when she tore off her wedding dress in The Garden of Eden *to emerge in diaphanous step-ins, the sensation was immense; leading writers in the daily press demanded to know how much further nudity could be carried before the Empire crumbled.*

Tallulah assaulting a cad—the not very alarmed-looking Eric Maturin—with an empty wine bottle. She is defending her virtue, and under the circumstances it is always wise to have drunk the wine first. (A puzzle: The wine in the glasses appears to be red, but the label on the bottle reads Moët et *Chandon.)*

"THE GARDEN OF EDEN."

At the Lyric.

Play in Three Acts, by R. Bernauer and R. Oesterreicher, adapted by Avery Hopwood, presented by Messrs Herbert Clayton and Jack Waller at the Lyric Theatre, on Monday, May 30.

Liane	Gladys Falck
Adele	Marcelle Roche
Cleo	Diana Caird
Call Boy	Arthur Holman
Rosa	Eva Moore
Revard	George Bellamy
Toni Lebrun	Tallulah Bankhead
Durand	Edward Irwin
Madame Grand	Barbara Gott
Henri Glessing	Eric Maturin
Count De L'Esterel	Herman De Lange
Count De Mauban	Ivo Dawson
Baron Lapereau	Robert English
Richard Lamont	Hugh Williams
Maître d'Hotel	Murri Moncrieff
Waiter	Arthur Ross
Professor Roasio	Dino Galvani
General Deval	Rex Caldwell
Aunt Mathilde	Annie Esmond
Uncle Herbert	Frederick Volpé
The Prime Minister	Robert Mawdesley
Prince Miguel De Santa Rocca	George Bellamy
Servant to the Prince	Roy Emerton

Miss Tallulah Bankhead is a good actress, as one discovered in "They Knew What They Wanted," when she was really given a character to play. Her part in "The Garden of Eden," adapted by Mr. Avery Hopwood for the English stage, is almost entirely characterless, and although Miss Bankhead acts with tremendous vigour and as skilfully as usual, one can take little interest in Toni Lebrun, the young Cabaret singer. Miss Bankhead looks attractive enough in her crêpe-de-chine undergarments, but her real admirers would surely prefer to see her in a part that was worth the name.

The purity of the heroine, with a soul as white as driven snow, is always over-insisted-upon by dramatists. In real life she is too commonplace to be noticed—even in Cabarets.

The only difference between Toni and a thousand other such heroines is that she doesn't marry the hero in the end. The authors could hardly put that over in a modern play, so they have resorted to a cynical device for disposing of her satisfactorily. There is a certain relief in the sketch of the old Prince who offers his fortune to her in return for marriage. He is a character drawn with cynical skill, and the piece assumed a touch of vitality when he was on the stage, although this was partly due to Mr. George Bellamy's fine acting.

The plot was fully detailed by our Edinburgh correspondent in the last issue. It is told slickly enough, but the dialogue is often weak and ineffective.

Miss Eva Moore was more at home as the Countess at the Hotel Eden than as the dresser in the Cabaret, because the part gave her more scope in the later scenes. Mr. Hugh Williams acted well as Richard Lamont, and Mr. Eric Maturin was good as ever in the part that was like a great many others of his parts. Miss Barbara Gott was sly and majestic as the proprietor of the disreputable cabaret and there was real, dry humour in Mr. Frederick Volpé's fussy Uncle Herbert. Mr. Herman de Lange, Mr. Ivo Dawson and Mr. Robert English were typical Riviera hotel loungers and Miss Annie Esmond did well in a small part. Mr. Dino Galvani put vitality into a dancing teacher and Mr. Edward Irwin acted well as the easily corruptible Police Inspector in the first act. There was excellent support from Miss Gladys Falck, Miss Marcelle Roche and Miss Diana Caird, as the dancing girls at the Cabaret, Mr. Robert Mawdesley, Mr. Murri Moncrieff and Mr. Roy Emerton.

The play was given an enthusiastic reception at the Lyric Theatre, where it opened on Monday of last week.

Tallulah prized John's oil portrait of her above all her other possessions. It made a great noise when it was exhibited at the Royal Academy, and one critic went so far —and far astray—as to call it the greatest portrait of a woman since Gainsborough. Oddly, the oil was nothing like as attractive as the John drawing shown here.

A letter from John, dated May 12, 1930. In it he says, "I have had many letters sent me in appreciation of your portrait; among them one from an American sculptor Enid Fowler—do you know her? She says the picture's 'fragile delicacy killed everything else in the whole show' and wants me to sit for her. Some of the papers publish a lot of drivel as usual. I am frightfully well now after a course of treatment and want to return to you before long like a giant refreshed. Are you working terribly hard? With love and admiration and gratitude." John's eagerness to return to Tallulah was presumably not in the role of a painter.

Stage Photo Co

MISS TALLULAH BANKHEAD
(Inset) COUNT ANTHONY DE BOSDARI

Miss Tallulah Bankhead's engagement to Count Anthony de Bosdari was announced last week, but it was stated at the same moment that this would not mean that the stage is to lose one of its most brilliant actresses. Miss Tallulah Bankhead has made a tremendous success in what has been probably justly designated her first real play, "Her Cardboard Lover," which last week reached its one hundredth performance at the Lyric Theatre, and is still a big draw

Tallulah's fiancé was evidently a charmer, but one soon saw that he would have drawbacks as a husband: when he gave her a present of a Rolls, it proved not to have been paid for; similarly with his gifts of jewels to her, which she later paid for herself. There was also the awkward matter of his turning out to be married to someone else. Tallulah would have liked a title, even a minor Italian one, but Tony had let the side down and was dismissed. All he asked of her was that she not break their engagement publicly until he had the use of her celebrated name in a certain business deal that he was engaged on in Germany. This was not exactly noblesse oblige, *but Tallulah bore him no grudge.*

Scenes from He's Mine.

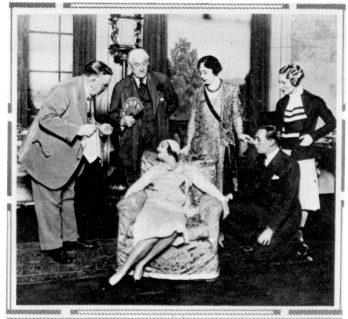

AFTER THE MOTOR ACCIDENT: THE MARQUIS (FREDERICK VOLPÉ), THE DUC (ALLAN AYNESWORTH), WANDA MYRO (TALLULAH BANKHEAD), THE DUCHESSE (HELEN HAYE), ETIENNE (GEORGE HOWE), AND SIMONE (SUNDAY WILSHIN).

WANDA FINDS THE VAMPING OF THE DUC DE BELLENCONTRE QUITE SIMPLE: MISS TALLULAH BANKHEAD AND MR. ALLAN AYNESWORTH.

AIMEE'S ACTRESS FRIENDS.

Tallulah Denies Story of Motor Joy-Ride.

"A GREAT WOMAN."

Why She Went to See the Evangelist.

Miss Tallulah Bankhead told an "Evening Standard" reporter to-day how she met Mrs. Aimee Semple McPherson, the evangelist, who left London at midnight last night for

MRS. AIMEE McPHERSON.

Glasgow, where she is beginning her provincial tour.

On Saturday she went with Mr. Leslie Howard, the young actor who plays the part of her husband in "Her Cardboard Lover," and Miss eatrice Lillie to call upon the evangelist at the Hotel Cecil.

One of the party stated afterwards that they had a long discussion about religious matters, and that they went away feeling that Mrs. McPherson was very sincere.

Miss Bankhead denied that she knew anything of any motor joy ride "to Southampton or anywhere else."

It had been stated that a party, including

The California evangelist Aimee Semple McPherson was a much lustier figure than the preachers of hellfire that America has been exporting to England in recent years. Evelyn Waugh made her a character in his early novel Vile Bodies *under the name of Mrs. Ape. In her entourage were a number of young women known as "angels" and bearing such appellations as Faith, Charity, Fortitude, and Chastity. Chastity had a tendency to get seasick and have carnal thoughts about men.*

Characteristic street scenes of the London period, when Tallulah and Leslie Howard were starring in Her Cardboard Lover, *at the Lyric Theatre. Having held up traffic along the way, Tallulah would arrive for a performance in her stylish green Bentley and at once be mobbed by her "gallery girls" and other fans. The gallery entrance to the Lyric can be seen in the photograph at the right.*

RIOTOUS SCENES AT A FIRST NIGHT.

POLICE CALLED TO DEAL WITH CROWD.

**The Play: "Blackmail."
Author: Charles Bennett.
Theatre: Globe.**

Extraordinary scenes took place last night before, during and after the first night of "Blackmail," a melodrama written by a young London actor of twenty-eight, discovered by Al Woods and cast by Tallulah Bankhead, who played the leading part.

Arnold Bennett saw Tallulah in The Lady of the Camellias. *Here she is kissing Armand (Glen Byam Shaw). Overleaf, in a chair, she is dying. Bennett was as thorough a journalist as he was a novelist, and he wrote this account of her "gallery girls":*

It begins on the previous afternoon. At 2 P.M., you see girls, girls, girls in seated queues at the pit and gallery door of the Tallulah theatre. They are a mysterious lot, these stalwarts of the cult. Without being penurious, they do not come from Grosvenor Square, nor even Dorset Square. They seem to belong to the ranks of the clerk class. But they cannot be clerks, typists, shop-assistants, *trottins*: for such people don't and can't take a day and a half off whenever their "Tallulah" opens. What manner of girls are they then?

Only a statistical individual enquiry could answer the question. All one can say is that they are bright, youthful, challenging, proud of themselves and apparently happy. It is certain that they boast afterwards to their friends about the number of hours they waited for the thrill of beholding their idol, and that those who have waited the longest become heroines to their envious acquaintances. Of course they do not sit and chatter and munch on those hired camp stools all the afternoon, all night, and all the next day. The queuing system has developed into a highly organized affair, with rules, relays, and a code of honour of its own. But at best, with all allowances made, the business of waiting must be very tedious and very exhausting, and none but the youthful or the insane-fanatical could survive it. Well, they obstinately wait for a century or so, and then the doors are unbolted and there is a rush of frocks. This is the first of the ecstatical moments.

I walk to the theatre one minute before the curtain is advertised to rise. But to get into the sacred fane is a feat. More girls, many more girls, with a few men, are trebly lined up in two groups across the pavement, and quite a number of policemen are urbanely but firmly employed in keeping the two groups apart. I have to force my way through one group and to convince policemen by a glance that I have a ticket. These girls are a little lower than the angels who by this time are already packed into the auditorium. They will not see Tallulah. The next best thing is to see the people who will see Tallulah.

The auditorium is crowded. And the price of seats has been doubled. You could buy a whole library of classics, you could go to the talkies every morning for a week, for the sum which you pay to see Tallulah on a first-night. For any ordinary first-night, twenty-five percent of the theatre-goers arrive either late, very late, or not at all. To be unpunctual and to disturb the rest of the audience is correct, then. To be punctual is to prove that you are of no account in the world. But for Tallulah everybody is in his seat when the band strikes up. No use pretending that you are superior, haughty, condescending! Because you aren't. You have paid, you feel excited; and you are there on time. Indeed, Tallulah makes you wait.

The play starts. Not a sound, or hardly a sound, of approving welcome. The programme, in which the names of the characters are printed in the

137

order of their appearance, lets you know that Tallulah is not yet. And until she comes the play is reduced to a mere prologue, has no general interest. Tallulah, and nobody and nothing else, is the play. Her entrance is imminent. The next second she will appear. She appears. Ordinary stars get "hands." If Tallulah gets a "hand" it is not heard. What is heard is a terrific, wild, passionate, hysterical roar and shriek. Only the phrase of the Psalmist can describe it: "God is gone up with a shout." The play stands still. Tallulah stands still. She is a little unnerved, and to be unnerved becomes her. The tumult dies. A number of impatient hiss for silence after there is silence. (And at frequent intervals throughout the performance these exasperating earnest ones continue to hiss for the very silence which their hissing destroys.)

The play resumes. You are startled when, on an exit, an actor gets a "hand," and a good one. Not because he has acted with great technical skill and so saved from derision a part which hovers forever on the edge of the preposterous. Not a bit. He gets a "hand" because he has uttered sentiments which appeal to the democratic heart of gold. For no other reason does a secondary actor get a "hand" at a popular performance.

I have never seen Tallulah in a good play. This play ("The Lady of the Camellias") is not bad. It is merely dead. It is one long demonstration that Dumas *fils* was not a patch on Dumas *père*. The dullness is epical. But no dullness of a play can impair the vogue of Tallulah. At every opportunity, and especially at the ends of the acts, the roars and shrieks recur in fullest volume. Hundreds and hundreds of robust young women are determined that this first night shall be a deafening success and it is. The play is the minor item of the entertainment.

What is Tallulah's secret? If she is beautiful, and she is, her beauty is not classical. How many wayfarers would look twice at her in the street? Her voice is not beautiful. It has, however, the slight seductive huskiness which lent so much enchantment to the acting of Pauline Lord. Her method of delivery is monotonous. Short rise—long fall. Short rise—long fall; endlessly. Rachel seldom understood the words she spoke; Sarah Bernhardt not always; and I doubt if Tallulah always understands hers. Anyhow, she simply threw away many points. Perhaps she could afford to be generous. For she has an exuberant, excessive vitality. She lives. True, she played Marguerite, the converted *cocotte*, with all the demeanour of a virginal soul. But she lived intensely. She never relaxed. Life radiated from her as it invariably does. I have seen Tallulah electrify the most idiotic, puerile plays into some sort of realistic coherence by individual force.

Then the end of the show. The loudest roar and shriek of all. Storms. Thunder and lightning. Gusts. And Tallulah, still virginal, withstanding everything with a difficult smile. I looked up at the gallery. Scores of lusty girls hanging over the rail and tossing their triumphant manes and gesticulating and screeching. A strange and disturbing sight. I wondered what these girls were in private life, in the prose of the day after. And the speech of thanks. Everybody was thanked; even the limited company which put the play on was thanked. And finally Tallulah steps forward into a new storm and thanks the thanker. God save the King! The Tallulah first-night is over.

But yet it is not over. One must positively go "behind." The stone stairs are blocked with the initiated and the inquisitive. I reach a landing and see an open door and a dressing room and a hot crowd within and Tallulah in the center. She breaks through the cordon and dashes out onto the landing.

"Are you coming to my party tonight?"

After all the terrible strain of rehearsals, of frock-fitting, of the dress rehearsal, of the first night, of the thunder and lightning and roaring of her reception, this astonishing, exhaustless creature is giving a party! Even now the hour is within a quarter of midnight, and she is still in her paint and her dying white nightgown. A difficult moment, for I am not able to go to her party; I am only able to go to bed. But she is full of tact. I love her. She returns to her worshippers. I fight my way to the stage-door. And lo! Scores and scores of girls waiting with everlasting patience to witness her departure, and Tallulah will have to face them before she goes to her party.

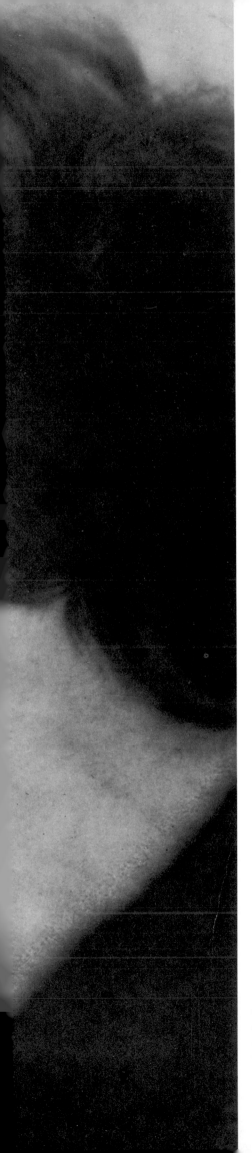

"Since I have a shorter time to live than others, I must live more rapidly."—Marguerite, in The Lady of the Camellias. *The portrait is by Dorothy Wilding.*

The picture opposite is of a scene from Let Us Be Gay, *a singularly complicated comedy by Rachel Crothers, who had given Tallulah her first speaking part in 1919, in* 39 East. Let Us Be Gay *was her last London play.*

To the left, Tallulah with a party identified as "The Countess Bosdari," but the chances are that it was her ex-fiancé, the amusing and unreliable Count.

Tallulah being sculptured by Frank Dobson. In all three pictures, Tallulah is, of course, smoking. At first glance, one would deduce that she had spared Dobson this iniquitous practice, but no— there on the curious stumplike object that serves to support her elbow rests the obligatory Craven A.

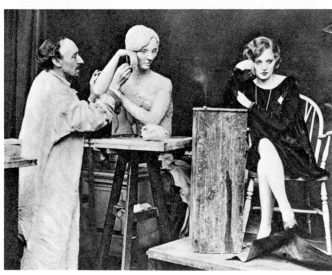

The Tatler

Vol. CXVII. No. 1523.   London, September 3, 1930   POSTAGE: Inland, 2d.; Canada and Newfoundland, 1½d.; Foreign, 4d.   **Price One Shilling**

Miss Bankhead Returns to Take Sound Film Role

Representative's Daughter Deserts London Stage to Play Lead in Local Picture

Quit Broadway 8 Yrs. Ago

Denies Reports of Romance; Thinks Englishmen 'Divine'

Tallulah Bankhead, the actress, paused long enough at playing Canfield on her return yesterday on the Aquitania, of the Cunard Line, to assert emphatically that it was sound motion pictures and not politics or romance that caused her to leave the London stage, where she attained distinction after deserting Broadway eight years ago. She was met by her father, Representative William B. Bankhead, of Alabama.

After explaining that her return to America made her extremely nervous, the slender actress said: "It's hackneyed to say I sacrificed all for my career, for that is a lot of rubbish. The truth is I have troubles enough of my own without a romance. It may be that I am going to find a beautiful man here.

"Oh, Englishmen are divine. Just divine. But I have seen and been with them so long the perspective gets dim. Now that I am away, I see Englishmen as even more divine than when I left them."

Miss Bankhead, who entered the theatrical profession after she secretly entered a beauty contest and won first prize, made little gestures with her hands and paused frequently to adjust a black and white knit cap on her blonde hair. In her suite was a small poodle.

For the edification of her small audience she gave a voice demonstration to prove that she had not acquired a decidedly English tone. After speaking in an Oxonian and then an American accent she said, "I am betwixt and between, a sort of international English. In England they think I talk very American and my American friends think I talk English. But I merely talk as I always have talked."

The report that Miss Bankhead would return to the stage in New York, where she appeared several times without much favorable comment before attaining her success as an emotional actress in London, was denied by her.

Miss Bankhead said she would begin work within a day or two on the motion picture entitled "New York Lady," which will be produced by Paramount. The scenario was written by Donald Ogden Stewart.

Miss Bankhead, who was dressed in black, fingered a turquoise bracelet and turquoise beads as she denied the accounts concerning the sale of her home in Berkeley Square, London. She said the incorrect reports were caused by her original idea of leasing the house.

Miss Bankhead, who was born in Jasper, Ala., is the niece of Senator John H. Bankhead, and the granddaughter of John Hollis Bankhead, who served as a Representative for twenty years. She returned to this country for three days several years ago for the only other time since she made her debut on the London stage.

Tallulah being made up somewhere on Long Island for her first American "talking" motion picture. The year was 1932 and Paramount still maintained Eastern studios in Long Island City. The original title of the movie was New York Lady, *later provocatively disimproved into* Tarnished Lady. *The script was the maiden screenwriting effort of the brilliant humorous writer Donald Ogden Stewart, who had much to learn. George Cukor was making his debut as a director, and he, too, had much to learn. The movie was very bad, and the critics tended to blame its failure on Tallulah, who had been given a great deal of advance publicity as a second Marlene Dietrich and who obviously wasn't a Dietrich at all.*

With Fredric March in My Sin. *Tallulah's movies in this period had optimistic titles, hard to live up to.* My Sin *and* The Cheat, *which followed it, were directed by George Abbott, who did not enjoy the experience.*

"There's only one thing I'd like to be sure of - that's you . ."   1309-38

On the left, a scene from Tarnished Lady. *The man in white tie and boiled shirt is Clive Brook, a debonair British actor much in demand for early talkies because he had been trained to speak English correctly, on a stage. Many popular American screen stars of the silent days did not so much speak as squeak.*

Lower left, Tallulah being branded by Irving Pichel in The Cheat. *Also, a glimpse of Tallulah striding down a street in Hollywood, in a photograph taken to illustrate the latest fashion in ladies' suits. By the standards of haute couture in the thirties, the skirt passed for short. The tradition that called for actors and actresses to dress more stylishly than ordinary mortals has long since vanished; now they wear soiled T-shirts and Levi's and go barefoot except in deep snow.*

Right, a classic courtroom vindication scene from The Cheat. *It was a good scene then and it is a good scene now. The heroine, having been gravely misunderstood, well deserves to be discovered to have been a perfect peach; no more branding for her, not in the midst of all those smiles.*

146

Silly, beautiful pictures. The dresses Tallulah was modeling have passed the test of time far better than the sculpture, which would have been well advised to be a cat. Even at the hands of inept sculptors, cats are almost foolproof.

Having made three miserable movies in the East, Tallulah was shipped West to start making miserable movies in Hollywood. Here she is on the set of Thunder Below, *with, for no reason respected by history, Rudy Vallee; with Charles Bickford, also in* Thunder Below *(Bickford, poor devil, is blind, and his wife is taking shameless sexual advantage of him); and with Robert Montgomery and Hugh Herbert in* Faithless. *Montgomery remembers Tallulah as having been very nice to him, a beginner.*

Upper right, a scene from The Devil and the Deep. *This was Charles Laughton's first American movie. He played a mad submarine captain, and there was nothing Laughton relished more than feigning madness: he could foam on cue as Tallulah's mother could faint on cue.*

Lower right, Gary Cooper and Tallulah in The Devil and the Deep. *Cooper would occasionally play the role of someone benignly daft but never mad. If it is a protestation of love that Tallulah is trying to keep him from uttering, what a waste of effort on her part! Under the best of circumstances, it would have taken him hours to blurt it out.*

Laughton, Tallulah, and Cooper at a sticky point in their triangle. As the billing indicates, Cary Grant was then comparatively small potatoes. As a passionate devotee of physical fitness, Grant regarded Tallulah's dissolute ways with awe. Old movie stills are a precious source of information concerning fashions in interior decoration as well as in dress. The silver teapot and demitasse cups are traditional, but the candlesticks are the last word in thirties chic.

Hollywood star-time. On the left, Tallulah on a movie lot with George M. Cohan, that often notably disagreeable man. It would be hard to imagine anyone with whom Tallulah had less in common; Cohan was Irish and puritanical and parsimonious, and nearly everything that Tallulah did in the course of an ordinary day would have struck him as fit matter for confession.

At a movie premiere with her friend and acting associate Anderson Lawlor. Lawlor is wearing that superlative nineteenth-century invention: the collapsible opera hat.

On a street corner with a guru named Mehir Baba, whom Tallulah regards with understandable skepticism. She was nominally an Episcopalian and was content to leave the religious mysteries of the East unexplored.

With the celebrated tennis champion "Big Bill" Tilden, whom Tallulah's usual cigarette threatens to do unusual injury to. Tallulah took up and quickly abandoned tennis. She is said to have played once or twice with Garbo, who took the game seriously and would have found Tallulah a pushover.

On the right, with Mrs. Lionel Barrymore. Two snappy dressers, plainly not dressed for the same occasion. Mrs. Barrymore has taken the precaution of keeping Tallulah's body between herself and the threat of being set afire.

Dammit! Write a Good Play! I'll Buy It! Shouts Tallulah

Miss Bankhead Gives Out an Interview— Or, Rather, a—" " ?—" ? " ! !

Lawlor, Tallulah, Ina Claire, and her unidentified escort. Miss Claire, one of the cleverest and most endearing of Broadway comediennes, is now living in retirement in California. The lady at the next table looks as if she would give anything to overhear what the four beautiful people are saying, which probably wasn't, to tell the truth, very much.

Tallulah at the fashionable nightclub El Morocco with Cecil Beaton.

Listening bemused to Michael Farmer, later a husband of Gloria Swanso

Drinking champagne with an unidentified companion somewhere in the depths of Ohio. Even on the road, she would take care to be well-companioned

...th the movie critic and newspaper columnist John S. Cohen at a Broadway opening. Cohen and Tallulah were old friends and not lovers, and they look it.

The New Play

Tallulah Bankhead Appears in 'Forsaking All Others," at the Times Square.

By RICHARD LOCKRIDGE.

Miss Tallulah Bankhead made her grand entrance last evening to considerable applause in an aimless three acts of chitter-chatter called "Forsaking All Others." Cheers rang out from the Times Square Theater, wherein this event occurred, and Miss Bankhead made a little curtain speech, saying that every one was very kind to her, as, indeed, every one was. Or, possibly, her authors might be excepted from that amiable conspiracy.

They have not, certainly, given Miss Bankhead much of a play. It is one of those fiercely smart little comedies, crowded and spilling over with wise-cracks of varied quality. Well dressed persons, few of them essential to the story, sit around in handsome interiors done by Donald Oenslager and quip. It is difficult to remember when so many quips have fallen in one evening —or when so many quick retorts seemed so essentially alien to the play in which they were embedded. Most of the best bits seem, indeed, not to have occurred to Edward Roberts and Frank Cavett; the original authors, and to have been thrust in later by other hands. And, every now and then, the jests, taken by themselves, are comic enough.

The play, however, remains an over-dressed wraith. Its plot has to do with a girl who was jilted at the altar. Her young man married another girl, straight-way repented and returned to her. "You're not very loyal, are you?" she inquired, understandably. "Now," said one of the prize oafs of dramatic literature, "what do you mean by that?" But he caught on, finally, and got a divorce. Then she married another man. A surprising number of characters are required to enact this tiny charade, which falls to pieces of its own lightness quite early in the first act. At no time does it remotely approach any human reality, in speech or motivation.

Miss Bankhead, doing her best, partially to redeem it. Certainly she has that strange gift of personality, which is possibly the one thing no actress can afford to be without. She crosses the footlights; when she is present you watch her, even on a crowded stage. She is, probably, a performer rather than an actress—a limber young woman with a husky voice, able to turn cart-wheels. It is difficult to guess what she might do in a play which required more than cart wheels. She is rather irregularly supported by a cast which, on its credit side, includes Cora Witherspoon, Donald Macdonald, Ilka Chase and, much of the time, Fred Keating (Mr. Keating does no tricks). Others in the cast are a little overwhelmed by the authors' longing for wicked witticisms.

> **'FORSAKING ALL OTHERS.'**
>
> A comedy in three acts by Edward Roberts and Frank Cavett. Staged by Thomas Mitchell; settings by Donald Oenslager; produced at the Times Square Theater by Arch Selwyn. The cast:
>
> Dent...............................Harlan Briggs
> Mrs. Paula La Salle...Cora Witherspoon
> Jefferson Tingle...........Fred Keating
> Shepherd Perry.........Donald Macdonald
> Mary Clay..........Tallulah Bankhead
> Dottie Winters................Nancy Ryan
> Arthur Smith..............Roger Sterns
> Dillon Todd............Anderson Lawlor
> Constance Barnes......Millicent Hanley
> Kilner Branch...............Ilka Chase
> Susan Thomas........Barbara O'Neil
> Maid...........................Ethel Remey
> Hooker Mason...........George Lessey
> The Reverend Duncan..Robert Hudson
> Eddie ....Harry Anderson
> Mr. Martin.......Delancey Cleveland
> A Lady...............Georgette Realin
> A Gentleman............Henry Fonda

THE PLAY

Tallulah Bankhead and Earle Larimore Appear in 'Dark Victory.'

> DARK VICTORY, a play in three acts by George Brewer Jr. and Bertram Bloch. Staged by Robert Milton; setting by Robert Edmond Jones; produced by Alexander McKaig. At the Plymouth Theatre.
>
> Dr. Frederick Steele.........Earle Larimore
> Miss Wainwright...........Mildred Wall
> Dr. Parsons...............Frederick Leister
> Judith Traherne.........Tallulah Bankhead
> Alden Blaine ....Ann Andrews
> Josie ....Myra Hampton
> Michael ....Edgar Norfolk
> Leslie Clark...............Dwight Fiske
> Miss Jenny...............Helen Strickland
> Postman ....Lewis Dayton

By BROOKS ATKINSON.

When Tallulah Bankhead finds the right sort of play for an American appearance she will be able to act it. "Dark Victory," in which she was acting at the Plymouth last evening, is not the play for which she has been waiting, although it is not destitute of quality. But Miss Bankhead infuses it with the odd sort of vitality that distinguishes her acting, and she plays with intuitive stage intelligence. According to the mood of the play, she can be reserved, terrified, resolute, tender, abandoned or plain floppy in style. She can shift styles with startling swiftness. It is not all pure gold, or at any rate not in this play, which is a curious stew of mixed vegetables. But Miss Bankhead has not only an interesting personality but a knowledge of her craft and a respect for her position in it. Obviously, she has prepared her appearance in "Dark Victory" as painstakingly as though the crises of the character were spontaneous.

George Brewer Jr. and Bertram Bloch have written a drama about a headstrong young lady who has only six months more to live. She is a dissolute member of the idle Long Island rich, who are never let off anything in our theatre. When she appears in Dr. Steele's office she does not know that she has tumor of the brain, but he knows that an operation will only postpone the day of her death and he does not tell her the whole truth. After she has recovered from surgical treatment she discovers by the reserve in his enthusiasm that her cure is only a reprieve. The rest of the play shows how she learns to be gallant before the end arrives. Since she has fallen in love with the doctor and marries him with the death sentence hanging over her head the play combines romance with valor.

The plot is something of a death sentence over the play. For once the date has been set for dying, the authors are imprisoned within their own invention. They have written a capital first act, where the characters are skillfully disclosed. But once the characters are introduced, "Dark Victory" drifts into the commonplaces of wickedness and morality; the writing lacks distinction, and, although the emotions are strong, you are likely to suspect them of being fraudulent. Before the day of darkness arrives their heroine is an unconscionable time a-dying.

The somber vivacity of Miss Bankhead's acting lays a spell on your sympathies, although your mind may be playing truant by the time the drama is half over. As the young doctor, Earle Larimore also plays with great conviction. When dramas are tying themselves up in knots you still have the privilege of admiring the actors. Mr. Larimore is worthy of admiration. He is neat, reticent and lucid; his emotions appear to be the fruit of concentrated thinking. He has the enviable faculty of inhabiting the stage. Although the play turns into a bedizened theatre piece after the first act and sometimes just avoids being maudlin, Miss Bankhead and Mr. Larimore have something to give that all of us are eager to accept.

Forsaking All Others was the play in which Tallulah returned to Broadway. It opened on March 1, 1933, when all the banks in the country were ordered closed. Tallulah backed the comedy herself; it was not a success and she claimed afterwards to have lost forty thousand dollars on it. She is seen, upper left, with Fred Keating in the telephone booth of a speakeasy, and, upper right, with Ilka Chase, who feels sorry for the newly jilted bride.

Lower left, Tallulah *in* Dark Victory, *a sad story about a girl who goes blind and dies; Tallulah consented to play in it only because its chief backer was her friend John Hay Whitney. The play later became a hit movie with Bette Davis.*

TALLULAH BANKHEAD

FORSAKING ALL OTHERS
TIMES SQUARE THEATRE

The New Play

'Something Gay,' Starring Miss Bankhead, Opens at the Morosco.

By RICHARD LOCKRIDGE.

Miss Tallulah Bankhead continued her rather gallant struggle against adversity and playwrights at the Morosco Theater last evening, bravely facing both as the star of a piece misleadingly called "Something Gay." "Something Gay" is by Adelaide Heilbron, and Miss Heilbron's slight inadequacy as a writer of witty comedies apparently results only from an inability to think up any witty dialogue.

As far as situation goes, the author has reared her comedy on a firm, if familiar, foundation. It is the one about the young wife who, suspecting her husband's dereliction, pretends to flirt with another man to arouse his jealousy. Since the other man is played by Hugh Sinclair, has all the better lines, and is, in addition, a former lover of the lady, it is evident almost from the beginning that their play acting will turn to earnest. It does so quite pleasantly, in a last act which is more ingenious than its predecessors, and is so brightly played as almost to make one think well of "Something Gay."

Before this point is reached, however, Miss Bankhead and Mr. Sinclair have anxiously tossed aside a whole haystack of dialogue, with hardly a glimpse of the needle of wit. To see them at it, carrying on by sheer dexterity and courage, vastly enhances one's respect for actors. It does, of course, make one wonder at the peculiar mismanagement which places two such engaging persons in so bad a spot.

Most of the action consists of the incessant lighting of cigarettes, several of which fell to the floor to

> **'SOMETHING GAY.'**
> A comedy in three acts by Adelaide Heilbron; staged by Thomas Mitchell; setting by Donald Oenslager; presented at the Morosco Theater by the Messrs. Shubert. The Cast:
> Hatters ....Percy Ames
> Nick ....Kent Thurber
> Herbert Grey ....Walter Pidgeon
> Julia Freyne ....Nancy Ryan
> Jay Cochran ....Hugh Sinclair
> Monica Grey ....Tallulah Bankhead
> Marie ....Elizabeth Dewing
> Dick Mathews ....Roy Gordon

smolder disconsolately, and pacing about. It is always a pleasure to watch Miss Bankhead pace, and one feels it is rather fine of her to go to so much trouble, and devote so much energy to a cause. There was some evidence last evening that the play had been under-rehearsed, but in spite of this the star acted with admirable ease and skill. Mr. Sinclair, who is one of the admirations of this department —he is one of the few actors who can read verse, for one thing—does an excellent job, although some of Miss Heilbron's lines must pain him. Nancy Ryan, Roy Gordon and Walter Pidgeon do, one supposes, all that is possible. There is an interesting set by Donald Oenslager, and for the evening's dustiness only the author seems at all to blame.

THE THEATERS
By PERCY HAMMOND

"RAIN," a revival by Sam H. Harris of the play by John Colton and Clemence Randolph, directed by Sam Forrest, settings by W. Oden Waller, at the Music Box with a cast as follows:

A Native Girl..........Elizabeth Dewing
A Native Policeman......K. A. Fernando
Two Natives..John Waller, Frank De Silva
Ameena..................Emma Wilcox
Private Griggs, U. S. M. C...Kent Thurber
Corporal Hodgson, U. S. M. C..Jack McKee
Sergeant O'Hara, U. S. M. C.
........................Walter Gilbert
Joe Horn...............Granville Bates
Mrs. Alfred Davidson.......Ethel Wilson
Doctor McPhail..........Nicholas Joy
Mrs. McPhail...........Ethel Intropodi
Quartermaster Bates (of the Orduna).
....................Harold De Becker
Sadie Thompson......Tallulah Bankhead
Reverend Alfred Davidson.Herbert Ranson

SYNOPSIS: Act I—Morning. Act II— Late Afternoon. Two Days Later. Act III Night. Four Days Later. Time: The present. The action of the play takes place in the hotel store of Trader Joe Horn, on the Island of Tutu'a, Port of Pago Pago, South Seas.

"Rain"

SADIE THOMPSON and the Reverend Mr. Davidson renewed their hostilities Tuesday night at the Music Box with Miss Tallulah Bankhead in a turbulent impersonation of the sad joy-girl of Pago Pago. Mr. Colton's "Rain," vigorously resisting the teeth of Time, showed no signs of its old age and seemed as fresh as if it had been written yesterday—which is something for its author and its director, Mr. Forrest, to boast about. It is possible that one errs in the suspicion that the cast was not so right as that which aided Miss Eagels in her fine performance. Loyalty to memories of its superb playing may interfere with judgment. But it was certainly good enough to repeat the story credibly; and with Miss Bankhead turning loose all her histrionic energies the revival became something in the nature of an occasion.

This Sadie Thompson, more physically glamourous than her predecessor, swaggers into Trader Horn's inn somewhere in the South Seas, swinging her rounded shanks in the wanton manner of Miss Mae West. As she laid her big eyes on a handsome leather-neck, and dropped husky wise-cracks from her full lips the resemblance to Miss West's art grew terrifying. However, when later the conflict began and she came to grips with "the mealy-mouthed hymn-hound," all the awful likeness vanished, and she was The Bankhead in a glorious simulation of fury. She damned her adversary as if she meant every blasphemous cuss-word she gave tongue to—and you may remember that Mr. Colton was not stingy in providing her with picturesque and, perhaps, unprintable profanity. It was in such scenes that Miss Bankhead was superior. When she got through with one of those gorgeous tantrums

the stage was littered with tatters from the torn passions. You felt that you had been eavesdropping on a four-square prostitute with her back to the wall, bawling out, if I may weakly paraphrase Miss Thompson's classic epithet, a psalm-singing son of a psychopath.

* * *

The intention was to hint above that Miss Bankhead's characterization was uneven, now deep then shallow. In the scene with Sergeant O'Hara, the sentimental devil-dog, after she had got religion from the Reverend Davidson, her acting was as pure as Duse's might have been in like circumstances. Elsewhere she seemed thoughtless and superficial. The inevitable comparison with Miss Eagels's steady characterization results in a belief that Miss Bankhead's performance is a splendid feat, distinguished by flashes of genius, and even in its least commendable moments a brilliant stunt.

* * *

Mr. Granville Bates as Joe Horn, the lazy South Sea trader, quotes Nietsche and Dr. Johnson indolently as the rain falls on Pago Pago; and Mr. Herbert Ranson as the fanatic man of God is as Mr. Maugham and Mr. Colton probably imagined him to be. Miss Ethel Wilson's gaunt playing of the missionary's wife was acclaimed last night as it deserved to be by an audience that was evidently happy in the enjoyment of a good old play vividly presented.

Tallulah was always admirably candid about her professional failures. In her autobiography, she refers to the brief run of Something Gay *as an entombment. She undertook the revival of* Rain *partly in order to rebuke Somerset Maugham for having kept her from playing the lead in the original London production. In the picture on the right, evidently taken during rehearsals, one notes the ever-present cigarette and the hand-cranked phonograph.*

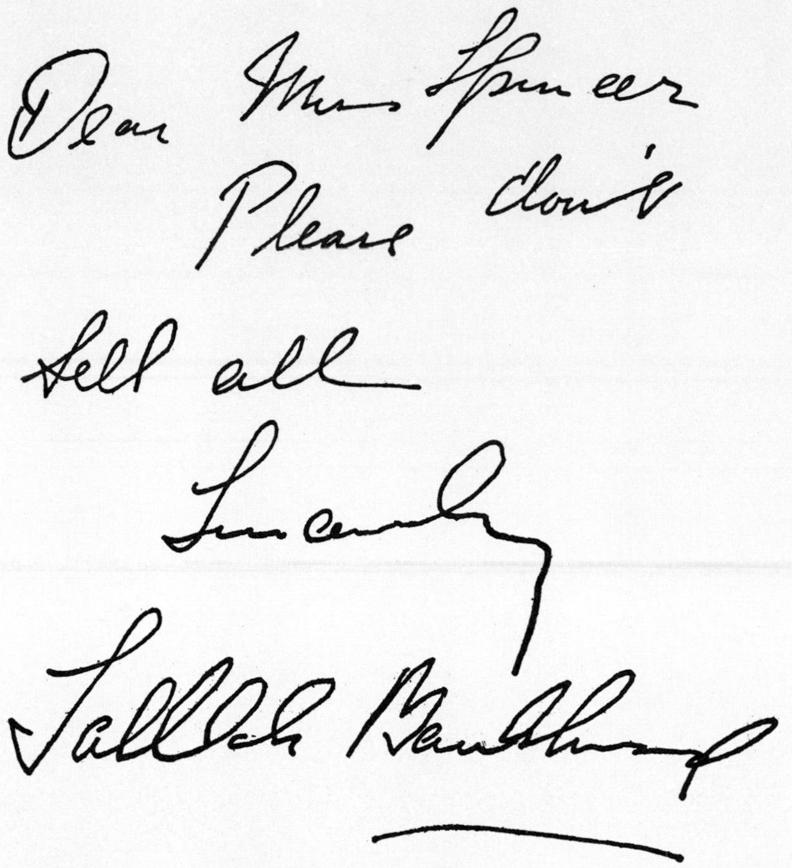

Dear Mrs Spencer

Please don't

sell all

Sincerely

Tallulah Bankhead

Analysis of Tallulah's Handwriting by Shirley Spencer
January 29, 1937, The Philadelphia Inquirer

    Tallulah Bankhead is really as temperamental as the actress she
portrays in George Kelly's latest play, "Reflected Glory." She has
an extraordinary handwriting, as individual as she is herself. It
slants far to the right at a hysterical angle, indicating her very
emotional nature. It is as natural for her to express herself as
for a river to flow to the sea. Her emotions overflow like a
turbulent stream.

    Her letters dwindle to a mere wavy line in between those tall,
inflated loops which she writes. This shows continuity of thought
and expression. Such writers are fluent talkers, expressing their
thoughts as they come to them.

    Combined with these extravagant loops, this feature reveals
that Miss Bankhead conveys her thoughts with imagination--vivaciously
and unconventionally. Her thoughts fly too rapidly for her pen to
follow. The pen movement is precipitous--a headlong flight disregard-
ing all stop signals.

*Above, an analysis of Tallulah's handwriting by a newspaper graphologist. Given
Tallulah's celebrity, Mrs. Spencer was not likely to go wrong.*

*On the right, Tallulah in a characteristic episode—being interviewed by a
reporter from some out-of-town newspaper. The reporter's shoes must have
caught Tallulah's eye without arousing envy.*

In Reflected Glory, *a play by George Kelly. One of the leading playwrights of the period, Kelly wrote* The Show-Off, Craig's Wife, *and a number of other successful plays.* Reflected Glory *is about an actress caught between the demands of marriage and a career; in the end—daringly, for the time—she chooses a career. Tallulah got excellent notices, though the critics disliked the play; it ran for sixteen weeks in New York, then took to the road. Tallulah admired Kelly in part because he was so unlike her in his shyness.*

Being greeted by Daddy when Reflected Glory *reached Washington. It was on this occasion that he gave her a rabbit's foot, which she carried everywhere.*

BROADWAY AGOGGIER THAN USUAL OVER TALLULAH'S WEDDING

She Falls for Handsome John Emery—Will Play Scarlett O'Hara, Says Variety

Tallulah Flies To Altar, Weds Actor in South

Jasper, Ala., Aug. 31.—Tallulah Bankhead, for years a mocker of marriage, flew to her wedding tonight. The blonde star of two continents came by plane from New York to become the bride of John Emery, handsome young scion of an

Tallulah and John Emery in Birmingham last night.

illustrious stage family and the man who will play "Caesar" this Fall to her "Cleopatra" in a new production of Shakespeare's "Antony and Cleopatra."

In the summer of 1937, Tallulah fell in love with a young actor named John Emery, took him home with her, and then took him down to her father's house in Jasper and married him, to the astonishment of her friends and the relief of her father, who henceforth invariably referred to her as Mrs. Emery. The improbable marriage ended in Reno, in 1941, after her father's death. Emery described their interlude as like the rise, decline, and fall of the Roman Empire. He intended this strange remark to be taken as a compliment to Tallulah's formidable powers; they remained friends until his death, in 1964. Emery's rather foppish good looks and gentlemanly manner are at present out of fashion.

Tallulah Bankhead in "Antony and Cleopatra"

Shakespeare's Tragedy Is Revived With a Cast Including Conway Tearle and John Emery

By JOHN MASON BROWN

Tallulah Bankhead barged down the Nile last night as Cleopatra—and sank. And with her sank one of the loveliest, most subtle, and most stirring of all Shakespeare's major tragedies.

As every reader knows who has responded to the pulse-beat of its verse, this drama of two lovers who considered the world well lost, when lost for love, is a magical script. It is a vigorous creation, world-wandering in its scenes and reckless in its splendid energy. Young love of the Romeo and Juliet kind is not its concern. Its story is no teary tale of youthful misfortune. It is an adult tragedy, as glorious in its maturity as is the sad saga of Verona's warring houses in its shimmering springlike qualities. Its final deaths are not brought about by tardy messengers and slow-footed friars. They are due to inner defects which eat like cancers into the careers of a grown man and a grown woman who are greatly placed.

This man and the woman he loves are not in love with love. They are oppressively in love with one another. They are weakened, almost sickened, by an affection they cannot control. Each is an addict to the drug of the other. Passion hovers like a thick cloud of incense over the text which lives because of their sacrifices and their deaths. These lovers are not trapped by coincidence in a tomb. They find their honor and themselves in the exultation of their dying. By so doing they lift the humor, the pathos, the sensuality, the verbal perfume, and the ubiquitous narrative of a passion-tossed tale into one of the supremest tragic flights of Shakespeare's genuis.

● ● ● ● ● ●

Then there are the actors. We must admit we never saw Miss Marlowe as Cleopatra, we admire her too much to regret having missed her. Nor did we see Miss Cowl. But for many years now we have been haunted by the vision of the queen and woman Shakespeare drew. His Cleopatra is not Miss Bankhead's.

Miss Bankhead can be a brilliant performer. She has many exciting gifts and often projects her glowing personality. But as the Serpent of the Nile she proves to be no more dangerous than a garter snake. As the tremulous, mercurial, arrogant, pleading, heart-sick heroine of the tragedy, she seems nearer to a midway than to Alexandria. She is beautiful. Yet her Cleopatra has no authority. Although she has a few, scattred moments of pathos toward the end, her performance is apparently designed without any dominating idea or any real comprehension of the character. She strikes some Egyptian poses. She screams termagant-wise when angry. But she cannot keep pace with Cleopatra's changing moods, or suggest her flaming tragedy. The truth is Miss Bankhead is never regal and seldom appears to have peeked with one eye closed into the complex and fascinating heart of Egypt's monarch.

As Shakespeare wrote his play,

"Antony and Cleopatra"

Shakespeare's play, adapted by William Strunk Jr. and presented last night at the Mansfield Theatre by Rowland Stebbins (Laurence Rivers, Inc.). Staged by Reginald Bach. Settings and costumes designed by Jo Mielziner. Music by Virgil Thomson.

THE CAST

Antony	Conway Tearle
Octavius Caesar	John Emery
Lepidus	J. Malcolm Dunn
Sextus Pompeius	Averell Harris
Domitius Enobarbus	Thomas Chalmers
Eros	Wilfrid Seagram
Scarus	Frederic Voight
Dercetas	Richard Ross
Demetrius	Charles Bowden
Philo	Henry Adrian
Thyreus	Stephen Fox
Agrippa	Ralph Chambers
Dolabella	Henry Saunders
Proculeius	Wilton Graff
Menas	John Parrish
Canidius	George V. Dill
Alexas	William Barwald
Mardian	Robert Williamson
Diomedes	Fred Hanschi
A messenger	Lawrence Fletcher
Cleopatra, Queen of Egypt	Tallulah Bankhead
Octavia	Regina Wallace
Charmian	Fania Marinoff
Iras	Georgia Harvey
A dancer	Kamila Staneska

and as history also dictates, Antony and Cleopatra are as necessary to one another "as the bow is to the arrow." If Miss Bankhead fails as Cleopatra, Conway Tearle fails even more distressingly as Antony. The Antony we see in our mind's eye, the Antony Shakespeare drew and his Cleopatra dreamed of, is not Mr. Tearle's mouthing and tired Marcus Antonius. He is the Anthony Mr. Shaw had his middle-aged Julius Caesar describe when he promised his kittenish Cleopatra that from Rome he would send her "a man, Roman from head to heel and Roman of the noblest; not old and ripe for the knife; not lean in the arms and cold in the heart; not hiding a bald head under his conqueror's laurels; not stooped with the weight of the world on his shoulders; but brisk and fresh, strong and young, hoping in the morning, fighting in the day, and reveling in the night."

Although John Emery is a pictorial Octavius, his Caesar is little more than that. As a picture it is moreover better as a silent than a talkie. Thomas Chalmers is disappointing in the strangely reduced role of Enobarbus. And the others, even more than the principals, are all so negative that it is impossible to realize the play being performed is "Antony and Cleopatra." No one would ever guess at the Mansfield that what is being so badly done and spoken there is one of the drama's greatest and most inflammable glories.

Right, Grace George and Tallulah in a revival of Maugham's The Circle. *Tallulah played the role that her friend Estelle Winwood had played in the original New York production. The critic Wolcott Gibbs objected that Tallulah seemed too attractive and intelligent to be altogether convincing—an objection that attractive and intelligent actresses find it hard not to consent to.*

Left, a pleasant fact about Chicago is that it has always been a great city for putting people's names in lights, the bigger the better. John Emery and Tallulah played in I Am Different *on the road and never brought it closer to New York than Washington, which was wise of them.*

Study in Jealousy

BY LLOYD LEWIS

"I AM DIFFERENT."

Adapted by Zoe Akins from a play by Lili Hatvany; presented by Lee Shubert at the Selwyn.

THE CAST.

Baroness Stephanie ....Fritzi Scheff
Jimmy, her son ....Walter Holbrook
Olga and Sara, her twin daughters..
. ...Charlotte and Shirley Cooper
Lou Hoeffler ....Hala Linda
Dr. Held ....Glenn Anders
Alex Toersen...............John Emery
Vera Nitzish ....Ada Gerald
Judith Held ......Tallulah Bankhead
Wilma Bernd............Dorothy Adams
"Provincial Penelope". Margaret Seddon

TALLULAH BANKHEAD opened her second theatrical visit to Chicago last night at the Selwyn in many long gowns and an even longer play. The former fit her better, although the latter probably will be all right by the time Lee Shubert has taken it in a little around the dialogue.

Mr. Shubert is here with the production, which started in California and is heading for a Broadway premiere. There is plenty of material in the play, which, although a comedy, is at the present moment standing with reluctant feet where old-fashioned romance and sophistication meet.

What it has not yet done is to make up its mind which way it will go. Miss Bankhead and the large and very capable cast are equal to the task of carrying it either way; the scenery is both expansive and expensive, and the story, as it stands, has the merit of giving an audience a lot of Miss Bankhead, herself.

Tallulah as Authoress.

The fair Tallulah is on the stage for almost two hours and a quarter, presenting the interesting moods, curves and wardrobe of an aristocratic Viennese authoress who starts out with a noble doctor-husband and high standing as a feminine psychologist and who winds up with a grouse-shooting lover and a syndicated column on "Lonely Hearts." Miss Bankhead tosses her coppery mane of hair excitingly, laughs her warm, contralto laugh very engagingly, and manages to temper voluptuousness with enough humor to make it believable, but she will be herself as an actress only when the play is, as has been said, taken in at the seams, as I am told the term has it.

You meet her as a guest in an uppercrust Austrian home where, a few minutes before her arrival, a jealous-mad actress has pinked her lover in the shoulder with a derringer. While Miss Bankhead's husband-in-name-only, Glenn Anders, doctors the wounded man Tallulah discusses the crime with the would-be murderess, hands down prescriptions as to the cure of jealousy and then proceeds in the very next act to fall in love with the wounded man.

Marital Geometrics.

He, played by John Emery (Miss Bankhead's husband in real life), is a gentleman-hunter with the brain of a wolfhound and the morals of an amiable rooster. His primitive simplicity and out-doors complexion lead the glamorous authoress to adopt him, shall we say, for a few trial months, her husband being a patient kind of cuckold who still maintains his residence with her. This triangle speedily becomes a quadrangle when there enters a vixen intent upon teaching the lady-psychologist to feel the jealousy which, in her books, is so loftily analyzed and minimized.

Then the vixen's husband enters the equation and the whole thing turns into a sextangle, if there is such a term in mathematics. The authoress, toppled from her academic height, experiences bitter pangs, and in the end is taught by one of her correspondence pupils, a quaint little old lady (Margaret Seddon from the movies), that it is best to tolerate a nitwit and unfaithful lover for life than to be bereft of love altogether.

Mr. Emery is excellent as the huntsman, and so is Miss Gerald as the lady who shoots him. Fritzi Scheff, once-famous for her "Kiss Me Again" in "Mlle. Modiste," received a long ovation when she entered in a minor part. Miss Hala Linda made vivid the vixen role, and Mr. Anders had little to do except to laugh as though he didn't mean it.

THE PLAY

Tallulah Bankhead Appearing in Lillian Hellman's Drama of the South, 'The Little Foxes'

THE LITTLE FOXES, a play in three acts, by Lillian Hellman. Setting by Howard Bay, costumes designed by Aline Bernstein; staged and produced by Herman Shumlin. At the National Theatre.

Addie	Abbie Mitchell
Cal	John Marriott
Birdie Hubbard	Patricia Collinge
Oscar Hubbard	Carl Benton Reid
Leo Hubbard	Dan Duryea
Regina Giddens	Tallulah Bankhead
William Marshall	Lee Baker
Benjamin Hubbard	Charles Dingle
Alexandra Giddens	Florence Williams
Horace Giddens	Frank Conroy

By BROOKS ATKINSON

As a theatrical story-teller Lillian Hellman is biting and expert. In "The Little Foxes," which was acted at the National last evening, she thrusts a bitter story straight to the bottom of a bitter play. As compared with "The Children's Hour," which was her first notable play, "The Little Foxes" will have to take second rank. For it is a deliberate exercise in malice—melodramatic rather than tragic, none too fastidious in its manipulation of the stage and presided over by a Pinero frown of fustian morality. But out of greed in a malignant Southern family of 1900 she has put together a vibrant play that works and that bestows viable parts on all the members of the cast. None of the new plays in which Tallulah Bankhead has acted here has given her such sturdy support and such inflammable material. Under Herman Shumlin's taut direction Miss Bankhead plays with great directness and force, and Patricia Collinge also distinguishes herself with a remarkable performance. "The Little Foxes" can act and is acted.

* * *

It would be difficult to find a more malignant gang of petty robber barons than Miss Hellman's chief characters. Two brothers and a sister in a small Southern town are consumed with a passion to exploit the earth. Forming a partnership with a Chicago capitalist, they propose to build a cotton factory in the South, where costs are cheap and profits high. The Chicago end of the deal is sound. But Miss Hellman is telling a sordid story of how the brothers and the sister destroy each other with their avarice and cold hatred. They crush the opposition set up by a brother-in-law of higher principles; they rob him and hasten his death. But they also outwit each other in sharp dealing and they bargain their mean souls away.

It is an inhuman tale. Miss Hellman takes a dextrous playwright's advantage of the abominations it contains. Her first act is a masterpiece of skillful exposition. Under the gentility of a social occasion she suggests with admirable reticence the evil of her conspirators. When she lets loose in the other two acts she writes with melodramatic abandon, plotting torture, death and thievery like the author of an old-time thriller. She has made her drama air-tight; it is a knowing job of construction, deliberate and self-contained. In the end she tosses in a speech of social significance, which is no doubt sincere. But "The Little Foxes" is so cleverly contrived that it lacks spontaneity. It is easier to accept as an adroitly designed theatre piece than as a document in the study of humanity.

* * *

One practical advantage of a theatre piece is the opportunities it supplies to the actors. In a perfectly cast performance, none of them fumbles his part. Sometimes our Tallulah walks buoyantly through a part without much feeling for the whole design. But as the malevolent lady of "The Little Foxes" she plays with superb command of the entire character—sparing of the showy side, constantly aware of the poisonous spirit within. As a neurotic victim of circumstances, Miss Collinge also drags the whole truth out of a character, and acts it with extraordinary lightness and grace. Frank Conroy plays the part of a tired man of the house with patient strength of character. Florence Williams is singularly touching in the part of a bewildered, apprehensive daughter of the family. There are also vivid characterizations in the other parts by Charles Dingle, Abbie Mitchell, Carl Benton Reid, Dan Duryea, Lee Baker and John Marriott.

* * *

Howard Bay has provided a setting that conveys the dark stealthiness of the story, and Aline Bernstein has designed suitable costumes for a period narrative. As for the title, it comes from the Bible: "Take us the foxes, the little foxes, that spoil the vines; for our vines have tender grapes." Out of rapacity, Miss Hellman has made an adult horror-play. Her little foxes are wolves that eat their own kind.

Tallulah as Regina Giddens in Lillian Hellman's The Little Foxes. *This was the finest role that she was ever to have and she made the most of it, thanks in large measure to the director, Herman Shumlin. On the right, she and Shumlin are talking things over during an early reading of the play; Lillian Hellman is listening hard. Shumlin was a sterner taskmaster than any Tallulah had hitherto encountered; he forced her to become a better actress than she then knew how to be. For nearly the first time, the full force of her energy and will to succeed went into the embodiment of a character wholly unlike herself.* The Little Foxes *gave her glory; it also gave her plenty of money, since her contract called for her to be paid 10 percent of the box-office gross and the play was a big hit.*

The settings for The Little Foxes *were by Howard Bay and the costumes by Aline Bernstein. Here Regina Giddens ("soulless and sadistic," Tallulah said of her, "an unmitigated murderess") cheerfully proposes a family toast. Her fellow celebrants are, from left to right, Lee Baker, Carl Benton Reid, Dan Duryea, and Charles Dingle. The play was revived in 1967 by the Repertory Theater of Lincoln Center. It was directed by Mike Nichols, and the cast included Anne Bancroft, George C. Scott, Margaret Leighton, and Austin Pendleton. The occasion proved to be like old times—Lillian Hellman and Tallulah in a brief newspaper quarrel and Tallulah ending by wishing everyone concerned with the revival a great success.*

Below, a card of good wishes from Katharine Hepburn, presumably accompanying flowers. Miss Hepburn's "there's only one of you and that is lucky for the rest of us" could be read two ways, but plainly it was intended to please Tallulah.

Right, a couple of letters to Eugenia Rawls's grandmother. Miss Rawls had first understudied and then assumed the role of Alexandra Giddens in The Little Foxes. *A lasting friendship sprang up between Tallulah and Eugenia Rawls. They had much in common besides their stage relationship as mother and daughter. Eugenia Rawls bore Tallulah's mother's and sister's name, she had lost her mother in infancy and been brought up by a grandmother, and she came from a small town in Georgia not unlike Jasper, Alabama. Tallulah took charge of Miss Rawls's marriage to Donald Seawell and subsequently became the godmother of the two Seawell children, Brook and Brockman, and made them heirs to a large portion of her estate.*

A party celebrating the five hundredth performance of The Little Foxes. *The place is Chicago, and among the guests are Katharine Hepburn, Ashton Stevens (drama critic of the Chicago* Tribune), *Tallulah, Cecil Smith, Eugenia Rawls, and Irene Castle. Since champagne is evidently available, the coffee urn looks unnecessarily large.*

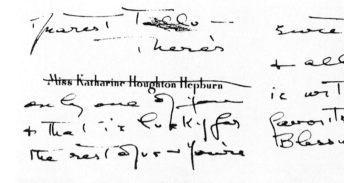

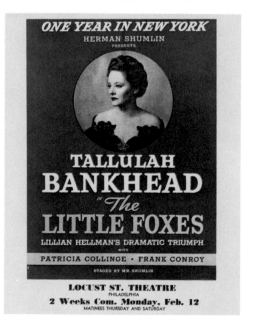

HOTEL ELYSÉE
60 EAST 54ᵀᴴ STREET
NEW YORK

TELEPHONE PLAZA 3-1066

CABLE ADDRESS
ELLEESAY, NEW YORK

December 2, 1939

Dearest Mrs. Rawls,

    I have heard so much about you from your baby, Eugenia, that I felt I must write and tell you how much we all love her. I think she has great talent and is as pretty as a picture; she has a wonderful sense of humor and is wise beyond her years. I sincerely believe that she will go very, very far in her profession and will one day become a great actress, because she has such courage.

    Everyone thinks she looks very like me and that her speaking voice resembles mine, which makes it a perfect combination in this particular play, as I am playing her mother. I can't wait for you to see her in this part. She has a scene where she is so touching that it almost breaks your heart; in fact, it is hard for me to keep in character when I watch her. (As you know, I am playing a very unsympathetic and cruel mother.)

    I hope that you will be able to come to New York soon and see for yourself, but if that is impossible, we will move the mountain to Mahomet!

    I had intended to write you a much longer and detailed letter but I've been caught in up in a maelstrom of duties and hectic obligations. When things have settled down a bit, I will take time off to write you again.

    My mother died when I was born and I was raised by my grandmother, so Eugenia and I have a great bond in common. I know that you are a wonderful person and I am looking forward with real joy to the time when I will have the privilege of meeting you personally.

    All good wishes, and if you will permit me to sign

With love

Tallulah Bankhead

HOTEL ELYSÉE
60 EAST 54ᵀᴴ STREET
NEW YORK

TELEPHONE PLAZA 3-1066

CABLE ADDRESS
ELLEESAY NEW YORK

December thirteenth
1939.

Dearest Eugenia's Grandmother,

    Thank you for the beautiful Cape jasmine you sent me. It was so fresh and lovely that if you weren't so far away, I'd have thought it had come straight from your Southern garden.

    I was so happy to receive your dear letter and deeply touched that my sincere admiration, affection and belief in your little Eugenia meant so much to you.

    I don't want you to bother to answer this letter as I know you've hurt your hand, and I think it too generous of you to have written me at all - not that I wouldn't love to hear from you again and often - but to me, writing letters is the most tedious business of all, even to those we love, - hence, the apparently cold-blooded typewritten letter. But I am sure you will forgive that when I tell you I write to my husband and my father the same way. It is perhaps half laziness on my part and half consideration of the recipient, because I fear my penmanship would never live up to your generous opinion of me and I should hate to disillusion such a valuable person as Eugenia's Grandmother.

    We will be coming South one of these days and no matter how crowded the house may be, Eugenia and I will be playing for you especially.

Love,

Tallulah

Roosevelt to Attend Bankhead Funeral After State Rites Today

WASHINGTON, Sept. 15 (A. P.). —President Roosevelt will attend funeral services Tuesday in Alabama for Speaker William B. Bankhead, who died of an internal hemorrhage early today.

The White House announced that the President would leave for Jasper, Ala., aboard his special train immediately after a state funeral for the Speaker in the House chamber tomorrow.

RAYBURN TO PRESIDE

Rep. Sam Rayburn, of Texas, now the House Democratic leader, will be elevated to the speakership and will preside over the services at the Capitol at 1 P. M. (E. D. T.).

The rites will be conducted by Rev. James Shera Montgomery, chaplain of the House, over which Bankhead had presided since 1936. Immediately afterward a special train will take the body to Alabama, accompanied by 60 of Bankhead's colleagues in the House and a number of Senators. The House will recess for three days.

The President will travel on another train. Dedicatory exercises for the new Washington airport Tuesday, at which Mr. Roosevelt was to have spoken, were postponed.

TRIBUTE FROM F. D. R.

The President paid tribute to Bankhead today in a message from the U. S. S. Potomac, returning to Washington from a cruise in Chesapeake Bay.

The President's message read:

"In the untimely death of the Speaker every American loses a tried and proven friend of our system of government. His experience, his fairness and his personality had endeared him to his colleagues and to all who knew him. I personally feel his loss deeply because for many long years his family and mine have been friends and he and I held each other in affectionate regard."

RITES AT JASPER

In Jasper, Mayor J. G. Burton, a close friend of the Bankheads for 25 years, said simple funeral services would be held from the First Methodist Church, of which the Speaker long had been a member. Dr. T. L. McDonald, the pastor, will conduct the rites. Burial will be in the Oak Hill Cemetery, where the late Senator John and Mrs. Bankhead, the Speaker's parents, are buried.

On arrival of the funeral train Tuesday at 11 A. M. from Washington, the Mayor said, the body would be taken to the church to lie in state until the hour of the services.

In the absence of a birth certificate, there can be no certainty about Tallulah's birth date. The family story held that it was January 31. This was enough to furnish her, in her mind, with a close tie to FDR, whose birthday was the thirtieth. Like all the Bankheads, Tallulah enjoyed feeling that she had ready access to the seats of the mighty. Eugenia and Tallulah going up the steps of the United States capitol, on the occasion of their father's state funeral, which FDR attended.

Former President Hoover with Tallulah at the opening of an art exhibition held to raise money for the Finns, during the Russo-Finnish War of 1940. Long after everyone else had given up starched collars and double-breasted suits, Hoover went on wearing them: emblems of the political conservatism that would have made him consider the Bankheads pernicious radicals. Tallulah and he are smiling together not because they like each other but because a photographer has told them to do so.

THE WHITE HOUSE
WASHINGTON

January 31, 1941

Dear Tallulah:

It was like you to do the thoughtful thing and send me that nice little message for my birthday. You know how deeply I appreciate it.

As ever yours,

Franklin D. Roosevelt

Miss Tallulah Bankhead,
Gotham Hotel,
New York, N. Y.

ALEXANDER WOOLLCOTT

Hoping you will remember
that your heart is God's little garden,
I beg to remain

Your affectionate uncle,

Alexander W.

Upper left, a fuzzy snapshot of Tallulah with
Alexander Woollcott and Jack Benny, at
the time she was playing in Rain, and a letter
from Woollcott to Tallulah, at the time he
was playing Sheridan Whiteside in The Man
Who Came to Dinner. The Whiteside
character was based on Woollcott and was sufficiently detestable for everyone, including
Woollcott, to enjoy the resemblance.

Lower left, with Robert Benchley and the
orchestra leader Paul Whiteman. Tallulah is
evidently telling Whiteman how mah-h-velous
he is, and Whiteman is not unwilling to agree,
simultaneously accepting congratulations
from an unseen friend.

Below, at a political rally, Tallulah
had many ties with England and
was even more eager to get the United
States into the war on England's side
than FDR was.

The New Plays

'Clash by Night,' Opens at the Belasco— 'In Time to Come,' at the Mansfield.

By RICHARD LOCKRIDGE.

All that good acting can do for a play, exceptional acting has done for Clifford Odets's "Clash by Night," which opened Saturday evening at the Belasco. Miss Tallulah Bankhead plays the familiar role of a woman disputed with sultry brilliance; Lee J. Cobb's performance as a betrayed husband is compelling; Joseph Schildkraut portrays an encroaching boarder with sharp clarity. And if the lesser characters of the play remain in the shadows, the fault is not that of the players.

The fault, along with the other faults which make of "Clash by Night" a major disappointment, is the fault of Mr. Odets. He has written a play which is at the same time convincing and uninteresting. He has worked over, methodically, familiar materials, employing essentially stock characters and adding nothing to their stature or to their breadth or depth. The dialogue displays many of his mannerisms and few of his talents and he has taken an inconsiderately long time to say what is obviously true.

'CLASH BY NIGHT.'

A play in two acts and seven scenes by Clifford Odets; directed by Lee Strasberg; settings by Boris Aronson; presented at the Belasco Theater on December 27, 1941, by Billy Rose. The cast:

Jerry Wilenski	Lee J. Cobb
Joe W. Doyle	Robert Ryan
Mae Wilenski	Tallulah Bankhead
Peggy Coffey	Katherine Locke
Earl Pfeiffer	Joseph Schildkraut
Jerry's Father	John F. Hamilton
Vincent Kress	Seth Arnold
Mr. Potter	Ralph Chambers
Tom	Art Smith
A Waiter	William Nunn
A Man	Harold Grau
Abe Horowitz	Joseph Shattuck
An Usher	Stephan Eugene Cole

Scenes from Clash by Night, *by Clifford Odets. The cast included Tallulah, Lee J. Cobb, Joseph Schildkraut, and Robert Ryan. Tallulah was supposed to portray a slatternly Staten Island housewife—a role as far beyond her as Cleopatra had been, though in the opposite direction. By the time the play reached Broadway, Tallulah, Cobb, and Schildkraut had nothing in common except their contempt for the producer, Billy Rose.*

Pinero's The Second Mrs. Tanqueray *was Tallulah's first venture into summer stock. She discovered to her surprise that she liked the hurly-burly of touring; having a low threshold of boredom, she preferred new faces in new places to the same faces in the same places. Moreover, when things went wrong on the road, it mattered less than on Broadway. The audiences relished watching a cast wrestle with imminent disaster. Once, on tour in a play with her old friend Estelle Winwood, Tallulah was dismayed to hear a telephone onstage start ringing at an unexpected moment. She said to Miss Winwood, "Answer it!" Miss Winwood picked up the phone, then turned with a smile to Tallulah: "It's for you."*

Below right, Colin Keith-Johnston, who played with Tallulah in The Second Mrs. Tanqueray. *He had by heart a large number of classic English poems, which he would recite in a grave, gentle voice as they drove through the long summer days from one theater to the next. Loving Tallulah, he composed poems to her, which he copied out by hand and sent to her one Christmas, in a schoolboy's blue-lined notebook.*

THE SECOND MRS. TANQUERAY, a play by Arthur Wing Pinero, opened last night at the Berkshire Playhouse under the direction of Romney Brent, with settings by Albert Ward with the following cast:

Aubrey Tanqueray .. Colin Keith-Johnston
Gordon Jayne, M.D. ...... Ralph Kellard
Morse .... Stephen Eugene Cole
Cayley Drummle .... James MacColl
Paula Tanqueray .... Tullulah Bankhead
Ellean .... Eugenia Rawls
Mrs. Alice Cortelyon ..... Leonore Harris
Sir George Orreyed .... Edmund George
Lady Orreyed .... Madeleine Clive
Captain Hugh Ardale .... Jess Barker

Director William Miles has brought something very special to the Berkshire Playhouse this week to win lends and influence people who are looking for some worthwhile way to pass the time between Beethoven and Beethoven, or even during Beethoven.

Miss Tallulah Bankhead is one of those rare individuals for whom the conventional supply of adjectives is depressingly unsatisfactory. She somehow transcends the tagwords of theatrical description to become a kind of dramatic experience. Her talent is great and her charm is undeniable, but the impact of her personality is more powerful still. To even the sorriest, most despicable character— Regina Giddens in the highly successful "The Little Foxes" is a handy case in point—she brings a certain majesty that even a playwright could not hope to create with words.

It is only natural then that for Paula Tanqueray, the tragic fallen angel with whom Arthur Wing Pinero shocked an earlier generation, Miss Bankhead should win sympathy and admiration. Her Paula is a vital, human character, strong in her weaknesses, vulnerble in her strength, a perform-

ance that no one who loves the theatre should miss.

Featured in the company with which Miss Bankhead is touring the summer circuit in "The Second Mrs. Tanqueray" is Colin Keith-Johnson, most vividly remembered for his Captain Stanhope in "Journey's End." Not having seen other performances of Aubrey Tanqueray, I assume that Mr. Keith-Johnson's interpretation was of the first order. At least it seemed right that Paula Tanqueray's husband should be a mild and considerably stuffy Englishman, gifted with infinite kindness and limited understanding; a well-meaning victim of circumstances over which he neither sought nor found control.

A special subsidiary honor of the evening goes to Eugenia Rawls, who seems to make a specialty of being estranged from Miss Bankhead. She played Alexandra Giddens in "The Little Foxes," avoiding her mother for three acts, and follows the same procedure, equally well, with her stepmother in "The Second Mrs. Tanqueray." She has a quiet charm which is not eclipsed even when competing with the brilliance of Miss Bankhead.

Despite the handicap of being saddled with most of Mr. Pinero cute and creaky epigrams, James MacColl makes Cayley Drummle, the family friend, emerge as less the P. G. Wodehouse character he might be under less competent treatment.

Albert Ward's sets are, of course, attractive, authentic and non-diverting. K. R. F.

After The Little Foxes, *Tallulah's most successful American play was* The Skin of Our Teeth, *by Thornton Wilder. She treated the play as a lark, coolly keeping her distance from the numerous roles she played in it, and this happened to be precisely what the author intended her to do. She was pleased to be called on to address the audience directly from time to time; it was what she often did, anyhow, by one trick or another, in plays that suffered from being lifted out of their conventional hermetic atmosphere. Tallulah would have been far more at home in the open, anything-goes theatrical merry-go-round of today than she was in the formal comedies and melodramas of the thirties and forties.*

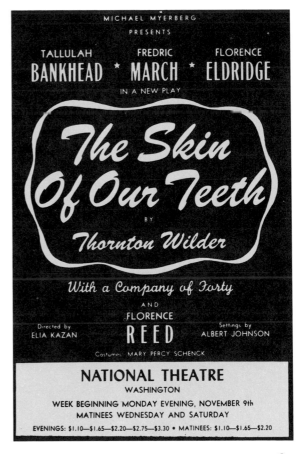

MICHAEL MYERBERG

PRESENTS

TALLULAH · FREDRIC · FLORENCE
BANKHEAD · **MARCH** · **ELDRIDGE**

IN A NEW PLAY

*The Skin
Of Our Teeth*

BY

Thornton Wilder

With a Company of Forty

AND

FLORENCE

Directed by **REED** Settings by
ELIA KAZAN ALBERT JOHNSON

Costumes MARY PERCY SCHENCK

NATIONAL THEATRE
WASHINGTON

WEEK BEGINNING MONDAY EVENING, NOVEMBER 9th
MATINEES WEDNESDAY AND SATURDAY

EVENINGS: $1.10—$1.65—$2.20—$2.75—$3.30 • MATINEES: $1.10—$1.65—$2.20

Tallulah in some of her many roles in The Skin of Our Teeth. *The young man with her below is Montgomery Clift, who subsequently became a celebrated movie star and died young. The letter is from a popular French dramatist, who lived in New York during the Second World War. As a dramatist, Bernstein saw at once what Wilder was attempting and how skillfully he had brought it off. The play became the occasion for a bitter literary quarrel when Henry Morton Robinson and Joseph Campbell, authors of* A Skeleton Key to Finnegans Wake, *accused Wilder of having plucked his play out of Joyce's novel.*

Rocevelt-Asteria
New York

November 20, 1942.

Dear Tallulah:

  I suppose the critics have
used up all the adjectives — so what
can I say, except that I have seen
the great actresses of our time on
two continents and don't remember
one performance more satisfying every
instant to the mind than yours in
that arresting and very beautiful
tragi-comedy.

  The direction too was subtile
and delightful, and the cast was
superb. This will be a great success.

  Do you by any chance remember
what an admirer of your unique gift
always has been

   Your old friend,

   Henri Bernstein

Miss Tallulah Bankhead

Backstage during the shooting of Tallulah's one good movie, Lifeboat. Among those present are Lena Horne, William Bendix, and Canada Lee, who died just as black actors were beginning to receive something like a fair chance in movies and plays.

Below, a scene from a performance at the Stage Door Canteen, in New York. Tallulah is questioning the Quiz Kids, a then popular group of intolerably intelligent and self-confident moppets.

Tallulah helping the war effort by having drinks at the Stork Club with a young soldier named Burgess Meredith. He was later to direct her in Midgie Purvis.

THE SCREEN IN REVIEW

'Lifeboat,' a Film Picturization of Shipwrecked Survivors, With Tallulah Bankhead, Opens at the Astor Theatre

LIFEBOAT, screen play by Jo Swerling from a story by John Steinbeck; directed by Alfred Hitchcock; produced by Kenneth Macgowan for Twentieth Century-Fox. At the Astor.
Connie Porter...........Tallulah Bankhead
Gus......................William Bendix
The German..............Walter Slezak
Alice Mackenzie..........Mary Anderson
Kovac....................John Hodiak
Rittenhouse..............Henry Hull
Mrs. Higgins.............Heather Angel
Stanley Garrett..........Hume Cronyn
Joe......................Canada Lee

By BOSLEY CROWTHER

That old master of screen melodrama, Alfred Hitchcock, and Writer John Steinbeck have combined their distinctive talents in a tremendously provocative film—indeed, a surprisingly unique one—titled "Lifeboat," which came to the Astor yesterday. With only nine characters under scrutiny within the limits of a standard ship's lifeboat—an area from which the camera never at any time departs—they have peeled off a tense and vital drama of survivors adrift from a torpedoed ship, absorbing in its revelations of character and its brilliantly pictorialized details. However, they have also given us an allegorical film with a theme which is startling in its broad implications, especially in this critical time.

For what the worthy gentlemen have given us, when you look closer than the surface aspects, is a trenchant and blistering symbolization of the world and its woes today. Within their battered lifeboat are assembled an assortment of folks who typify various strata of a free, democratic society. There is, first, a parasitic woman, representative of the luxury fringe, who is opportunistic and cynical—a picturesque trifler in every respect. Then there is an American business tycoon, likewise opportunistic and cynical; two meek and pathetic women and four men of the torpedoed ship's crew. These latter are two tough but aimless fellows, a Cockney dreamer and a pensive Negro—all of them clearly indicative of an inarticulate class.

In the boat, also, is a German, lone survivor of the submarine which fired the fateful torpedo and was in turn sunk from the stricken ship. And very soon it is this German—commander of the sub, it transpires—who assumes command of the lifeboat when the others cannot choose their own leader. It is this resourceful German who amputates the leg of one of the men when none of the other survivors is up to this harrowing task. In short, it is this German, personification of the Nazi creed, who proves to be the only competent leader in a boat full of ineffectuals.

John Hodiak, Tallulah Bankhead, William Bendix and Mary Anderson in "Lifeboat."

Lifeboat *was an immediate critical and popular success. Jo Swerling had written the screenplay, from a story by John Steinbeck, and Alfred Hitchcock had directed it with a skill so familiar that Bosley Crowther, of the* Times, *was already describing him as the "old master."*

The cast of Lifeboat *was indeed all-star. Besides Tallulah, Bendix, and Lee, it included Walter Slezak, Mary Anderson, Hume Cronyn, John Hodiak, Heather Angel, and Henry Hull, with whom Tallulah had acted on Broadway in the early twenties.*

Crowds lining up on Times Square to see Lifeboat. The scene strikes the contemporary eye as mysteriously older than its time; at a glance, one would guess that it dated back to the First World War and not to the Second. The Times Square depicted here was roundly deplored by men of the cloth and editorial writers, but when the present Times Square is being deplored by the same parties, it turns out that it is to this Times Square that they speak wistfully of returning.

By Otis L. Guernsey Jr.

"A Royal Scandal"—Roxy

"A ROYAL SCANDAL," a screen play by Edwin Justus Mayer, adapted by Bruno Frank, from a play by Lajos Biro and Melchior Lengyel, directed by Otto Preminger, produced by Ernst Lubitsch, presented by Twentieth Century-Fox Pictures at the Roxy Theater with the following cast:

The Czarina................Tallulah Bankhead
Chancellor ....Charles Coburn
Anna ....Anne Baxter
Alexei ....William Eythe
Marquis de Fleury..........Vincent Price
Captain Sukov..............Mischa Auer
General Ronsky.............Sig Ruman
Malakoff...................Vladimir Sokoloff
Drunken General...........Mikhail Rasumny
Boris ....Grady Sutton
Variatinsky ....Don Douglas
Countess Demidow...........Eva Gabor
Wassilikow ....Egon Brecher

DESPITE such glittering collaborators as Tallulah Bankhead, Charles Coburn, Ernst Lubitsch and Otto Preminger, "A Royal Scandal" is one for the jaybirds. This new Twentieth Century-Fox film at the Roxy is a broad burlesque of the court of Catherine the Great, outlined in skits whose buffoonery is reminiscent of the stylized operetta plot. Though there are occasional flashes of expert clowning in some of the scenes, the screen play yearns for farcical wit and artful twists of situation. Comfortable only when it is kidding itself, "A Royal Scandal" is the sort of picture which offers a better laugh to the actors in the making than to the audience in attendance.

Miss Bankhead does what she can by raising her eyebrows and lowering her voice from time to time, but the humor is too heavy-handed to be upheld by a mere performance. She is a roguish Other Woman as she goes on the prowl for a handsome young officer and lures him away from his maid-in-waiting. The best scene is the one in which the czarina attains her purpose in a silk-and-satin boudoir with champagne to match, a fine background for the predatory Bankhead manner. The actress is not so fortunate in other sequences; the rest of the "off-with-his-head!" nonsense about war, love, plotting generals and palace guards does not allow Miss Bankhead enough adult material to sustain good fun.

After Lifeboat *came* A Royal Scandal, *produced by Ernst Lubitsch and directed by Otto Preminger. The movie received little praise and did badly at the box office; perhaps the time for a touch of Viennese schmaltz had passed. The settings were sensationally attractive. They had a kind of confectionary opulence, characteristic of Hollywood in its golden prime. In the Lubitsch world, sex was a comic game, played according to rules the very breaking of which was subject to rules; one was always scheming to make love in big, silken beds or to be waltzing till daybreak over shining parquet floors. In the informal photograph taken on the set, Tallulah is entertaining a young American officer; the cigarette in her hand goes ill with her costume as Catherine the Great. The wonder is that she didn't set fire to herself and others more often than she did.*

The country place in Westchester that she named "Windows" because it had so many of them. She might also have called it "Chimneys."

Tallulah and her sister, Eugenia, with a couple of younger playmates. Their revels, such as they were, must have been fairly simple-minded.

Striking a pose with her friend Edie Smith in the living room at "Windows." The piled-up newspapers and portable radio are characteristic.

Her worshipped household gods were furniture, faithfully carried from place to place, and pets, whether dogs, cats, birds, monkeys, or lions.

Tallulah was never much of an outdoor
girl, and a long hike through the woods
would not be her notion of a jolly time.
Nevertheless, here she is gathering
firewood for one or another of the many
fireplaces at "Windows" and looking
plausible enough in a novel role. An
outdoor appearance more bizarre and
therefore more convincing came about
when an errand boy whom Tallulah used
as her local bookie contrived, on his way
to "Windows," to knock down a portion
of stone wall at the entrance to a
neighbor's place. The neighbor notified
Tallulah of the damage. Late that night,
hearing strange sounds at the end of the
driveway, the neighbor armed herself
with a flashlight and traced the sound to
its source. She discovered Tallulah and
Estelle Winwood engaged in restoring
the wall with their bare hands, heaping
up stones in the dark and chattering away
in bibulous contentment at their task.

The group of stars above are attending some sort of grisly theatrical luncheon and bearing up well: Tallulah, Helen Menken, Beatrice Lillie, and Paula Lawrence.

The Theatre Guild sponsored Tallulah in a troubled and not very successful production of Philip Barry's Foolish Notion. Again, as so often, the critics praised Tallulah and blamed Barry for having written an unresolved and perhaps unresolvable play.

Left and right, Tallulah in The Eagle Has Two Heads, which someone quickly renamed The Turkey Has Two Heads. The man on the stairs is Helmut Dantine; on the road his part had been taken by a young unknown named Marlon Brando, who did everything in his power to get fired and got fired. His next role was in A Streetcar Named Desire. Tallulah fell the full length of that long flight of stairs at every performance. When the occasion demanded, she was still a superb tomboy-acrobat, trained on the sidewalks of Montgomery.

Tallulah arriving at the theater on one of her national tours of Private Lives. *She played in the Coward comedy for years, at a personal profit of around five thousand dollars a week. In Tallulah's version, it was not the play that Coward had written for Gertrude Lawrence and himself to star in, but its structure is so strong that it appears able to withstand almost any amount of actors' mayhem. Out-of-town audiences were delighted with Tallulah's volcanic rambunctiousness.*

With Donald Cook, romping. Cook was Tallulah's equal as a drinker and was less disciplined about not drinking before going on; it was sometimes remarkable that, having reached the floor, they were able to get up again.

Greeting Patricia Neal at the start of her career. Miss Neal was playing the Regina Giddens of The Little Foxes *at an earlier age, in* Another Part of the Forest.

This photograph, which might well put one in mind of Rembrandt's "The Anatomy Lesson," is actually of Tallulah playing cards with stagehands during a performance of Private Lives. Not being any sort of a "method" actress, Tallulah never felt it necessary to get into the mood of a role and remain there throughout a performance. When she wasn't needed onstage, she would sit in the wings gossiping or reading magazines—anything to keep herself occupied. Backstage, she was probably the most admired performer of her time.

Noël Coward must have known perfectly well what Tallulah was doing with his play, but as an old friend he wasn't saying a word. When he finally got around to seeing it, Tallulah was ready for him—she played it as quietly as possible, almost demurely, and Coward again affected to be pleased.

Al Hirschfeld drew many caricatures of Tallulah, of which this one, with three Nina's, is typical. Over the years, Hirschfeld has sketched uncounted thousands of actors and actresses. His likenesses are always precise and without malice; the theater he sees and draws is a joyous one, full of promise.

BANKHEAD'S 'LIVES' CUES CANADA TOUR

Toronto, June 25.

Tallulah Bankhead, here with Donald Cook in the Ernest Rawley revival of Noel Coward's "Private Lives," broke all summer theatre records in the 39-year history of the Royal Alexandra with a complete sell-out for the week, grossing $17,-200, with the 1,525-seater scaled at a light $2.50 top. Advance sale was $6,300, with whole week seeing hundreds of turnaways at every performance.

Because of this business, Rawley will send the production on a quick Canadian tour after the fortnight's engagement of "Lives" at Greenwich, Conn. Troupe will do a one-night performance at the Capitol, Ottawa, July 8, when the Gov. Gen. of Canada will be present; five nights at His Majesty's, Montreal, starting July 9; and week of July 15 at the Royal, Toronto, for return engagement. Director is Robert Henderson.

22, PLACE VENDÔME

4th December, 1948.

It was very sweet of you darling,
to send me your lovely and very welcome
cable.

My opening was delayed for a few
days by a beastly attack of laryngitis, but
I am now quite well and acting away in French
as if I had been born to it.

My love to you, as always.

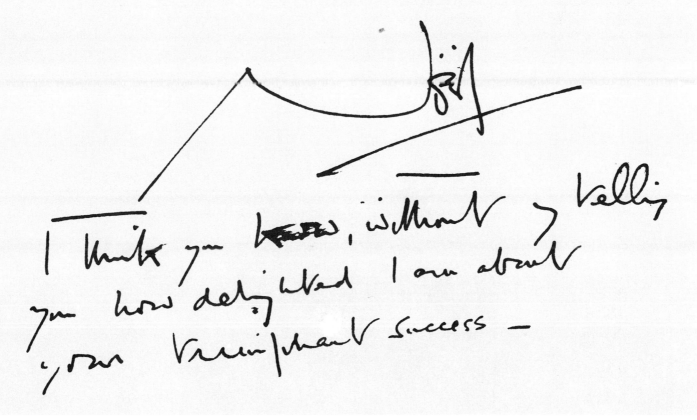

I think you know, without my telling
you how delighted I am about
your triumphant success —

A photograph by Richard Avedon of Tallulah at her dressing table. Reflected in the mirror is the ghostly image of her dresser-secretary-maid, Evyleen Cronin, who was later discovered to have been regularly kiting Tallulah's bank checks up to a total of some fifteen thousand dollars.

If Tallulah was an unlikely figure tramping the woods, she was a still more unlikely figure as a sailor. She would go aboard a boat not in order to get from one place to another but in order to enjoy a party.

Below, Tallulah introducing President Truman on a coast-to-coast broadcast, during the presidential campaign of 1948. She made the broadcast from her dressing room at the Plymouth Theatre, during an intermission of Private Lives.

Right, greeting President Truman at a rally held in Madison Square Garden. Tallulah followed the President's speech with a short one of her own. She had been warned that the audience might walk out on her, since it was Truman they had come to hear; the audience stayed.

Marlene Dietrich, John Huston, and
Tallulah celebrating an award by New
York movie critics to Huston for his
direction of the movie The Treasure
of Sierra Madre. *He later won two
Oscars for* Treasure—*one for his
direction and one for his screenplay.
His father, Walter Huston, also won
an Oscar for best supporting
actor in* Treasure.

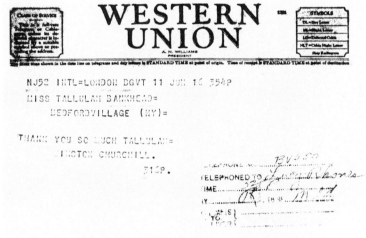

*Much of Tallulah's life at this time centered on "Windows," and at
"Windows" it centered on the pool. Ordinarily, she preferred to
swim naked, but there were occasions when she wore a swimsuit
and other occasions when it seemed sensible to jump in fully clothed.*

*A cable from Churchill. Though they met but once, they felt
themselves to be old friends.*

THE WHITE HOUSE
WASHINGTON

May 8, 1951

Dear Miss Bankhead:

You certainly did beat me to the punch. I
couldn't get through on the phone that night
so I didn't pursue the matter with enough
persistence I suppose to get a chance to talk
with you and Margaret. I thought it was a
grand show. I appreciate very much your
kindness to Margaret and her mother joins
me in that appreciation.

I hope you have a most pleasant and profitable
summer.

Sincerely yours,

Harry Truman

Miss Tallulah Bankhead
Hotel Elysee
60 East 54th Street
New York, New York

*"The Big Show" was the last big gun fired by radio
before it surrendered most of the night air to television.
The show had an unprecedentedly high budget and
gathered in star performers from all over the world.
Tallulah acted as master of ceremonies, and a formula
was soon developed by which the expected thing was
for Tallulah to trade insults with her peers.*

*Upper far left, at a "Big Show" party with Bob Hope,
Fred Allen, and Sid Caesar. Fred Allen said of the sound
of her voice that it was like a man pulling his foot out
of a pail of yogurt.*

*Lower far left, with Laurence Olivier and his then wife,
Vivien Leigh.*

*Left, singing with Margaret Truman (whose father
wrote to say how pleased he was) and Louis Armstrong
and admiring, with Gary Cooper, the clowning of
Danny Kaye.*

*The telegram from Ed Murrow led to Tallulah's
appearance on his TV program "Person to Person."*

*Overleaf, a letter to Dee Engelbach, the producer of
"The Big Show," intelligently complaining that she is
given too little to do.*

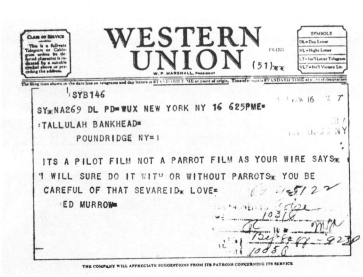

ITS A PILOT FILM NOT A PARROT FILM AS YOUR WIRE SAYS
I WILL SURE DO IT WITH OR WITHOUT PARROTS YOU BE
CAREFUL OF THAT SEVAREID. LOVE=
ED MURROW

Hotel Elysée

60 EAST 54TH STREET, NEW YORK 22, N. Y.
TELEPHONE PLAZA 3-1066

December 1st
1951

Dee:

I don't know how to begin this.

Please don't be mad or tewibbly, tewibbly hurt, because I know I will never get this letter finished -
as of Now I'm reminded of once in the middle of a
blizzard Bob Benchley came to my hotel in the wee
sma' hours dressed in such peculiar garb that my Edie
thought he was W. C. Fields, and his opening remark
was, "I'm not hurt - I'm just tewibbly, tewibbly cold."
So don't be mad, don't be hurt, and never be cold - not
to me.

If you will recall, the last time we were in Hollywood
I was genuinely and deeply distressed about the
material, and you asked me to bear with the situation.
I did and would have, without being asked, what with
Judy falling out at the eleventh hour and the unfore-
seen but unimportant contretemps with ze dainty
Hungarian and the gentleness and unselfishness of
X Mary the spot.

Being the Queen of Non Sequitor, I press on. I know
what pressure the authors are under from week to week
to write for and please all the stars on The Big Show,
and although I've said this many times, I will repeat
for the record that if the stars were not pleased by
their material or placated by you, there would be no
Bit Show, because there ain't that many animals to go
around. There are only a few handfuls of top-flight
stars in each category.

Why are they on The Big Show? Because of their extra-
curricular activities. They have their Ph.D.s whether
of the theatre, screen, radio, television, nightclubs,
records - what have I got to lose - or rockets to the
moon? I never graduated from grammar school. Teacher,
how do you pronounce Patrice Munsell?

Hotel Elysée

60 EAST 54TH STREET, NEW YORK 22, N. Y.
TELEPHONE PLAZA 3-1066

I'm sincere when I say I'm grateful and lucky that I don't have to play eight times a week, but I'm not yet so old, fat and tired that integrity doesn't rear its ugly head. I have felt humiliated and depressed many times on The Big Show, and I feel that I should make a formal feeble or feeble formal protest. How feeble can I get? My word is my bond; therefore my bond is my word.

To go back to the first show, if you remember, I didn't mind what I had to do, until I saw the national press: "All this and Tallulah too," and you will recall I strongly objected when we began the new season to being introduced as the star of The Big Show. The scripts I have been given do not warrant these eulogies. I know Goody Ace is the Tower of Pisa and the Mona Lisa and in spite of his pontifical and withdrawn attitude he is a wise and kindly man. I know that Mort, in spite of his beard, which is so clean there can be no Communist hiding behind it - I can half close my eyes and still think he's pretty. As for Selma and George, they are too close to home. They would cry, too, if my dog --- oh, skip it.

Dee - Oh Dee, Dee, what a cue for Meredith -

I am not quoting my fans, nor my fans' fans, nor my friends nor my friends' friends, when they say, "I love the Big Show, but you don't have enough to do." My darlings, how wrong you are! I have too much to do, but what I have to do is not enough.

Forgive me, Dee, if I'd had more time I'd have written a shorter letter.

Bless you,

Tallulah,

P.S. Dee, you know I wouldn't hurt a fly......did I?

J. N. -

Federal Bureau of Investigation
United States Department of Justice
Washington 25, D. C.

February 11, 1949

Miss Tallulah Bankhead
Hotel Elysee
60 East 54th Street
New York, New York

Dear Tallulah:

I have received your kind letter of
February 9 and was very glad indeed to hear from
you. Your kind comments are greatly appreciated,
and I trust that you will not hesitate to call on
me at any time you think I might be of assistance
to you.

Hoping to see you in the not too distant
future and with kindest regards,

Sincerely,

J. Edgar Hoover

Tallulah had written to J. Edgar
Hoover on some trifling matter,
and he sent her this trifling reply.
Little did he know Tallulah: he
had no idea that she would take
his "do not hesitate to call on me
at any time" literally. When,
shortly afterwards, she learned
that her friend Billie Holiday had
been arrested on a drug charge,
she immediately got in touch
with Hoover and managed to
secure Billie Holiday's release.
One imagines that Hoover
took care to write her no
more civil letters.

Left, in a TV sketch with Bert
Lahr. Lahr is playing Rembrandt,
and who better for the part?

Right, the town house on East
Sixty-second Street, in Manhattan,
to which Tallulah moved after
reluctantly selling "Windows."
Running a country place had
proved too difficult for her, and
after a few years the town house
would also prove too difficult.
Eventually, she moved into
an apartment on East Fifty-
seventh Street.

Right, Tallulah lecturing in Texas: "Dahlings, I've dieted a week to bring you this figure." Sipping often from a glass as she talked, she said, "I'll bet you think it's gin." The audience, of course, laughed. "I wish it were," Tallulah added. It was.

Having discovered that her dresser-secretary, Mrs. Cronin, had stolen thousands of dollars from her, Tallulah decided to go to court. Most performers who lead unconventional lives are blackmailed into keeping silent by the threat of revelations injurious to their careers. Tallulah was confronted by just such threats, and when the case came to trial Cronin's lawyer introduced as much scandal into the testimony as he could. Tallulah was unabashed. Mrs. Cronin was found guilty, upon which Tallulah begged for clemency on her behalf.

Left, Tallulah being lifted over a snowbank by her attorney, Donald Seawell, on their way to court. The tabloids enjoyed every moment of the case. The caption for this picture was, of course, "Legal Aid."

TALLU UPHELD, MAID CONVICTED

During court recess, Tallulah alternately . . .   registers grim expression and . . .   smile of firm confidence as she . . .

assures gathering of reporters . . .   in between cigaret chain-smoking that . . .   she'll "disprove" every charge made.

Tallulah Bankhead emotes off-stage at trial of her former secretary-maid.   (Story, P. 3. Other Photos, P. 3. Back Page)

TALLULAH BANKHEAD

Darling Sophie and Alan:

I can't be clever or wise or witty - I can only apologize for taking so long to return your embrace. Come and see me, and a kiss for whatever's the name for a cello's Stradivarius.

Love,

Tallulah

November 1st 1954

Mr. and Mrs. Alan Shulman
20 Weyburn Rd.
Scarsdale, N. Y.

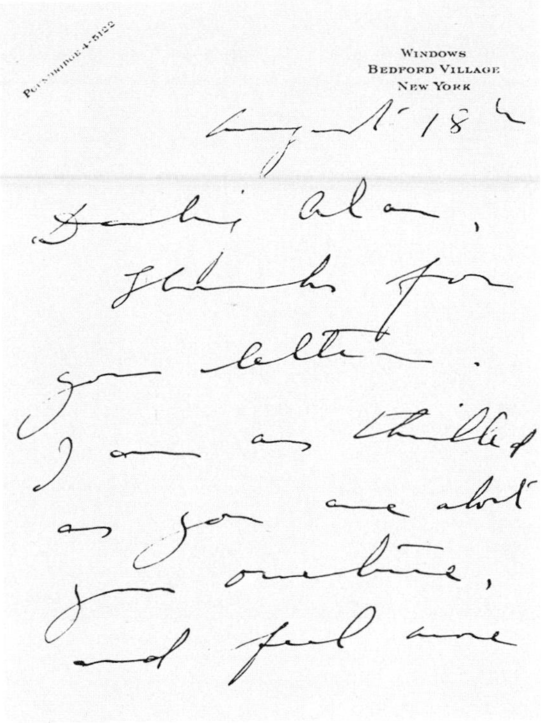
WINDOWS
BEDFORD VILLAGE
NEW YORK

A cellist in the orchestra that played for "The Big Show" dedicated an overture to Tallulah.

Watching the Giants at the Polo Grounds. For many years, Tallulah was preoccupied with baseball, though she admitted that she never understood the game as well as her friend Ethel Barrymore. Once, when Jackie Robinson was running to catch a ball that would turn a home run into an out, Tallulah shouted, "Catch it, you bastard!" and, in the same breath, "Don't hurt yourself, dahling!"

Music-Loving Tallulah Bankhead Delighted By the Dedication of a New Overture to Her

Tallulah Bankhead, who admits to loving music and grows especially voluble in discussing it, will be one of the more interested listeners at tonight's Philharmonic-Symphony concert. Guido Cantelli will conduct the première of Alan Shulman's "A Laurentian Overture," which Mr. Shulman has dedicated to Miss Bankhead.

The actress was asked yesterday about the sequence of events leading to the dedication.

"We met each other on the Big Show program," she explained. "Alan is a brilliant 'cellist. I'm simply devoted to him. He's a darling. We talk music all the time."

Mr. Shulman, she said, had been working on his overture for some time.

"He said he'd dedicate it to me if it turned out well. I guess it did. No. I haven't heard it yet, I'm sorry to say. I couldn't get to the dress rehearsal. Maybe it's just as well. Alan phoned me today and told me he had butterflies."

The dedication is something of a novelty to Miss Bankhead.

"Some popular pieces have been written for me, you know—not classical," she went on. "Certainly this is the first time a classical composer has given me a dedication. I'm terribly flattered and honored."

Had she ever studied music?

"But of course, darling! I took piano and violin when I was at school. I even played pieces for commencement. Things like Sinding's 'Rustle of Spring.' And then there was a Chopin nocturne—how does it go? Dah dah, da da DAAAH da.

"I never kept it up, of course. But I love music. My favorite composer, however, is not the musician's favorite. Wagner!"

She was assured that some of the most eminent living musicians considered Wagner among the elect.

"Not really!" she said in delight. "Most musicians tell me that Mozart is the greatest. I adore him, too. But me, I'm an emotional gal, and Wagner's music sweeps me away. But really, darling, I don't know anything about music at all. I'm always listening, though. I keep my radio tuned to WQXR all day."

Since she comes from Alabama, what was her opinion, she was asked, of being associated with the Laurentians by dedication.

"The Laurentians? I don't even know what they are."

When they were identified she said:

"Oh? Of course, now I remember. Good! Some of my best friends are Canadians."

*Right, contact prints by Richard
Avedon of Tallulah in a classic
posture: in bed, smoking, telephone
at the ready, a couple of woolly dogs
nuzzling her, and books scattered all
around—in this case, copies of her
newly published autobiography.*

*Below, the autobiography caused a
certain amount of trouble in England.
Tallulah had written of the London
production of* Rain, *which starred
Olga Lindo, "It was an immediate fail-
ure." That was a wishful recollection on Tallulah's
part (she had sought the role for herself), and almost thirty years later Miss Lindo was rightly
determined to set the record straight. The
five words were expunged. Newspaper
readers must have assumed that the "offending
passage" was much more wicked than it actually was.*

*Tallulah at the Little Church Around the Corner, in
her role as godmother to Master Brockman
Seawell. Beside her are his parents, Donald
and Eugenia Rawls Seawell. Of the baby's tears,
Tallulah said, "I'd cry, too! Think of all the lovely
sins we've just renounced in his name!"*

A fan letter from a celebrated bookworm.

Olga Lindo Settles Libel Suit

LONDON, Feb. 10 (AP)—Olga Lindo, British actress, today settled her libel action over five words in Tallulah Bankhead's autobiography. The amount the publisher, Victor Gollancz, will pay to Miss Lindo, a veteran of thirty-seven years on the British stage, was not disclosed. The publisher's counsel told the court the offending passage would be dropped from future editions.

THE WHITE HOUSE
WASHINGTON

Kansas City, Missouri
August 4, 1952

Dear Tallulah:

The proof copy of your book arrived a day or two ago and I haven't been able to put it down. It is undoubtedly the most interesting book I've had in my hands since I have been President of the United States. You say in that book that you are a professional actress and have no idea of becoming anything else. It is my opinion that the demand on you for more books in the same vein as this one will undoubtedly be your profession from now on.

I hope you will find it convenient before the time comes for me to vacate the White House to make a call on Mrs. Truman and myself.

Thanks again for your thoughtfulness in sending me an advance copy of your wonderful book. As soon as I get back to Washington I will send you a special copy of Bill Hillman's book which came out a few months back.

Sincerely yours,

Harry Truman

Miss Tallulah Bankhead
Hotel Elysee
60 East 54th Street
New York, New York

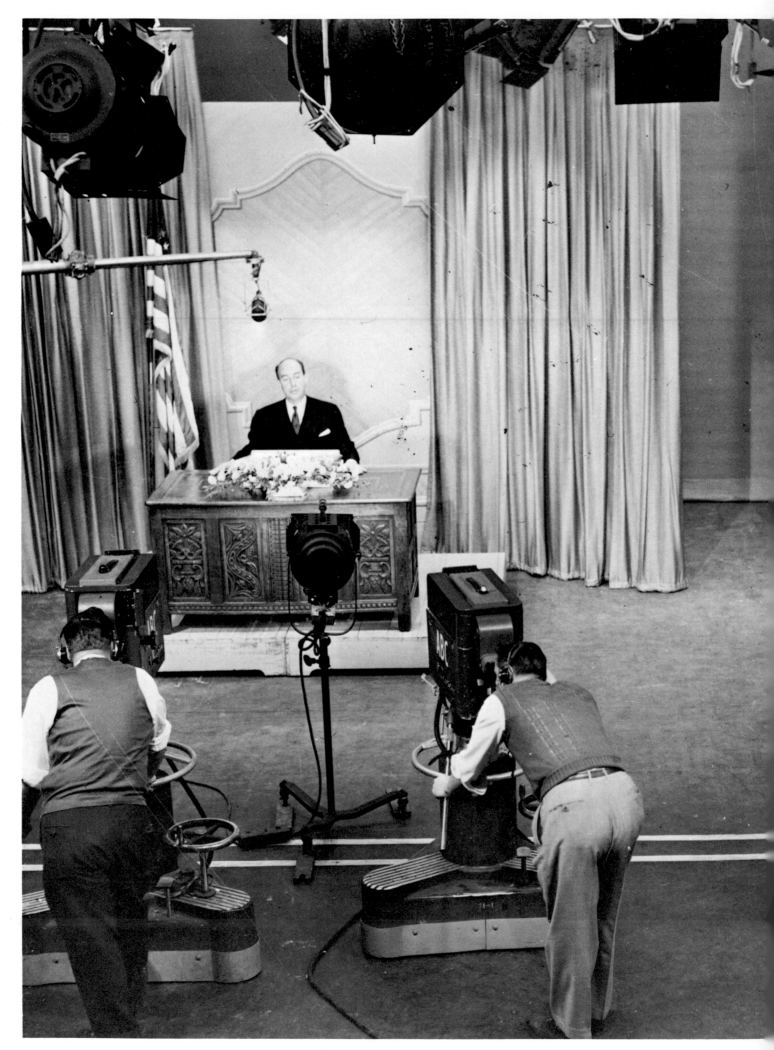

It happened by chance that Tallulah and Adlai Stevenson turned up at the same TV studio at the same time. Tallulah was plugging her book; Stevenson was making a campaign address. As an ardent Democrat and friend of Stevenson's, Tallulah was delighted to stand by and offer encouragement. She had helped put Truman in the White House— why not Stevenson?

Below, Richard Rodgers, George Ball, Irene Selznick, Henry Fonda, Robert E. Sherwood, and Ethel Barrymore join Tallulah in endorsing Mr. Stevenson.

Tallulah introduces Cobina Wright to the merrymakers.

Eddie Arcaro gives tip on a horse to Dorothy Hart and Nina Foch ...ght

A Tallulu of a Party

The words flowed like champagne . . . and so did the champagne. The occasion for all the gaiety was party thrown in honor of Tallulah Bankhead at the Pen and Pencil Club. It celebrated Tallulah's foray into the book-writing business and her departure for Hollywood. All the "dahlins" were there and many of them didn't leave until 5:30 A.M.

Tallulah raids kitchen to see how the steaks are coming along.

Sid Caesar of television fame offers champagne for connoisseuse Bea Lillie's consideration. Mrs. Caesar and film comic Reginald Gardiner share the table The guest list read like a "who's who" of show business.

"Come get it," bawls Tallu . . . and Eve Gabor heeds call with J. M. Seabrook.

The guest of honor shares the mike with crooner Johnny Johnston as the party moves into the wee hours.

(NEWS fotos by Ebbs Brewer)
Dave Garroway's kisse night by the

Tallulah was at her noisy worst at parties of this sort. She was expected to get drunk and sing and shout and talk dirty and exchange broad insults and broader compliments, and so she did. The occasion was the publication of her autobiography, and her publisher, Cass Canfield, in the picture to the right, looks as if he had his eyes fixed on the nearest exit. Eugenia Rawls once told Tallulah of how, on a flight between Washington and New York, she overheard two men seated directly behind her discussing Tallulah. One of the men wound up the discussion by remarking, "I have never heard anybody say something against Tallulah Bankhead in any bar in the world that somebody else didn't rise to defend her." Tallulah looked at Eugenia for a moment, then shook her head and said, "Any bar in the world."

Tallu's Party Like Tallu—Uninhibited

By NANCY RANDOLPH

"Dahlin', people have such shockin' manners these days. They just don't listen—shut up, all of you. I mean, shut up, dahlins!"

Thus spake Tallulah Bankhead from time to time above the incredibly dahlin' celebrity-packed party.

It was a champagne supper given strictly for the actress-author—midnight Saturday until 5:30 A.M. yesterday — and was liberally strewn with diamonds, dahlins and damns. The host: Bruno of the Pen and Pencil Club. The idea: to celebrate Tallulah's new book, "Tallulah," and also her departure yesterday for Hollywood to make a new picture.

The evening began with champagne and casual curses, and started to end about 3:45 with hymns in an honest-to-goodness community sing.

Songs by Tallulah.

When La Bankhead led off in "Silent Night, Holy Night" in her best Alabama baritone, following up with "I'll Be Seeing You" (in all the old familiar places), it seemed like a broad hint to get-the-heck out and go home. Like the "Good Night, Ladies" orchestral farewell. But that couldn't have been more wrong.

"Dahlin', don't go! When all these g——d—— people leave, a few of us can settle down to a real jam session. WHY DON'T A LOT OF YOU GO????"

Several persons, including your correspondent went—merely as far as the bar. Not what you think! For an aspirin. A jumbo-size bottle of same was there, waiting.

"Lend me a comb, someone, my hair's gone wild," Tallulah cried. Eva Gabor obliged.

Now several hundred champagne-filled guests were joining in with the guest of honor in "May The Good Lord Bless and Keep You Until We Meet Again."

Handsome Cobina Wright, under pressure, got up and sang "Besame Mucho."

And when Fritzi Scheff sang the song that long ago made her famous, "Kiss Me Again", Tallu-

(NEWS foto by Ebbs Breuer)

Reginald Gardner, Bea Lillie, publisher Cass Canfield and Tallulah split a bottle of champagne at midnight supper party.

lah rushed over to drop a curtsey and kiss the singer's hands.

Other performers were: Beatrice Lillie, Reginald Gardiner and Vivian Blaine—in the midst of it all Tallulah was heard in a ringingly clear answer to a question. "My love life? I just haven't got any! How can you, in my racket?"

Down from the walls of Bruno's club, gazed framed prints depicting authors of far sterner nature than the guest of honor: Henry Wadsworth Longfellow, Mark Twain, George Bernard Shaw. Walt Whitman alone seemed to approve.

Tallulah's little sister Eugenie, with a close friend, Louise duPont Carpenter, was observed to drop in briefly and drop out again.

Among those present were: Mr. and Mrs. Edward Douglas

(Janet) Madden, with Mrs. Cobina Wright and Luther Reed; Thyra Samter Winslow; Ed and Pegeen Fitzgerald, Abel and Grace Green, Ceil Chapman and her husband, Tom (MGM) Rogers, Paula Lawrence, Joe Bushkin and his heiress-wife the former Francice Netcher; two of the glamorous Gabors, Zsa Zsa and Eva, publisher Cass Canfield and Sammy Colt, son of Ethel Barrymore. Tallulah vehemently kissed Cass: "I've got to get you switched to Adlai."

About 4:15, Cy Coleman began to pound out "Why try to Change Me Now?"—his own new composition—and the jam session was on for 25 durable remaining dahlin' guests.

(Other pictures in centerfold)

235

One afternoon in the fifties, Tallulah went to the studio of Philippe Halsman to have her portrait taken. She sat on the floor and talked and smoked and drank Old Grand-Dad glass after glass, as Halsman snapped picture after picture. It is Halsman's custom, at the end of a session, to ask his subjects to consent to being photographed in the act of leaping into the air. This request has produced remarkable results over the years, and none more remarkable than the leap achieved by the late literary critic Stanley Edgar Hyman, who was known to be one of the most intransigently sedentary men alive. On being asked to make a leap, Tallulah did her best, but in vain—of all Halsman's subjects, she alone remained anchored to the ground. A strange fate for someone whose cartwheels and back somersaults had once brought down the house in London.

*Rather to her surprise, Tallulah
turned out to be a smash hit as a
nightclub performer. Here she is at
the Sands, in Las Vegas, entertaining with songs and assorted one-
liners an audience that includes
Montgomery Clift, Jane Powell,
Lucille Ball, and Desi Arnaz. (The footlights are worth noticing. Long after most
other performers had given them up,
Tallulah insisted upon them in every
contract.) Tallulah earned up to thirty
thousand dollars a week at Vegas—a then
formidable sum—and spent much of it at the
gambling tables. Her attorney, Donald
Seawell, once arranged with Jack Entratter,
the manager of the Sands, that Tallulah's
chips, which she assumed were worth a dollar,
would by secret arrangement between Entratter
and Seawell be worth only a penny. This did wonders for Tallulah's losses, but what would she
have said if she had been, for a change, a big winner?*

A tiny part in a tiny movie, Main Street to
Broadway. *Assisting is Rose Riley.*

Overleaf, the finale of The Ziegfeld Follies, *a
show that was notable for the opulence of its settings
and its poverty in every other particular and that
closed out of town, at a loss of half a million dollars.*

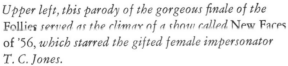

Upper left, this parody of the gorgeous finale of the Follies served as the climax of a show called New Faces of '56, which starred the gifted female impersonator T. C. Jones.

Lower left, a scene from the doomed Follies.

Above, Tallulah in the Follies and Jones in one of his remarkable takeoffs of Tallulah. Jones, who died in 1971, at the early age of 50, was the only female impersonator in recent years to receive high praise on Broadway. Wolcott Gibbs said of him in The New Yorker, "If anybody had told me a couple of weeks ago that I was shortly to spend a large part of an evening happily watching a female impersonator imitate Miss Tallulah Bankhead, I would have said that the world was certainly coming to a pretty pass. This, however,

was precisely what happened last Thursday evening, when Leonard Sillman's New Faces of '56 opened at the Ethel Barrymore. The performer's name is T. C. Jones, and the chances are that without a wig and other accessories he resembles Miss Bankhead very little more than I do; his work is the broadest possible burlesque of a set of mannerisms never too far from burlesque in the original; and yet somehow the effect is as hilarious as anything I have seen this year. The technique that achieves this unlikely miracle is far beyond my talent to analyze, and I think we will just have to let it go as a simple statement of fact: T. C. Jones is a brilliantly accomplished mimic, and if some of his material is a little special (a good deal of the humor depends on knowing what happened to The Follies in Boston), that seems all right with me."

Scenes from Welcome, Darlings, *some of which was plundered from the wreck of* The Ziegfeld Follies *and which Tallulah took on the summer circuit, where audiences are expected to be tolerant. The scene from* Peter Pan *is memorable only for the fact that it permitted Wendy to announce, "I am Wendy Moira Angela Darling," and for Tallulah to reply, "I am Peter Pan, darling."*

Opposite, a scene from A Streetcar Named Desire. *Tennessee Williams had said that in composing the play he had had Tallulah in mind for the role of Blanche DuBois, but by the time Tallulah got around to playing it, she was both too old and too celebrated as a public clown; the most touching lines she had to utter were greeted by certain sections of the opening-night audience in New York as if they were raunchy Tallulah-isms. She struggled heroically but in vain to silence the laughter of admirers who, perhaps unconsciously, were bent upon destroying her.*

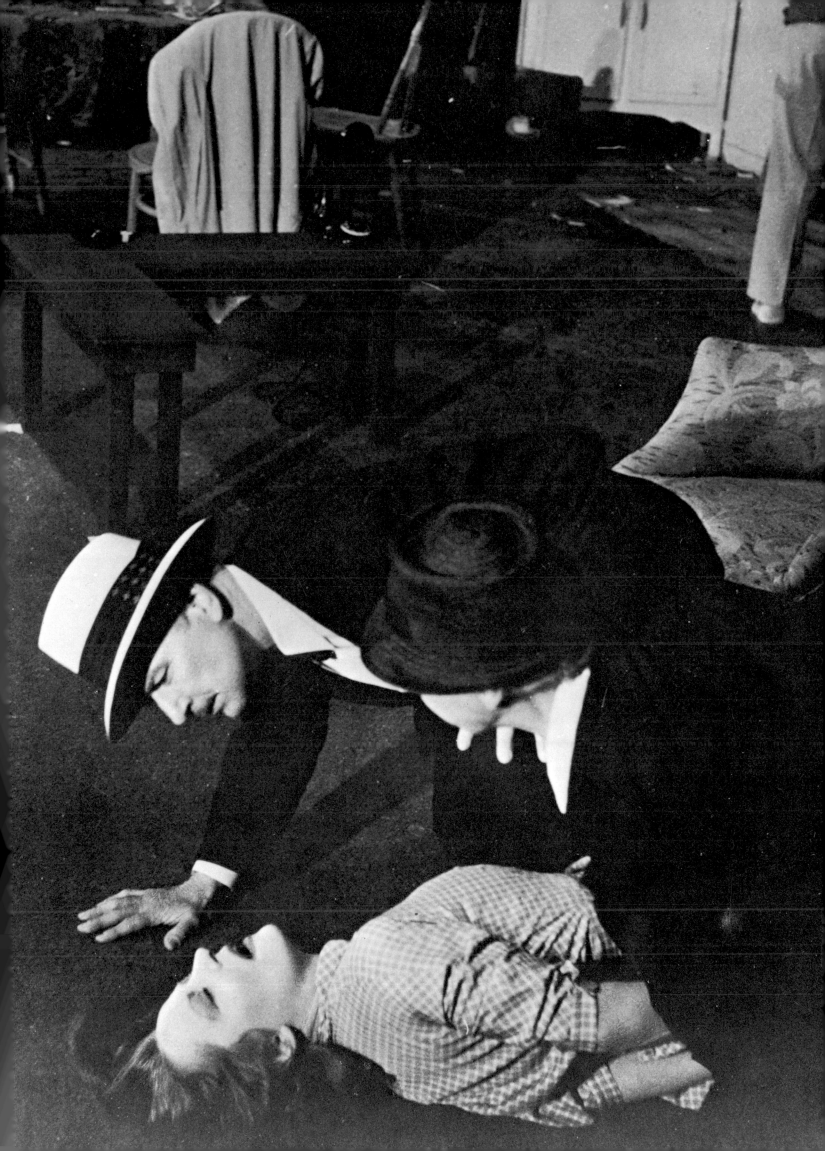

Welldahlingitwaslike this, thislampwasbymy..

By THEO WILSON

Tallulah had just been through one blankety-blank of an evening, complete with cops, doctors, five stitches in her arm, a house guest with hepatitis and no sleep—but she came roaring on the phone yesterday with a full head of steam and went right into a magnificent denunciation of those "fantastic" reports that she had tripped and fallen on a "blankety-blank vase."

The indestructible Miss Bankhead—who else at 56 could carry on like this after a night like that?—told THE NEWS:

"Dahling, I never trip, not even the gay fantastic! I had at my bedside this porcelain lamp with curleycues on it. I've been trying for two days to get my doctor, for my house guest who has hepatitis, and we just couldn't find him!

She Reached, Lamp Fell

"Well, I went to bed at 11 or 12:30 and then I woke up and I was reaching over to turn on the light and the lamp fell over and broke and cut my arm. They said my maid panicked but she didn't. We couldn't get my doctor—we haven't been able to find him, I told you—and so this ambulance came.

"That other newspaper got the whole bloody thing wrong," Tallulah said. "They've mixed me up with my sister who has race horses. She fell over a blankety-blank bridge lamp and got two black eyes and a bloody nose."

(Tallulah was referring to her seven-times-married sister, Eugenia Bankhead. She didn't explain where Eugenia and the lamp collided, and since she talks as fast as her sister's racehorses run, we never had a chance to ask.)

Well, after the maid called an ambulance, said Tallulah, "these three enchanting policemen came, and then there was this perfectly charming doctor who put five stitches in my arm. I didn't have a thing while it was done. I was noble."

Tallulah insisted she was not ill. "If I were, no one would dare to call me at this blankety-blank time of the day."

"Why, there were reports that I was murrrrrrrderrrrred," she roared, "when I became ill with acute nephritis last year and had to be carried from the house." There was some more roaring, and Tallulah hung up after telling the reporter: "God bless you, dahling."

That's Tallu's story. The E. 49th St. police station house report reads, however: "At 12:30 A. M. a call was received from 230 E. 62d St., asking for an ambulance for an injury.

"One Tallulah Bankhead, age 56, at residence 230 E. 62d St. Subject fell over vase and cut left forearm. Subject refused medical aid of Beth-David ambulance." Signed: Radio Car Patrolman Thomas Murray.

(Picture on page 1)

Tallulah Is Hospitalized, Hospital Tallulahized

Tallulah Bankhead has entered Flower-Fifth Avenue Hospital for a "general checkup" and some of the other patients there are positive that the doctors aren't going to find anything wrong with the lady's lungs.

One patient called THE NEWS yesterday to say that he knew Tallu was on the floor, on account of "I could hear her bellowing that she wanted an air-conditioner pronto."

"Did she get one?"

"I guess so," said the patient. "From the hammering and noise going on in that room, she's getting everything she's hollering for."

As she grew older Tallulah was subject to more and more accidents, which she feared would threaten her career. She tried to keep news of her misadventures out of the papers, but she had early mastered the art of making headlines, and now it was too late to master the art of keeping out of them.

Right, Estelle Winwood, Tallulah, and Joan Blondell in a disastrous comedy called Crazy October, *by James Leo Herlihy. After a long tryout on the road, it closed in San Francisco, as far as possible from New York. Tallulah's face has become a tragic mask, and it is hard to tell what thoughts are being entertained behind those dark eyes.*

A number of Tallulah's old friends among the critics were delighted with her performance in Midgie Purvis, *a play by Mary Chase. In it she played a fifty-year-old woman who frequently disguised herself as an eighty-year-old in order to have more harum-scarum fun with children. The play was a ramshackle affair, and despite the best efforts of its producers, Robert Whitehead and Roger L. Stevens (seen with Tallulah below), its director, Burgess Meredith, whom Tallulah had entertained at the Stork Club long ago, and Tallulah herself, it did not succeed. Walter Kerr said of her, "She is serving notice that an actress is back in town," but what Tallulah needed and couldn't find was a play worthy of her talents.*

A telegram from Tallulah to Katharine Hepburn, at the time of Miss Hepburn's father's death: "Dear Katy I loved him too and your Mother whom I did not know about until long after—I am truly sorry bless you Tallulah."

48 • DAILY NEWS, FRIDAY, FEBRUARY 3, 1961

Fine Comedy Blend: Bankhead & Chase

By JOHN CHAPMAN

(Reprinted from yesterday's late editions.)

Putting playwright Mary Chase and actress Tallulah Bankhead together is an inspiration, like inventing the martini. Mrs. Chase is daffy and sweet and Miss Bankhead is realistic and tart. The blending of these two remarkable women took place at the Martin Beck Theatre last evening with the premiere of Mrs. Chase's comedy, "Midgie Purvis."

As a dramatic structure, "Midgie Purvis" is rickety now and again—but I, for one, do not intend to make picky complaints about a slow spot here and there. I'd rather dwell on such moments as the time when Miss Bankhead, as an 80-year-old baby sitter for two small boys and a girl, is indignant at hearing that the children have to go back to school this week when they've been there all last week. "They're running school into the ground," she says.

Whistler's Mother

I'll give you the start of the plot but no more. The curtain rises on a grand staircase and

Tallulah Bankhead
A darling old lady

"MIDGIE PURVIS"
Comedy by Mary Chase, produced by Robert Whitehead, Roger L. Stevens and Alfred R. Glancy Jr. at the Martin Beck Theatre, Feb. 1, 1961.

THE PRINCIPALS

Mrs. Durkee	Mary Farrell
Canfield Purvis	William Redfield
Edwin Purvis	Russell Hardie
Midge Purvis	Tallulah Bankhead
Dorothy Plunkett	Alice Pearce
Luther Plunkett	John Cecil Holm
Vivian Stubbs	Janie Mars
Althea Malone	Nydia Westman
Emma Pasternack	Jane Van Duser
Cleo June	Pia Zadora
Wesley	Paul Mace
Harry	Joseph Grassi
Dr. Sidensticker	Clinton Sundberg

bulk of the comedy is about Miss Bankhead's mad adventures with the moppets.

A Warning, Too

Miss Bankhead's performance is a joy to behold and hear, for it bubbles with the comic spirit and falls in perfectly with the playwright's nutty notions. But "Midgie Purvis" is not just a slight comic invention; like such other Chase plays as "Harvey" and "Mrs. McThing," it carries a gentle warning to the human race that it should act more human.

Burgess Meredith has directed the play most charmingly, and has invented a maneuver with the inevitable long telephone cord which should put the long cord people right out of business. And the cast, including Alice Pearce, John Cecil Holm, Clinton Sundber, and Nydia Westman, is all for fun.

For fun, too, are Ben Edwards' settings — particularly old lady Bankhead's hideout apartment behind the Wee Wee Candy Shoppe in a town which I suspect is Denver.

RIDER TO EQUITY STANDARD RUN-OF-THE-
PLAY CONTRACT DATED December 26, 1962,
BY AND BETWEEN TALLULAH BANKHEAD (HERE-
INAFTER REFERRED TO AS THE "ACTOR") AND
BROCK-CARSON (HEREINAFTER REFERRED TO AS
THE "MANAGER") WITH RESPECT TO "HERE TODAY"
(HEREINAFTER REFERRED TO AS THE "PLAY"

TERMS:

Notwithstanding anything herein contained to the contrary the
Actor shall have the right to terminate her services hereunder
on June 1, 1963, or any time thereafter by giving the management
four weeks prior written notice.

BILLING:

The Manager agrees that the Actor shall receive sole star billing
above the title of the Play in type not less than 100% of the size
of the largest letter used for the title of the Play with respect to
size, boldness, thickness, color and prominence of type.

The name of no other person either directly or indirectly connected
with the Play shall receive equal or superior billing to that accorded
the Actor with respect to size, thickness, prominence, boldness and
color, except the name of Estelle Winwood which may appear in type
equal to that of the actor with respect to size, thickness, prominence,
boldness and color.

The Actor's name shall appear as outlined above in all paid advertising and publicity and promotional media released or authorized
to be released or under the control of the Manager, including but
not limited to programs, billboards, houseboards, signs, marquees,
periodicals, and newspaper advertising of every kind and nature.

APPROVAL:

The Manager agrees that the Actor shall have the right of approval
of the cast and director.

MAID:

The Manager agrees to pay the sum of One hundred ($100) dollars per
week to the Actor's maid. The Manager also agrees to provide at
his expense the transportation of the actor's maid, which transportation shall be on the same conveyance as that used to transport
the Actor if the Actor so desires.

SECRETARY:

The Manager agrees to pay the transportation of the Actor's secretary,
which transportation shall be on the same conveyance as that used to
transport the Actor if the Actor so desires.

INITIAL HERE

COMMISSION:

There shall be no deduction from the Actor's weekly salary due the
agent; said commissions due hereunder shall be paid directly to the
agent by the Manager.

Tallulah was a stern bargainer with producers, and one of the reasons that she did less and less work as she grew older was that she insisted upon terms much more onerous than other actors of the time were asking. Aside from a very high salary, she would take care to add certain other provisos, as in the rider on the left. Her loyalty to her old friend and champion, Estelle Winwood, is worth noting; only Miss Winwood was ever allowed equal billing. The reference to first-class transportation for a maid goes back to the days when her dresser, Rose Riley, being black, occasionally ran into difficulties on the road.

Below left, a bill for Tallulah's costume expenses for Here Today. By current standards—and by Tallulah's standards at any time—the charges are astonishingly low.

Below right, Estelle Winwood making up for Here Today. Tallulah quoted a critic as saying of Miss Winwood that she looked as if a snowflake could give her a concussion, but how tough she was and is! She was at least eighty when this photograph was taken and would have many years of acting before her.

GUY M. KENT
SUTTON TERRACE EAST
450 EAST 63RD STREET
NEW YORK, NEW YORK

June 22, 1962

Miss. Tallulah Bankhead
447 East 57th St.
New York, 21, N.Y.

COSTUME EXPENSES FOR MISS. BANKHEAD'S WARDROBE FOR "HERE TODAY"

8 yds red silk chiffon @ $2.50	$20.00
8 yds silk crepe @ $6.50	$52.00
Dyeing charges on silk crepe	$ 7.50
1 yd. beige moss crepe @ $2.00	$ 2.00
7 yds. Kabuki silk @ $4.00	$28.00
2½ yds India silk @ $6.50	$16.25
2½ yds. Siamese silk @ $9.00	$22.50
NYC tax on above fabrics	$ 4.44
2 yds. extra India silk @ $6.50 plus tax	$13.39
1 white silk blouse (Ohrbach's)	$ 3.13
1 pr straw sandals (A.S. BECK)	$ 3.00
1 natural Milan straw hat	$ 4.50
1 pink straw hat (Ohrbach's)	$ 2.99
2 pr slacks 1 blue, 1 white (Lido sportswear)	$27.77
2 purses 1 leather, 1 straw (Dexter & Co.	$18.28
6 pr silk tights, 1 pr "Peds" (La Ray Boot Shop)	$31.15
Costume design fee, @ $100. per costume for 3 costumes	$300.00
TOTAL	$558.92

Note to accountant:

All sales slips are made out to either Guy Kent, or NBC, for

the purpose of obtaining the above articles at either a

wholesale price, or a discount price.

251

THE MILK TRAIN
DOESN'T STOP HERE ANYMORE

*David Merrick, Tallulah, and Tab
Hunter backstage at* The Milk Train
Doesn't Stop Here Anymore. *Tennessee
Williams had openly based his play
on Tallulah—its protagonist, Flora
Goforth, is an aging Southern narcissist
who feeds more and more feverishly on
a beautiful young man—and Tallulah, with
her usual courage, had been eager to star in it.
An early version of the play, with Hermione
Baddeley, having failed, Williams offered it to
Tallulah in a revised version, which reached
New York in 1964. The play was again pronounced
a failure, and Merrick closed it after five performances.
It was Tallulah's last appearance on Broadway.*

Tallulah returned to London in 1964 to play a role in a horror movie that was eventually entitled, over her protests, Die! Die! My Darling! *She put up at the Ritz, because it was where she had stayed on her first visit to London over forty years earlier, knowing the name of no other hotel. Going up the steps, she caught her heel in a rubber mat and fell; she was sure that everyone would say of her that she had been drinking and, sure enough, almost everyone did. Old and ill as she was, she worked hard at the movie and had a miserable time. Though a failure, the movie sometimes turns up at a late hour on TV.*

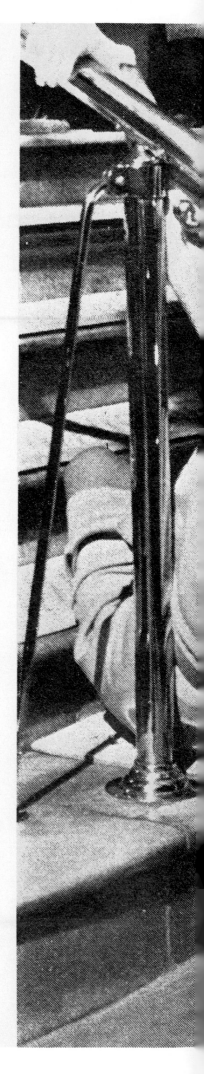

Tallulah Who?

London, Oct. 19 (AP) — Actress Tallulah Bankhead gave this explanation today as to why she calls everybody "dahling":

"Because all my life I've been terrible at remembering people's names. I once introduced a friend of mine as Martini. Her name was actually Olive."

Tallulah takes a London tumble

Never, absolutely never, in all of her 61 years of ups and downs had anything so positively ghastly befallen Tallulah Bankhead. There she was, posing sedately at the steps of the Ritz in London, where she had gone to make a movie. An instant later it happened. But no one could dispute that Tallu took her tumble with a dramatic flair.

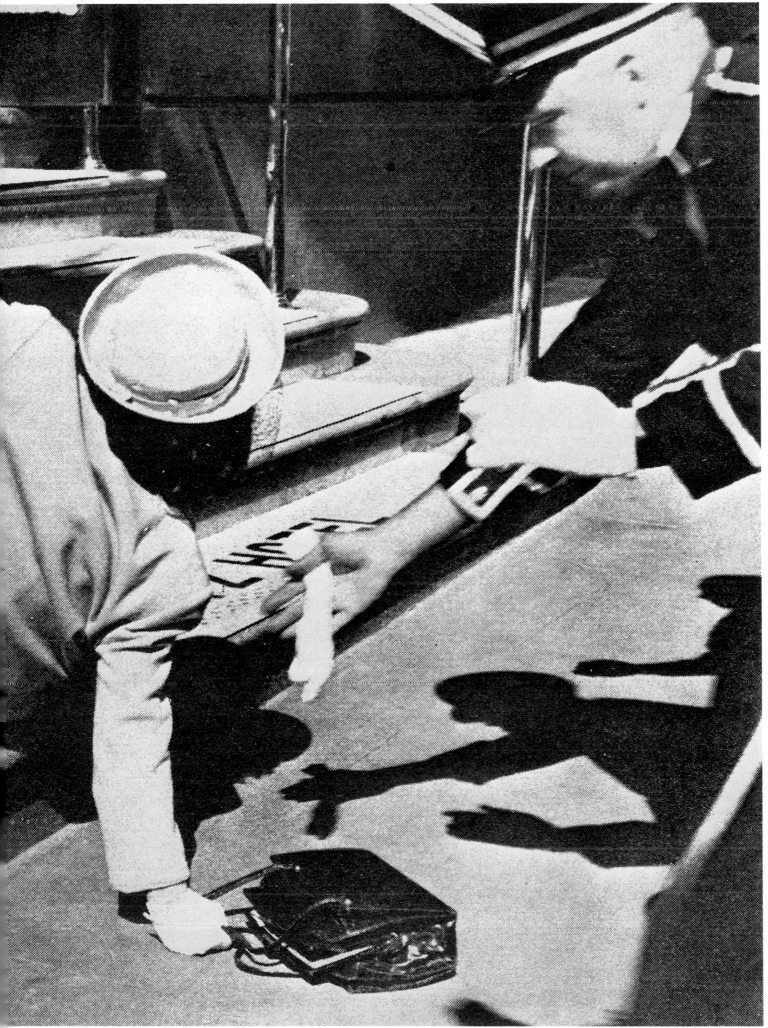

Tallulah in a scene from Die! Die!
My Darling! *She played a religious
fanatic—hard though it may be to believe
—and is seen conducting a service.
Among the demented servants gathered
for prayer is Donald Sutherland.*

*One of the happy occasions of the final years of
Tallulah's life was the famous masked ball
that Truman Capote gave at the Plaza
in honor of Katharine Graham. Tallulah spent
weeks getting ready for it, in spite of a
curious premonition that, once there, nobody
would speak to her. It turned out that scores of old
friends were delighted to see her. She had a fine time.*

*Tallulah and Jesse Levy, with whom she renewed
an old acquaintance at the Capote ball. He became her
secretary-companion and tended her faithfully until
her death. As a party gag, she is wearing a sash
that bears the name of her purported rival.*

256

In 1967 Tallulah and Jesse
flew out to Hollywood, where
she acted in two episodes of the
"Batman" series for a fee of
twenty thousand dollars. As usual,
she pretended she needed the
money. (Her estate was to total
nearly two million dollars, all of her
own earning.) In Hollywood, she
had dinner at the house of George
Cukor, who had directed her in
Tarnished Lady, her first American
talkie. What a terrible movie
it had been! Katharine Hepburn
came by and they had a long,
merry talk. More than a year later,
she made her last TV appearance;
it was on Johnny Carson's "Tonight
Show." She said that going on the show
was a way of proving to people that
she wasn't dead.

Greeting Patricia Neal at Sardi's, after the premiere of the movie version of
The Subject Was Roses, *starring Miss Neal. For a wonder, it is Miss Neal
who is smoking and not Tallulah. This was Tallulah's last public appearance.*

*At her dressing table with the collection of oddments that accompanied her
everywhere. The cherished rabbit's foot that her father had given her
was to be slipped into her coffin on the day of her burial, December 14, 1968,
in the churchyard of Old St. Paul's, in Rock Hall, on the Eastern Shore.*

Tallulah's will, which contains few surprises. Most of the legatees are members of her family—old friends like Estelle Winwood and the Seawells; male companions like Philip Hall and Ted Hook; faithful employees like Rose Riley; and faithful former employees like Edie Smith and the Underdowns, who had kept house for her in the happy London days. Tallulah was characteristically precise in the disposition of her personal effects and in her precautions in regard to her sister. They had often gone separate ways, not without anger, but Tallulah was determined to protect Eugenia as well as possible after death. For they were not only sisters but Bankheads, and that was a bond stronger even than envy, even than love.

I, TALLULAH BROCKMAN BANKHEAD, residing in the City, County and State of New York, do hereby make, publish and declare this to be my Last Will and Testament, hereby revoking all wills and codicils by me at any time heretofore made.

FIRST: I direct that my just debts and funeral expenses be paid as soon as practicable after my death.

SECOND: I give and bequeath to each of the following named persons who survive me, the legacy stated after his or her name:

A. To WILLIAM BROCKMAN BANKHEAD, the sum of Five Thousand ($5,000.00) Dollars.

B. To BROOK SEAWELL, the sum of Ten Thousand ($10,000.00) Dollars.

C. To BROCKMAN SEAWELL, the sum of Ten Thousand ($10,000.00) Dollars.

D. To ROSE RILEY, the sum of Two Thousand ($2,000.00) Dollars.

E. To PHILIP HALL, the sum of Ten Thousand ($10,000.00) Dollars.

F. To ESTELLE WINWOOD, the sum of Ten Thousand ($10,000.00) Dollars.

G. To EDIE SMITH, the sum of Ten Thousand ($10,000.00) Dollars.

H. To KENNETH CARTEN, now residing in London, England, the sum of Ten Thousand ($10,000.00) Dollars.

I. To MARIE RICKENBACH, the sum of Five Hundred ($500.00) Dollars.

J. To ALAN VINCENT, the sum of One Thousand ($1,000.00) Dollars.

K. To ROBERT WILLIAMS, the sum of Five Hundred ($500.00) Dollars.

L. To ELIZABETH LOCK, now residing in London, England, the sum of Five Hundred ($500.00) Dollars.

M. To JOHN UNDERDOWN, now residing in London, England, the sum of Five Hundred ($500.00) Dollars.

N. To MARY UNDERDOWN, now residing in London, England, the sum of Five Hundred ($500.00) Dollars.

O. To KITTY LINI, the sum of Five Thousand ($5,000.00) Dollars.

P. To JAMES E. HERLIHY, the sum of Two Thousand Five Hundred ($2,500.00) Dollars.

Q. To EMMA ANTHONY, the sum of Two Thousand ($2,000.00) Dollars.

R. To GEORGE HYLAND, the sum of One Thousand ($1,000.00) Dollars.

S. To LAURA MITCHELL, the sum of One Thousand ($1,000.00) Dollars.

T. To JESSE W. LEVY, the sum of Ten Thousand ($10,000.00) Dollars.

U. To DANIEL SHINE, the sum of Five Thousand ($5,000.00) Dollars.

V. To TED HOOK, the sum of One Thousand ($1,000.00) Dollars.

W. To EUGENIA BANKHEAD, the sum of Five Thousand ($5,000.00) Dollars.

In the event that any of said persons shall predecease me, his or her legacy shall be added to and become part of my residuary estate and shall be distributed as hereinafter provided.

THIRD: I give and bequeath to each of the following named persons who survive me, the bequests stated after his or her name:

A. To BROOK SEAWELL, my diamond earrings and my eighteenth century dressing table

B. To ESTELLE WINWOOD, my diamond and sapphire pendant.

C. To EUGENIA BANKHEAD, my mink coat.

D. To EUGENIA RAWLS SEAWELL, my Renoir, my mink cape, my aquamarine and diamond ring, my six pointed aquamarine and diamond brooch and, except for the film print of "Lifeboat", all of my films and my 16 mm. movie projector.

E. To KENNETH CARTEN, now residing in London, England, the portrait of me by Peter Sheil.

F. To PHILIP HALL, my pair of white jade vases, the painting by me with a red staircase entitled "Room at the Top" and the two paintings executed by him which I possess.

G. To DONALD SEAWELL, my two (2) Eisendeck paintings.

H. To EDIE SMITH, my gold necklace, my gold and moonstone brooch and my moonstone and sapphire bracelet.

I. To JUDY JOY, niece of DOLA CAVENDISH, my star sapphire ring with diamonds.

J. To LOUISA CARPENTER, my pink shell brooch with gold and diamonds.

K. To MILDRED DUNNOCK, my white porcelain tulips.

L. To GEORGE CUKOR, the portrait of me by Ambrose McEvoy.

M. To EDIE VAN CLEVE, my gold weave cigarette case.

N. To RUTH MITCHELL, my white jade statuette with teak base and the film print of "Lifeboat" which I own, if the same can be found among my effects.

O. To TED HOOK, the painting by Grandma Moses which I possess.

P. To ELLIOTT REID, also known as TED REID, the painting entitled "Harbor of Dieppe" by Max Bond.

Q. To CHARLES REDFERN, the four (4) etchings and paintings executed by him, which I possess.

R. To JESSE W. LEVY, my Baldwin grand piano and bench.

S. To my namesake, TALLULAH BROCKMAN BANKHEAD, my gold Cartier dressing table set inscribed "Tallulah".

T. To KITTY LINI, all articles of clothing not otherwise bequeathed herein.

In the event that any of said persons shall predecease me, his or her bequest shall be added to and become part of my residuary estate and shall be distributed as hereinafter provided.

FOURTH: My sister, EUGENIA BANKHEAD, is presently indebted to me, said indebtedness being evidenced by a promissory note and secured by the pledge of a diamond ring. If at my death my said sister shall be indebted to me in any amount, I direct my Executor to cancel such indebtedness and return to her all property belonging to her pledged as security therefor together with all evidence of indebtedness, hereby discharging my sister from all liability in respect thereto.

FIFTH: If my sister, EUGENIA BANKHEAD, survives me, I bequeath to her an annuity at the rate of Two Hundred Fifty ($250.00) Dollars per month so long as she shall live. To provide for the payment of said annuity, I direct my Executor to purchase from a life insurance company of good standing, licensed to do business in the State of New York, a non-assignable, non-cancellable, single premium, commercial annuity con-

tract, without cash value or refund provisions and without any term certain, providing for the payment, monthly if possible but at least quarter-annually, of said annuity and to deliver the annuity contract so purchased to my said sister, which delivery shall constitute complete satisfaction of this bequest. Until such annuity contract has been purchased, I direct my Executor to pay the annuity in monthly installments out of the net income and, to the extent necessary, the principal of my residuary estate.

I direct that this bequest for my sister shall take effect in preference to all other gifts, devises and bequests made in this Will.

SIXTH: All the rest, residue and remainder of my said estate, real, personal and mixed, of every kind and nature and wheresoever situate, of which I may die seized or possessed or to which I may be entitled at the time of my death, including, without limitation, all property over or concerning which I may have any power of appointment and all property herein attempted to be disposed of, the disposition of which shall fail to take effect by reason of lapse or other cause, and the proceeds of any policy or policies of life insurance payable to me or to my estate (all of which is herein termed my "residuary estate"), I give, devise and bequeath in equal shares of such number that there will be one (1) such share for the children (taken collectively) of WILLIAM BROCKMAN BANKHEAD who survive me, and one (1) such share for

I direct that my said Executor and his successor or successors shall serve, whether in the State of New York or elsewhere, without being required to give bond or other security for the faithful performance of his duties as such.

IN WITNESS WHEREOF, I have hereunto set my hand and affixed my seal this 24ᵗʰ day of November, 1967.

Tallulah Brockman Bankhead (L.S.)
TALLULAH BROCKMAN BANKHEAD

SIGNED, SEALED, PUBLISHED AND DECLARED this 24ᵗʰ day of November, 1967, by the above named Testatrix, TALLULAH BROCKMAN BANKHEAD, as and for her Last Will and Testament, in the presence of us, and the undersigned, who were all together with her at such time, and thereupon we, at her request and in her presence, and in the presence of each other, hereto subscribe our names as witnesses thereto.

Sydney A. Curia residing at 56 Elizabeth Road New Rochelle, N.Y

_____ residing at _____ Ave. Oceanic, N.J

Harry McPherson residing at 75 East End Ave. New York City

TALLULAH BANKHEAD: A Chronology of Her Professional Career

BY HUGH BEESON, JR.

P—play, MP—motion picture, N—nightclub

1918

THE WISHFUL GIRL (MP)

Produced by Edna Goodrich for Empire-Mutual Productions. Directed by Del Henderson and John B. O'Brien. Screenplay by John B. O'Brien. *This is the film in which Tallulah was cast as a result of her winning the* Picture-Play *contest. With her in the film was François du Barry of Fairfield, Conn., another of the twelve winners.*

THE SQUAB FARM (P)

Tryout: New Haven. Produced by the Messrs. Shubert at the Bijou Theatre, New York, March 13. 45 performances. A comedy by Frederic and Fanny Hatton. Directed by J. C. Huffman. Tallulah played Gladys Sinclair; others in the cast were Lowell Sherman, Harry Davenport, Raymond Bloomer, G. Oliver Smith, Helen Barnes, Alma Tell, William L. Gibson, and Marie Centlivre.

Tallulah auditioned for Maeterlinck's The Betrothal, *but was turned down by Winthrop Ames, the producer, and Guthrie McClintic, the casting director, who decided that she was "far too mature." She was sixteen years old.*

WHEN MEN BETRAY (MP)

Produced by Ivan Abramson for Sterling Film Company. Screenplay by Louise Abramson, based on a short story by Clark Jefferson Winston. Directed by Ivan Abramson.

Tallulah's first review in which she was cited individually appeared shortly after the film opened in the spring of 1919: "Miss Tallulah Bankhead is new to the screen and she proves the truth of the theory that brains are better than experience." She was described as "exquisite of feature, dainty of form, deliciously feminine. . . . Her appearance brings with it the feeling that the very atmosphere is surcharged with energy."

THIRTY-A-WEEK (MP)

Produced by Samuel Goldwyn for Goldwyn Pictures, Inc. An original screenplay by Thompson Buchanan. Appearing opposite Tallulah was Tom Moore.

1919

39 EAST (P)

Produced by the Messrs. Shubert at the Broadhurst Theatre, New York, March 31. 160 performances. A comedy by Rachel Crothers. Directed by Rachel Crothers. Tallulah played Penelope Penn; *she was a replacement for Constance Binney, who was taking weekend vacations. Tallulah appeared only six times (the weekends of July 25-26 and August 1-2), when the play was closed because of the actors' strike.* Others in the cast were Henry Hull, Sidney Blackmer, Alison Skipworth, John Morris, and Lucia Moore.

FOOTLOOSE (P)

Produced by George C. Tyler at the Greenwich Theatre, New York, May 10. 32 performances. A comedy by Zoë Akins, adapted from *For-Get-Me-Not* by Herman Merivale and F. C. Grove. Directed by George C. Tyler. Tallulah played Rose de Brissac; others in the cast were Emily Stevens, Norman Trevor, Lillian Brennard, Robert Casadesus, John Webster, and Elizabeth Risdon.

THE VIRTUOUS VAMP (MP)

Produced by Joseph M. Schenck for Gladstone Productions. Based upon a short story, "New York Lady." Directed by John Emerson. Tallulah was an extra; the stars of the film were Constance Talmadge and Conway Tearle.

Tallulah "idled through most of the summer," though she did spend two weeks in summer stock as an apprentice in Somerville, Mass., and another two in Baltimore.

1920

A leading role in The Hottentot, *a comedy by Victor Mapes and William Collier, was assigned to Tallulah in February. In the cast were Ann Andrews, William Collier, and Donald Meek. The producer, Sam H. Harris, had set the opening for March 1; but after the second day of rehearsals, Tallulah was dismissed ("We are very sorry, but we don't think that your voice is strong enough. . . .").*

1921

NICE PEOPLE (P)

Produced by Sam H. Harris at the Klaw Theatre, New York, March 2. 120 performances. A comedy by Rachel Crothers. Directed by Rachel Crothers. Tallulah played Hallie Livingston; others in the cast were Rod La Roque, Katharine Cornell, Francine Larrimore, Hugh Huntley, Merle Maddern, Henry Hull, and Charles Gibney. *Tallulah left the play before the end of its run to go into* Everyday, *written expressly for her by Rachel Crothers.*

EVERYDAY (P)
Produced by Mary Kirkpatrick at the Bijou Theatre, New York, November 16. 30 performances. A comedy by Rachel Crothers. Directed by Rachel Crothers. Tallulah played Phyllis Nolan; others in the cast were Henry Hull, Minnie Dupree, Lucille Watson, and Mary Donnelly.

DANGER (P)
Produced by Carle Carleton at the Thirty-ninth Street Theatre, New York, December 22. 79 performances. A domestic drama by Cosmo Hamilton. Replacing Kathlene MacDonnell, Tallulah played Mary Hubbard; others in the cast were Leslie Howard, Ruth Hammond, H. B. Warner, Know Orde, Gilda Leary, Stapleton Kent, and Marie Goff.

1922

NO, SIRREE! (R)
Produced by the "Vicious Circle" (the Algonquin Round Table) at the Forty-ninth Street Theatre, New York, April 30. 1 performance. An "anonymous entertainment," *No, Sirree!* was a parody of *Chauve-Souris;* sketches were written by George S. Kaufman, Ring Lardner, Robert Benchley, Marc Connelly, Dorothy Parker, Franklin Pierce Adams, Alexander Woollcott, Heywood Broun, and Robert E. Sherwood; with the exception of Lardner, all appeared in the production. Others in the cast were Lenore Ulric, Helen Hayes, Brock Pemberton, Donald Ogden Stewart, Alice Duer Miller, Neysa McMein, Ruth Gillmore, Harold W. Ross, Sidney Blackmer, and Mary Brandon. Tallulah played an ingenue in a sketch entitled *He Who Gets Flapped.* Jascha Heifetz provided the music, and Laurette Taylor wrote a review, which appeared the next day in the *Times.*

HER TEMPORARY HUSBAND (P)
Produced by H. H. Frazee at the Frazee Theatre, New York, August 31. 92 performances. A comedy by Edward A Paulton. Directed by H. H. Frazee. Tallulah played Blanche Ingram; others in the cast were Ann Andrews, Henry Mortimer, Selena Royle, and William Courtenay.

THE EXCITERS (P)
Produced by the Selwyns at the Times Square Theatre, New York, September 22. 43 performances. A comedy by Martin Brown. Directed by Edgar Selwyn. Scenic production and art decoration by Clifford B. Pember. Tallulah's gowns by Madame Francis. Tallulah played "Rufus" Rand; others in the cast were Aline MacMahon, Enid Markey, Allen Dinehart, Chester Morris, Robert Hyman, Thais Lawton, Florence Flinn, and Echlin Gayer.

1923

THE DANCERS (P)
Produced by Sir Gerald du Maurier at Wyndham's Theatre,

London, on February 15. 344 performances. A play by "Hubert Parsons" (Viola Tree and Sir Gerald du Maurier). Directed by Sir Gerald du Maurier. Tallulah played Maxine; others in the cast were Sir Gerald du Maurier, H. W. Furniss, Audry Carten, Nigel Bruce, and Lilian Braithwaite.

1924

CONCHITA (P)
Produced by Jeffry Lowden at the Queen's Theatre, London, March 19. 37 performances. A play by Edward Knoblock. Directed by Edward Knoblock. Tallulah played the title role.

THIS MARRIAGE (P)
Produced by E. Holman Clark at the Comedy Theatre, London, May 7. 53 performances. A play by Eliot Crawshay Williams. Directed by J. E. Vedrenne, assisted by José G. Levy. Tallulah played Yvonne Taylor; others in the cast were Cathleen Nesbitt, Herbert Marshall, Auriol Lee, A. Bromley Davenport, and Thomas Reynolds.

THE CREAKING CHAIR (P)
Produced by C. Aubrey Smith at the Comedy Theatre, London, July 22. 235 performances. Directed by C. Aubrey Smith. Tallulah played Anita Latter; others in the cast were Nigel Bruce and C. Aubrey Smith.

1925

FALLEN ANGELS (P)
Produced by Noël Coward and others at the Globe Theatre, London, April 21. 158 performances. A comedy by Noël Coward. Directed by Noël Coward. Tallulah played Julia Sterroll; she replaced Margaret "Bunny" Bannerman in the role and learned the part in four days.

THE GREEN HAT (P)
Produced by Gerald Hopkins, Jr., at the Adelphi Theatre, London, September 2. 128 performances. A drama by Michael Arlen, adapted from his novel *The Green Hat.* Tallulah played Iris March; others in the cast were Leonard Upton and Robert Horton.

1926

THE SCOTCH MIST (P)
Produced by Sir Patrick Hastings, K. C. and M. P., at the St. Martin's Theatre, London, January 26. 117 performances. A play by Sir Patrick Hastings. Tallulah played Mary Denvers; playing opposite her was Godfrey Tearle.

THEY KNEW WHAT THEY WANTED (P)
Produced by Basil Dean at the St. Martin's Theatre, London,

May 18. 108 performances. A drama by Sidney Howard. Directed by Basil Dean. Tallulah played Amy; others in the cast were Glenn Anders and Sam Livesay.

THE GOLD DIGGERS (P)
Produced by William Mollison, in association with Jack Waller and Herbert Clayton, at the Lyric Theatre, London, December 14. 180 performances. A comedy by Avery Hopwood. Tallulah played Jerry Lamar; others in the cast were Jobyna Howland, Dorothy St. Elmo, Madge Aubrey, Marjorie Brooks, Hugh Williams, Ruth Terry, Joan Barry, Joan Clarkson, Ian Hunter, Fred Kerr, David Wilton, John Perry, Charles Carson, and Sidney Seaward.

1927

For the benefit of the King's College Hospital, Tallulah produced, on April 5, "a special cabaret and gala night entertainment" at the Café de Paris in London. She performed in a sketch, entitled "Always Apologize," written by Audry and Waveney Carten.

GREAT LOVERS OF ROMANCE
Produced and staged by Olga Lynn at the New Theatre, London, May 6. 1 performance. Replacing the Baroness Ravensdale, Tallulah played Cleopatra in this tableau, presented during the matinee of Marie Tempest's *London Pride;* the presentation was a benefit performance for the Leicestershire Nursing Association.

THE GARDEN OF EDEN (P)
Produced by the Messrs. Herbert Clayton and Jack Waller at the Lyric Theatre, London, May 30. 232 performances. A play by R. Bernauer and R. Oesterreicher, adapted by Avery Hopwood. Directed by Herbert Clayton. Tallulah played Toni Lebrun; others in the cast were Hugh Williams, Eric Maturin, Arthur Ross, George Bellamy, Marcelle Roche, Eva Moore, Barbara Gott, Robert English, Rex Caldwell, Annie Esmond, and Arthur Holman.

On June 14, Young Men in Love, Michael Arlen's seventh novel, was published by George H. Doran. Ysabel Fuller, a primary character in the fiction, was based upon Tallulah: "Her eyes were remarkable. They were blue, they were violet, they were beautiful. They radiated the gentle insolence of a child of nature . . . the sophisticated innocence of trans-atlantic virginity. . . . Her legs were American, slender, eager, destructive, delicious." Ysabel, an actress, had a following not unlike Tallulah's: "several of Ysabel's faithful gallery-girls had waited for a glimpse of her. . . . They waited for her every night. They loved everything about her. . . ."

1928

BLACKMAIL (P)
Produced by Raymond Massey, in association with Alfred Butt and A. H. Woods, at the Globe Theatre, London, February 28. 42 performances. A melodrama by Charles Bennett. Directed by A. H. Wood. Tallulah played Daphne Manning; others in the cast were Frank Vosper, Amy Veness, Alexander Onslow, Alfred Clark, Henrietta Watson, James Rennie, Reginald Gardiner, and Julian Hamilton.

In a feature "devoted to short articles and paragraphs on a variety of household interests," the March issue of The Sphere presented an article by Tallulah entitled "The Fun of Open House." Tallulah wrote that "it can be done on next to nothing." The hostess should have open house "only on certain days of the week. Then your friends are more likely to co-ordinate and get together, instead of straggling in, two one day, and one the next." Guests should bring "gramo-phone records, sandwiches, fruit salads, lime juice, soda-water, and gin. . . ."

MUD AND TREACLE (P)
Produced by Frederick Lonsdale at the Globe Theatre, London, May 9. 46 performances. A play by Frederick Lonsdale. Tallulah played Polly Andrews. According to one critic, the play was "full of stimulating dialogue. It might have been by Bernard Shaw and Noël Coward." Among its memorable lines: "The only place where men and women can usually meet is in bed."

Using Eugenia Hoyt as her professional name, Sister made her London debut in The Barker, on May 12, at the Playhouse Theatre. Her leading man was James Kirkwood, Sr. One critic wrote, "Eugenia Hoyt disturbs masculine hearts;" she has a "husky drawing voice to betoken the passionate nature which she throws wholeheartedly into her acting." Eugenia left the company, without notice, two weeks after the play opened. "Sister was later to give some spectacular performances," Tallulah said afterwards, "—but not on the stage."

The Evening Standard, of London, announced on August 3 that Sister, using the name Sally Bankhead, would make her film debut as a French maid in Mayfair, a production of the New Era Film Company.

HER CARDBOARD LOVER (P)
Produced by Jack Middleton at the Lyric Theatre, London, August 21. 173 performances. A comedy by Jacques Deval and P. G. Wodehouse. Tallulah played Simone; others in the cast were Leslie Howard, Jack Melford, and Elizabeth Arkell. After the played closed in London, it toured the provinces, opening in Glasgow on April 15, 1929.

On October 17, Tallulah signed a contract with Ideal Films, Ltd. Her salary, £500 a week, was reputed to be the highest paid to any actress in England. Replacing Gladys Cooper, Tallulah began work on her first English movie, His House in Order, *based upon the play by Sir Arthur Wing Pinero.*

HE'S MINE (P)

Produced by William Mollison at the Lyric Theatre, London, October 29. 98 performances. A comedy adapted from a French farce. Tallulah played Wanda Myro ("a fake Serbian princess"); others in the cast were Frederick Volpe, Helen Haye, Allan Aynesworth, and George Howe.

1930

THE LADY OF THE CAMELLIAS (P)

Produced by the Daniel Mayer Company (T. E. Adams, Ernest W. Parr, Anthony Eustrel, and W. Macqueen-Pope) and Nigel Playfair at the Garrick Theatre, London, March 5. 136 performances. Directed by Nigel Playfair. Sets by George Sheringham. Incidental music by Alfred Reynolds. Costumes by Mrs. Gordon Craig, Mrs. Lovat Fraser, and George Sheringham. Tallulah played Marguerite; others in the cast were Glen Byam Shaw, Cecil Humphreys, D. A. Clarke-Smith, Winifred Evans, Joan Matheson, Violet Marquesita, Renée de Vaux, Terence de Marney, C. V. France, Angus L. MacLeod, H. Scott Russell, Marcus Barron, Joan Sutherland, Ellen Pollock, Richard Goolden, and Harold Warrender.

Tallulah recorded "Don't Tell Him" and "What Do I Care?" (H.M.V., Number B-3687) on June 11. (In 1972, "Don't Tell Him" was rereleased in an album entitled Nostalgia's Greatest Hits, *Stanyan Records, Number 10055, and "What Do I Care?" was included in an album entitled* A Nostalgia Trip to the Stars: 1920-50, *Monmouth-Evergreen Records, Number MES/7030.)*

LET US BE GAY (P)

Tryout: Birmingham. Produced by Gilbert Miller and Rachel Crothers at the Lyric Theatre, London, August 18. 128 performances. A comedy by Rachel Crothers. Tallulah played Kitty Brown; others in the cast were Arthur Margetson, Sybil Carlisle, Bellenden Powell, Ernest Haines, Helen Haye, Walter Fitzgerald, Joan Matheson, Ronald Ward, Francis Lister, Cecily Byrne, and Eric Cowley.

1931

TARNISHED LADY (MP)

Produced by Paramount Pictures. Opened at the Rivoli Theatre, New York, April 29. Screenplay by Donald Ogden Stewart, adapted from his story. Directed by George Cukor.

Tallulah played Nancy Courtney; others in the cast were Clive Brook, Phoebe Foster, Alexander Kirkland, Osgood Perkins, and Elizabeth Patterson.

MY SIN (MP)

Produced by Paramount Publix. Opened at the Times Square Paramount and the Brooklyn Paramount, New York, September 11. Screenplay by Owen Davis and Adelaide Heilbron from a story by Fred Jackson. Directed by George Abbott. Tallulah played Carlotta (Ann Trevor); others in the cast were Fredric March, Harry Davenport, Scott Kolk, Lily Cahill, Ann Sutherland, and Margaret Adams.

THE CHEAT (MP)

Produced by Paramount Publix. Opened at the Times Square Paramount and the Brooklyn Paramount, New York, December 11. Adapted from a story by Hector Turnbull. Directed by George Abbott. Tallulah played Elsa Carlyle; others in the cast were Irving Pichel, Harvey Stephens, Jay Fassett, Ann Andrews, William Ingersoll, Henry Warwick, Robert Strange, and Hanaki Yoshiwara.

1932

THUNDER BELOW (MP)

Produced by Paramount Publix. Opened at the Times Square Paramount and the Brooklyn Paramount, New York, June 17. Screenplay by Josephine Lovett and Sidney Buchman, adapted from a novel by Thomas Rourke. Directed by Richard Wallace. Tallulah played Susan; others in the cast were Charles Bickford, Paul Lukas, Eugene Pallette, Ralph Forbes, Leslie Fenton, James Finlayson, Edward van Sloan, Mona Rico, Carlos Salazar, and Gaby Rivas.

MAKE ME A STAR (MP)

Produced by Paramount Publix. Opened at the Times Square Paramount and the Brooklyn Paramount, New York, July 1. Screenplay by Sam Mintz, Walter DeLeon, and Arthur Kober, adapted from Harry Leon Wilson's novel *Merton of the Movies,* and the play by George S. Kaufman and Marc Connelly. Directed by William Beaudine. Tallulah was an unbilled guest star; others in the cast were Stuart Erwin, Joan Blondell, Zasu Pitts, Ben Turpin, Charles Sellon, Florence Roberts, Ruth Donnelly, and Oscar Apfel.

THE DEVIL AND THE DEEP (MP)

Produced by Paramount Publix. Opened at the Times Square Paramount and the Brooklyn Paramount, New York, August 19. Adapted from a story by Harry Harvey. Directed by Marion Gering. Tallulah played Pauline Sturm; others in the cast were Gary Cooper, Charles Laughton, Cary Grant, Paul Porcasi, Juliette Compton, Henry Kolker, Dorothy Christy, and Arthur Hoyt.

FAITHLESS (MP)
Produced by M-G-M. Opened at Capitol Theatre and Loew's
Metropolitan Theatre, New York, November 18. Adapted
from "Tinfoil," a story by Mildred Cram. Directed by
Harry Beaumont. Tallulah played Carol Morgan; others in
the cast were Robert Montgomery, Hugh Herbert, Maurice
Murphy, Louise Closser Hale, and Anna Appel.

1933

FORSAKING ALL OTHERS (P)
Tryout: Boston, Providence, Wilmington, Washington.
Produced by Archie Selwyn at the Times Square Theatre,
New York, March 1. 110 performances. A comedy by Edward
Barry Roberts and Frank Morgan Cavett. Directed by
Thomas Mitchell (after Harry Wagstaff Gribble, Frank
Morgan Cavett, and Arthur J. Beckhard). Sets by Donald
Oenslager. Tallulah's costumes by Hattie Carnegie. Tallulah
played Mary Clay; others in the cast were Ilka Chase, Fred
Keating, Cora Witherspoon, Barbara O'Neil, and Henry
Fonda. (Tallulah produced the play, which, she said, lost
$40,000. "Since I was in the contrary position of being my
own employer, I worked for a new minimum wage—
nothing a week.")

Tallulah was cast to play Julie Kendrick in Jezebel, a play by
Owen Davis which was to be produced and directed by
Guthrie McClintic. The play was scheduled to open at the
Martin Beck Theatre on September 25; Tallulah was
hospitalized on August 26, rejoined the company on
September 5, collapsed, and returned to the Doctors Hospital,
where she was confined for four weeks. She underwent
surgery on November 4 and, in all, was hospitalized for
fifteen weeks.

1934

THE RUDY VALLEE SHOW (NBC radio). February 15.
The Affairs of Anatol, a comedy by Arthur Schnitzler.
Appearing with Tallulah were Horace Braham and Porter
Hall; this was her debut on American radio.

DARK VICTORY (P)
Produced by Alexander McKaig at the Plymouth Theatre,
New York, November 9. 51 performances. A drama by
George Brewer, Jr., and Bertram Bloch. Directed by Robert
Milton. Sets by Robert Edmond Jones. Tallulah played Judith
Traherne; others in the cast were Earle Larimore, Frederick
Leister, Ann Andrews, Myra Hampton, Dwight Fiske, Helen
Strickland, Lewis Dayton, and Mildred Wall.

1935

RAIN (P)
Tryout: Philadelphia. Produced by Sam H. Harris at the

Music Box Theatre, New York, February 12. 47 performances. A play by John Colton and Clemence Randolph,
based on a story by W. Somerset Maugham. Directed by
Sam Forrest. Sets by W. Oden Waller. Tallulah played
Sadie Thompson; others in the cast were Kent Thurber,
Granville Bates, Herbert Ransom, Ethel Wilson, Nicholas
Joy, Jack McKee, Emma Wilcox, and Ethel Intropodi.

SOMETHING GAY (P)
Tryout: Boston. Produced by the Messrs. Shubert at the
Morosco Theatre, New York, April 29. 56 performances.
A comedy by Adelaide Heilbron. Directed by Thomas
Mitchell. Sets by Donald Oenslager. Tallulah played Monica
Grey; others in the cast were Walter Pidgeon, Nancy Ryan,
Hugh Sinclair, Kent Thurber, Percy Ames, Elizabeth Dewing,
and Roy Gordon. (Tallulah's opinion of Something Gay
was succinct: "as misleading a title as ever was hung on
two hours of plot and dialogue.")

1936

REFLECTED GLORY (P)
Tryout: San Francisco, Los Angeles. Produced by Lee
Shubert (by arrangement with Homer Curran) at the
Morosco Theatre, New York, September 21. 127 performances. A comedy by George Kelly. Directed by George Kelly.
Sets by Norman Rock. Tallulah played Muriel Flood; others
in the cast were Ann Andrews, Clay Clement, S. T. Bratton,
Alden Chase, Phillip Reed, Robert Bordoni, and William
Brisbane. (Reflected Glory toured after its Broadway run;
among the cities it played were Boston, Detroit, Chicago,
Birmingham, and Washington.)

THE RUDY VALLEE SHOW (NBC radio). September 24.
Tallulah performed Dorothy Parker's "The Waltz."

On Monday, December 21, Tallulah reported to the Selznick
International Studios in Hollywood to make screen tests
for the role of Scarlett O'Hara in Gone With the Wind.
She made three tests, two of which were in Technicolor,
wearing costumes which Greta Garbo had worn in Camille.
Tallulah's tests were directed by George Cukor, at that time
the director of GWTW. Portions of the tests (as well as an
earlier one) were shown on Hollywood: The Selznick Years
on ABC Television on March 21, 1969.

1937

RCA MAGIC KEY (NBC radio). January 10. Tallulah
performed a scene from Reflected Glory.

THE RUDY VALLEE SHOW (NBC radio). June 17. With
Florida Freibus, Tallulah enacted "Advice to the Little
Peyton Girl" by Dorothy Parker.

RADIO PLAYHOUSE (CBS radio). August 30. Portraying Viola, Tallulah appeared in *Twelfth Night* with Orson Welles, Estelle Winwood, Helen Menken, Conway Tearle, and Sir Cedric Hardwicke.

On Tuesday, August 31, Tallulah married John Emery. Her father was startled, she said, "when he learned I was to marry. He thought Sister had a monopoly on the sacrament." Edie Smith, her secretary, commented: "I've always wanted to make a trip to Reno."

THE KATE SMITH SHOW (CBS radio). September 30. With Henry Fonda as Armand, Tallulah presented a brief version of *Camille*—twelve minutes, a feat of condensation!

ANTONY AND CLEOPATRA (P)
Tryout: Pittsburgh. Produced by Lawrence Rivers, Inc., at the Mansfield Theatre, New York, November 10. 5 performances. A tragedy by William Shakespeare, adapted by William Strunk, Jr. Directed by Reginald Bach. Sets by Jo Mielziner. Costumes by Jo Mielziner and Cecil Beaton. Music by Virgil Thomson. Tallulah played Cleopatra; others in the cast were John Emery, Conway Tearle, Regina Wallace, Thomas Chalmers, Fania Marinoff, and Stephen Fox. (*"Since there was nothing in the penal statutes to cover my offense," she said, "I was let off with a reprimand."*)

1938

Wilella Waldorf reported in The New York Post *on January 25 that Tallulah had decided to accept the leading role in* By Candlelight, *a comedy-with-music by Cole Porter. Rehearsals were to begin in two weeks, followed by an extended pre-Broadway tour. Retitled* You Never Know, *the musical—without Tallulah—opened at the Winter Garden in New York and ran for 78 performances. In the cast were Clifton Webb, Libby Holman, and Lupe Velez.*

FOR MEN ONLY (NBC radio). February 21. Tallulah chatted about baseball with two members of the New York Yankees.

THE CIRCLE (P)
Produced by William A. Brady at the Playhouse Theatre, New York, April 18. 72 performances. A comedy by W. Somerset Maugham. Directed by Bretaigne Windust. Sets by Donald Oenslager. Tallulah's costumes by Hattie Carnegie. Tallulah played Elizabeth; others in the cast were John Emery, Grace George, Bramwell Fletcher, Cecil Humphreys, Dennis Hoey, May Marshall, and Audry Ridgwell.

THE RUDY VALLEE SHOW (NBC radio). June 23. *"L" Is for Love*, a comedy by Howard Paris. Tallulah played Jill Dean; opposite her, as Jim Dean, was John Emery.

I AM DIFFERENT (P)
Produced by Lee Shubert in association with Joseph M. Gaites. A comedy by Zoë Akins, translated from a play by Lili Hatvany. Tallulah played Judith Held; others in the cast were John Emery, Glenn Anders, Margaret Sedden, Ara Gerald, and Fritzi Scheff. The play opened in Los Angeles in August and then toured, closing in Washington, on November 26.

1939

THE LITTLE FOXES (P)
Tryout: Baltimore, Pittsburgh. Produced by Herman Shumlin at the National Theatre, New York, February 15. 408 performances. A drama by Lillian Hellman. Directed by Herman Shumlin. Sets by Howard Bay. Costumes by Aline Bernstein. Tallulah played Regina Giddens; others in the cast were Abbie Mitchell, John Marriott, Patricia Collinge, Carl Benton Reid, Dan Duryea, Lee Baker, Florence Williams, Charles Dingle, and Frank Conroy. *The Drama Critics Circle Award for Best Play was not given for the 1938-39 season because the required three-fourths agreement was not reached by the eleven members;* The Little Foxes *received six votes, and Robert E. Sherwood's* Abe Lincoln in Illinois *drew five. Tallulah received the* Variety *citation for Best Performance by an Actress During the 1938-39 Season.*

THE KATE SMITH HOUR (CBS radio). March 16. Tallulah performed "Sentiment," a monologue by Dorothy Parker.

THE GREATER NEW YORK FUND ALL-STAR SHOW (NBC radio). April 23. Tallulah read "The Waltz," by Dorothy Parker.

THE NEW YORK DRAMA CRITICS CIRCLE AWARD PROGRAM (NBC radio). April 23. Tallulah appeared in two scenes from *The Little Foxes*.

THE PEOPLE'S PLATFORM (CBS radio). August 20. With Ford Frick, Lyman Brasson, Bill Corum, and Ed Ferguson, Tallulah talked about baseball.

On December 8, The Theatre Handbook and Digest of Plays, *edited by Bernard Sobel, was published by Crown Publishers. Included was an article by Tallulah entitled "The Stage as a Career" ("I think direction is the most valuable thing in the theatre, apart from good play or type casting. The more talent you have, the more discipline you need.").*

1940

The national company of The Little Foxes *opened its tour in Washington on February 5. The play was presented in twelve cities before it closed, for the summer, in Detroit on April 15. Box-office records were set in Boston, Philadelphia, Hartford, and Toronto.*

THE SECOND MRS. TANQUERAY (P)
Produced by Cheryl Crawford, Leo Bulgakov, and Proctor Jones, at the Maplewood Playhouse, Maplewood, N.J., on July 1. A melodrama by Sir Arthur Wing Pinero. Directed by Romney Brent. Sets by Albert Ward, Ralph Alswang, Herbert Andrews, and others. Tallulah's costumes by Madame Karinska. Tallulah played Paula Tanqueray; others in the cast were Stephan Eugene Cole, Leonore Harris, Madeleine Clive, Colin Keith-Johnston, James MacColl, Eugenia Rawls, Jess Barker, Ralph Kellard, and Edmund George. This was Tallulah's first appearance in summer theater; the company appeared in Amherst, Taunton, Harrison, Stockbridge, Dennis, White Plains, Cedarhurst, and Marblehead.

The national company of The Little Foxes *reopened in Princeton, N.J., on September 14, 1940, and closed in Philadelphia on April 5, 1941. The company traveled more than 25,000 miles and appeared in 104 cities.*

By a margin of 10 votes, Tallulah, the sole opposition nominee, failed of election to the Council of the Actors' Equity Association on May 24. She was defeated by Sam Jaffe, who polled 256 votes. John Emery, who ran for the council on the regular ticket, was elected.

1941

On January 21, it was announced in Hollywood that Jack Warner was considering Tallulah for the role of Fanny Skeffington in Mr. Skeffington. *Bette Davis, who earlier turned down the part, played it in the film.*

THE CAMPBELL PLAYHOUSE (CBS radio). April 18. Tallulah starred in a play titled *The Talley Method.*

TIME TO SHINE (NBC radio). April 23. Tallulah appeared opposite Eddie Cantor and received the following telegram from Anita Loos: "You are an absolute raving sensation. All but died of convulsions. The day you go on the air permanently should be declared a legal holiday."

YOUR HAPPY BIRTHDAY (NBC radio). April 25. Tallulah wished birthday greetings with the co-host, Axton Fisher.

LINCOLN HIGHWAY (NBC radio). April 26. Interviewed by Hector Prod, Tallulah discussed her "already lengthy" career, spoke out against Hitler, and read a love poem.

GREATER NEW YORK FUND VARIETY PROGRAM (NBC radio). April 27. Tallulah was introduced by Mayor Fiorello La Guardia as she and other Broadway stars aided in New York City's annual pledge drive for its social agencies.

HER CARDBOARD LOVER (P)
Produced by Cheryl Crawford, Dorothy and Julian Olney, and others. A comedy by Jacques Deval and P. G. Wodehouse. Directed by John C. Wilson. Sets by Raymond Sovey. Tallulah's costumes by Hattie Carnegie; make-up and coiffure by Elizabeth Arden. Tallulah played Simone; others in the cast were Harry Ellerbe, Fred Keating, Stephan Eugene Cole, Viola Frayne, and Sandy Campbell. A summer stock production, the play opened in Westport, Conn., and then was performed in Brighton, Mass.; Maplewood, N.J.; Marblehead, Mass.; Ogonquit, Me.; and White Plains and Cedarhurst, N.Y.

On August 17, Tallulah entertained soldiers at Camp Langdon, N.H. She received a citation from Major William F. Nee and was commissioned a second lieutenant in the 22nd Coast Artillery by Colonel Walter Dunn.

PHILIP MORRIS PLAYHOUSE (CBS radio). October 10. *The Little Foxes, with members of the Broadway cast, was performed.*

CLASH BY NIGHT (P)
Tryout: Detroit, Baltimore, Philadelphia. Produced by Billy Rose at the Belasco Theatre, New York, December 27. 49 performances. A drama by Clifford Odets. Directed by Lee Strasberg. Sets by Boris Aronson. Tallulah played Mae Wilenski; others in the cast were Lee J. Cobb, Robert Ryan, Katherine Locke, Joseph Schildkraut, Stephan Eugene Cole, Joseph Shattuck, Art Smith, John F. Hamilton, Harold Grau, and William Nunn.

1942

LISTEN, AMERICA (NBC radio). January 18. Tallulah urged Americans to buy war bonds and stamps.

Under the headline "Tallulah Bankhead to Start Series . . . Salary Reported to be Highest in Radio World," Mary Gaunt West proclaimed in the Courier-Journal *in Louisville, Ky., on January 30 that Tallulah would begin her own series on NBC on February 3.*

PHILIP MORRIS PLAYHOUSE: JOHNNIE PRESENTS (NBC radio). February 3. *Suspicion,* adapted from a story by Dorothy Sayers, presented Tallulah in her first radio mystery; Ray Bloch's Orchestra provided the music.

TIME TO SMILE (NBC radio). March 5. Tallulah was co-host with Fred Allen.

Impersonating Ethel Barrymore as the schoolteacher in

The Corn Is Green *for a $10,000 purchase of defense bonds (and then buying $5,000 worth herself after making the audience "promise" not to tell anyone), Tallulah helped Danny Kaye set a sales record in his one-night stand for the war effort at La Martinique in New York on April 5.*

WAR BOND DRIVE (NBC radio). April 11. With a bevy of stage and screen stars, Tallulah read listeners' pledges on a New York program.

LISTEN, AMERICA (NBC radio), April 26. Tallulah read "The Roots of a Tree" by Carl Bixby.

PHILIP MORRIS PLAYHOUSE: JOHNNIE PRESENTS (NBC radio). May 19. Dorothy Parker's soliloquy "The Telephone Call" was read by Tallulah; she was backed by Ray Bloch's Orchestra.

STAGE DOOR CANTEEN (CBS radio). September 10. Helen Menken, Ethel Barrymore, Sir Cedric Hardwicke, and Charles Laughton were among Tallulah's all-star cast.

THE SKIN OF OUR TEETH (P)
Tryout: New Haven, Baltimore, Philadelphia, Washington. Produced by Michael Myerberg at the Plymouth Theatre, New York, November 18. 359 performances. A play by Thornton Wilder. Directed by Elia Kazan. Sets by Albert Johnson. Costumes by Mary Percy Schenck. Tallulah played Sabina; others in the cast were Fredric March, Florence Eldridge, Montgomery Clift, Florence Reed, E. G. Marshall, Frances Heflin, Stanley Prager, and Andrew Ratousheff. *Tallulah left the cast on May 29, 1943, having given 229 performances; she was replaced by Miriam Hopkins. For her portrayal of Sabina, Tallulah won the New York Drama Critics Award for "Best Actress of the Year"; she received a similar citation from* Variety *and from the Barter Theatre in Abingdon, Va.*

1943

MILK FUND FOR BABIES (NBC radio). January 10. Again offering her support for a charitable cause, Tallulah appeared on the program with Mayor La Guardia and staff members from the city hospitals.

THAT THEY MIGHT LIVE (NBC radio). April 18. The leading role in a war drama, *I Served on Bataan,* was played by Tallulah.

RADIO READER'S DIGEST (CBS radio). May 2. With Conrad Nagel as narrator, Mrs. Johnny "Leadville" Brown was acted by Tallulah in a "radio playlet," *The Unsinkable Mrs. Brown.* Bob Nolan directed; Don Bryan and Kenn Sisson provided music.

NEW YORK PHILHARMONIC SYMPHONY (CBS radio). May 30. A tribute to Memorial Day, "The Blue and the Grey," was rendered by Tallulah.

STAGE DOOR CANTEEN (CBS radio). June 10. Guests with Tallulah were Fred Allen, Portland Hoffa, Jimmy Durante, Bob Hope, and Tom Howard.

STAGE DOOR CANTEEN (MP)
Produced by Sol Lesser, in association with the American Theatre Wing, for United Artists. Opened at the Capitol Theatre, New York, June 24. Screenplay by Delmer Daves. Directed by Frank Borzage. Songs by Al Dubin, Richard Rodgers, Lorenz Hart, Johnny Green, and Gertrude Lawrence. Tallulah appeared as herself; others in the cast were Katharine Hepburn, Lynn Fontanne, Alfred Lunt, Ina Claire, Gypsy Rose Lee, Judith Anderson, Elsa Maxwell, Paul Muni, Yehudi Menuhin, Franklin Pangborn, George Raft, Elliott Nugent, Cornelia Otis Skinner, Merle Oberon, Lon McCallister, Helen Hayes, Humphrey Bogart, Ethel Merman, Martha Scott, and Katharine Cornell.

1944

LIFEBOAT (MP)
Produced by Kenneth Macgowan for 20th Century-Fox. Opened at the Astor Theatre, New York, January 12. Screenplay by Jo Swerling, based on a story by John Steinbeck. Directed by Alfred Hitchcock. Tallulah played Connie Porter; others in the cast were William Bendix, Walter Slezak, John Hodiak, Henry Hull, Hume Cronyn, Mary Anderson, Canada Lee, and Heather Angel. Tallulah received the New York Film Critics Award for "Best Actress of the Year" for her portrayal.

STAGE DOOR CANTEEN (CBS radio). January 21. After performing Dorothy Parker's monologue "The Little Hours," Tallulah shared the radio stage with Count Basie, Lena Horne, Elsa Maxwell, and George Jessel.

WORDS AT WAR (NBC radio). February 29. A rebroadcast of *I Served on Bataan* was presented.

MILLION DOLLAR BAND (NBC radio). May 6. Tallulah promised to sing but didn't; instead, she introduced two songs and joked with Harry James.

TIME TO SMILE (NBC radio). May 10. A special program was broadcast from Fort Monmouth, N.J., with Tallulah serving as mistress of ceremonies.

STAGE DOOR CANTEEN (CBS radio). June 10. Harpo Marx, Gypsy Rose Lee, Mike Todd, Otto Kruger, and Katharine

Cornell were among the stars. Tallulah read Joyce Kilmer's "Trees" and participated in a comedy sketch.

ONE THOUSAND CLUB OF AMERICA (NBC radio). November 6. Tallulah urged all Americans, "Democrats and otherwise," to vote for Franklin Delano Roosevelt.

THE RUDY VALLEE SHOW (NBC radio). November 16. Tallulah read a poem and acted in a short play.

THE FRANK SINATRA SHOW (CBS radio). December 4. Again Tallulah promised to sing, and again she did not; instead, she exchanged quips with Frank Sinatra, "whose voice is almost as low as mine."

THIS IS THE WORD (CBS radio). December 16. The word was "Buy Bonds," and she encouraged all Americans to do so.

1945

THE RALEIGH ROOM WITH HILDEGARDE (NBC radio). January 2. At the impetus of Anna Sosenko, the producer, Tallulah made her singing debut on network radio. "I'm not sure that America is ready for this, dahlings," she said as she warbled, with Clifton Webb, "I'll Be Seeing You."

WAR BOND SHOW (NBC radio). January 6. *These Are Our Men*, a drama, starred Tallulah and Walter Huston.

THE RALEIGH ROOM WITH HILDEGARDE (NBC radio). January 16. Brought back by popular demand, Tallulah sang "I'll Be Seeing You."

FOOLISH NOTION (P)
Tryout: New Haven, Boston, Baltimore, Washington. Produced by the Theatre Guild (Theresa Helburn–Lawrence Langner) at the Martin Beck Theatre, New York, March 13. 104 performances. A comedy by Philip Barry. Directed by John C. Wilson. Production supervised by Armina Marshall. Sets and lighting by Jo Mielziner. Music by Arthur Norris. Tallulah's costumes by Mainbocher. Tallulah played Sophie Wing; others in the cast were Mildred Dunnock, Donald Cook, Aubrey Mather, Henry Hull, Barbara Kent, Joan Shepard, and Maria Manton (Marlene Dietrich's daughter). After closing on Broadway, the play had an extensive tour. *On May 15, Tallulah received a note from David O. Selznick: "I did want you to know that, more and more, I am convinced you are the great actress of our time."*

A ROYAL SCANDAL (MP)
Produced by Ernst Lubitsch for 20th Century-Fox. Opened at the Roxy Theatre, New York, April 11. Screenplay by Edwin Justis Mayer, adapted by Bruno Frank from Lajos Biro and Melchior Lengyel's play, *The Czarina*. Directed by Otto Preminger. Tallulah played Catherine the Great; others in the cast were Anne Baxter, Vincent Price, Sig Ruman, Charles Coburn, William Eythe, Mischa Auer, Vladimir Sokoloff, Grady Sutton, and Eva Gabor. Miss Gabor's part was deleted in some released versions.

CURTAIN TIME ON BROADWAY (NBC radio). April 14. In a tribute occasioned by the death of Franklin Delano Roosevelt, Tallulah read Nathaniel A. Benson's "Elegy of Remembrance." Appearing with her on the broadcast were Ethel Barrymore and Elliott Nugent.

THE MARY MARGARET McBRIDE SHOW (NBC radio). April 20. Tallulah discussed the loss of F.D.R., the status of the war, and the importance of presenting a united effort for President Truman.

ATLANTIC SPOTLIGHT (NBC radio). April 28. Again, a sense of patriotism was Tallulah's theme; she urged all who loved freedom to show their "colors and stripes" for the benefit of America and the world.

THE KATE SMITH HOUR (CBS radio). April 29. Tallulah appeared in a comedy sketch and then delivered Dorothy Parker's monologue "The Waltz."

On May 18, Tallulah recorded two broadcasts—one in English, the other in French—for the Radio Program Bureau of the Office of War Information.

THE JERRY WAYNE SHOW (CBS radio). June 15. As the "incomparable voice of wonder," Tallulah quipped with her host and then picked the best of the currently popular records.

THE NAVY HOUR (NBC radio). August 14. The title role of Helena was taken by Tallulah in a dramatization titled *A Salute to the U.S. Cruiser Helena.*

THE RALEIGH ROOM WITH HILDEGARDE (NBC radio). September 11. Tallulah sang "Don't Fence Me In."

1946

THE EDGAR BERGEN–CHARLIE McCARTHY SHOW (NBC radio). February 24. "Imitating" W. C. Fields, Tallulah parried with Charlie before succumbing to the flattery of Mortimer Snerd, whom she threatened later to reduce to sawdust or firewood.

THE RALEIGH ROOM WITH HILDEGARDE (NBC radio). March 13. Tallulah sang "Always," after which Hildegarde jibed, "Never again."

CHESTERFIELD SUPPER CLUB (NBC radio). March 29.

Perry Como was the host; Tallulah and Jack Smith were the guests.

THE FRED ALLEN SHOW (NBC radio). May 5. Among the regulars—Titus Moody, Mrs. Nussbaum, *et al.*—Tallulah went "slumming" in Allen's Alley.

THE PENGUIN ROOM WITH HILDEGARDE (NBC radio). May 15. Tallulah was cited as the "most popular guest."

RADIO READER'S DIGEST (CBS radio). May 26. Tallulah played the title role in *The Story of Helen Zabriskie.*

WE, THE PEOPLE (CBS radio). August 18. As moderator and guest star, Tallulah presided over a discussion on "the throes and joys of summer theater."

THE CAMPBELL ROOM (CBS radio). October 6. Hildegarde and Tallulah sang "Anything You Can Do."

THE FRED ALLEN SHOW (NBC radio). October 27. Fred Allen and Tallulah performed for the first time a skit— "The Mr.-and-Mrs. Breakfast Broadcasting Satire"—which became a radio classic. (*In 1972, a recording of the sketch was released in an album entitled* The Golden Age of Comedy, *Volume I, Evolution Records, Number 3013.*)

THE EDGAR BERGEN—CHARLIE MCCARTHY SHOW (NBC radio). November 17. Charlie McCarthy kidded Tallulah about being "the highest paid guest star in radio."

THE CAMPBELL ROOM (CBS radio). November 24. Tallulah and Hildegarde chatted about fashions and men; Tallulah sang scattered bits of "Some of These Days."

In an interview with Elinor Hughes, published in Boston on December 10, Tallulah said that "one studio" was interested in having her appear in a filmed version of Christopher La Farge's The Sudden Guest.

1947

THE EAGLE HAS TWO HEADS (P)
Tryout: Washington, Boston, Hartford, Providence, Philadelphia, Baltimore, Pittsburgh, Cleveland, Montreal, Toronto, Buffalo, Detroit. Produced by John C. Wilson at the Plymouth Theatre, New York, March 19. 29 performances. A romantic melodrama by Jean Cocteau, adapted by Ronald Duncan from *La Mort Ecoute aux Portes.* Directed by John C. Wilson. Sets by Donald Oenslager. Costumes by Aline Bernstein. Tallulah played the Queen; others in the cast were Eleanor Wilson, Kendall Clark, Helmut Dantine, Cherokee Thornton, and Clarence Derwent. The title was changed from *Eagle Rampant* while the play was in tryouts,

during which time—15 weeks—Colin Keith-Johnston left the cast, and Marlon Brando was replaced by Helmut Dantine.

While onstage in her revue at the Blue Angel, in New York, impressionist Florence Desmond ad-libbed with Tallulah, who was in the audience on March 29. Tallulah played Tallulah while Miss Desmond played Katharine Hepburn; then Tallulah gave her impression of Gracie Fields. Columnist Bert McCord noted with glee the following Tuesday that it was "the best intimate show in town."

THE CAMPBELL ROOM (CBS radio). March 30. Hildegarde sang; Tallulah read Dorothy Parker's "Here We Are."

KRAFT MUSIC HALL (NBC radio). April 17. Al Jolson and Tallulah gibed to determine "who was quicker on the Southern drawl." She won. He sang special lyrics in her honor, and she countered by imitating him in "Swanee."

INFORMATION, PLEASE (ABC radio). April 23. Answering questions with Tallulah were Franklin P. Adams, Jackie Robinson, Dr. Rufus Clement, and John Kiernan.

KRAFT MUSIC HALL (NBC radio). May 1. Tallulah tried a duet ("Carolina in the Mornin'") with Al Jolson, then recited a monologue by Dorothy Parker.
June 5. Tallulah sang "When the Blue of the Night" with Bing Crosby.

WE, THE PEOPLE (CBS radio). June 24. The discussion centered on baseball, and Tallulah centered on the Giants.

1948

PRIVATE LIVES (P)
Produced by John C. Wilson at the Plymouth Theatre, New York, October 4. 248 performances. A comedy by Noël Coward. Directed by John C. Wilson. Sets by Charles Elson. Tallulah's costumes by Mainbocher. Tallulah played Amanda Prynne; others in the cast were Donald Cook, Barbara Baxley, William Langford, and Therese Quadri. At the end of its lengthy run—the play toured prior to opening on Broadway and then took to the road again after its New York engagement—*Private Lives* had been on the boards for 204 weeks. The final performance was in Passaic, N.J., on June 3, 1950. Among its directors were Robert Henderson and Martin Manulis, and other members of the cast, at various times, were Buff Cobb, Phil Arthur, and Eugenia Rawls. The original production of *Private Lives* (it opened at the Phoenix Theatre, London, on September 4, 1930, with Gertrude Lawrence and Noël Coward) ran for 101 performances. Tallulah boasted—justifiably—that the play had been in nearly every state (only Maine, Nevada, and Florida were untouched) and had grossed more than a million and a half dollars.

THE FRED ALLEN SHOW (NBC radio). October 17. Tallulah and Fred Allen again did the "Mr.-and-Mrs. Breakfast Broadcasting Satire."

From her dressing room in the Plymouth Theatre, in New York, during an intermission of Private Lives, *Tallulah introduced President Harry S. Truman on October 21 in a major campaign address. Her three-minute speech was broadcast on ABC "to the largest audience ever to hear the voice of an actress." Ten days later, Tallulah followed Truman on the platform at Madison Square Garden, where she addressed an audience of 20,000.*

HI, JINX! (WNBC radio). December 13. On the "Tex and Jinx" show, Tallulah talked about the election and her recent cover story in *Time* magazine.

1949

In an unusual editorial faux pas, Tallulah was given second billing in a Variety *headline of March 23: "Sherwood, Bankhead Aid Sought on Govt. Legit Bill"—but she was in top form in the story that followed: "Tallulah Bankhead and Robert E. Sherwood are being sought as members of the legit legislative committee which will go to Washington to work for a $1,000,000 bill for a $300,000,000 federal appropriation for education." She and Sherwood were "figured naturals for the group on the strength of their influence with the Administration."*

On May 22, Governor William Tuck of Virginia presented Tallulah her second Best Actress Award—an acre of farm land, a ham, and a "platter to eat it off of"—from the Barter Theatre. She won for her performance in Private Lives, *which never played the Barter Theatre.*

Sam Zolotow announced in The New York Times *on August 10 that Tallulah had decided to appear in* Lily Henry, *a play by Mae Cooper and Grace Klein. Basil Dean was named as the director, and the Broadway opening was set "for the fall or early 1950."*

Tallulah spent three days, August 22 through August 24, before the cameras, making screen tests for the role of Amanda Wingfield in The Glass Menagerie. *Directed by Irving Rapper, she was photographed by Karl Freund in six scenes. "I was absolutely floored by her performance," said Rapper. "It's the greatest test I've ever seen. . . . I couldn't believe I was seeing such reality. I'll go so far as to say she was giving as brilliant if not a greater performance than Laurette Taylor." The role went to Gertrude Lawrence.*

Marie Torre wrote in The New York World-Telegram *that Tallulah would not appear in* Lily Henry. *She added, in her*

column of September 28, that the play "still might be produced on Broadway in the fall by Richard Aldrich, Richard Myers, and John C. Wilson."

"Bankhead Decision Today" was a headline in The New York Times *on September 30, indicating that producer Leland Hayward would soon announce whether Tallulah would appear in Garson Kanin's new play,* The Rat Race. *Tallulah liked the script; Mr. Hayward did not like her salary demands (15 percent of the weekly box-office receipts and 25 percent of the profits). "As things stand at the moment, Miss Bankhead is thinking of going out on the road again with 'Private Lives' on October 17." She did, and* The Rat Race *opened and quickly closed, "boiled in oil," she said, "by the critics, one of the most pretentious flops of the generation."*

On Christmas Eve, Tallulah gave a dinner party at Antoine's, in New Orleans, for the Private Lives *company. The next day she received holiday greetings from John C. Wilson, the producer, who also told her that he "had heard of a new French play that would be magnificent for her."*

1950

In March, the National Newspaper Service, of Chicago, promised Tallulah (and her lawyer, Donald Seawell) that the name of the secretary in its new comic strip would be changed from Tallulah to Jezebel. "Jezebel!" laughed Tallulah. "That's a good one, dahling, on that woman!"

On May 13, Tallulah received from the Night Hawks Social Club in Washington, D.C., a citation "for her democratic stand, opposing discrimination in the theatre arts, and her inimitable acting skill, thus making her a golden inspiration to aspiring, talented persons of all races and religions."

From her dressing room in the Central Theatre in Passaic, N.J., Tallulah announced on June 3 that she was retiring from the stage, that she "would never act in the theater again." She kept her word until September 12, 1954, when she let it be known that she was returning to Broadway in Dear Charles.

From Time, *September 4: "Manhattan's Station WNBC was looking for a sponsor for its new World Series commentator: Broadway's tumultuous Tallulah Bankhead. 'It will cost somebody $25,000 to get me on the air,' said the New York Giants' No. 1 fan, 'but if the Giants win, I'll do the show for nothing.' "*

THE BIG SHOW (NBC radio)
Produced for NBC by James Harvey. Individual programs produced and directed by Dee Engelbach. Written by Goodman Ace, Selma Diamond, George Foster, Mort Green,

Welbourn Kelley, Joel Murcott, and Frank Wilson. Special material by Fred Allen. Music directed by Meredith Willson. Chorus directed by Max Teer and Ray Charles. Special lyrics by Sammy Kahn, arranged by Sidney Fine and Phil Moore. Announcers: Bert Cowlan, Ben Grauer, Ed Herlihy, and Jimmy Wallington. Mistress of ceremonies: Tallulah.

November 5. Guests were Fred Allen, Mindy Carson, Jimmy Durante, José Ferrer, Portland Hoffa, Frankie Laine, Paul Lukas, Ethel Merman, Russell Nype, and Danny Thomas. *In its review on November 8,* Variety *was enthusiastic: "They don't come any bigger than this one and it rates Nielsen's best."*

The New York Herald Tribune *announced, on November 10, that Tallulah had optioned Edwin J. Mayer's comedy* I'm Laughing *and that Lee Shubert would produce the play on Broadway; in the same article it was noted that Tallulah might star in Arthur Curran's film adaptation of S. N. Behrman's play* Biography.

THE BIG SHOW (NBC radio)
November 12. Guests were John Agar, David Brian, Fanny Brice, Frank Lovejoy, Groucho Marx, Ezio Pinza, Jane Powell, and Hanley Stafford.

SCREEN DIRECTOR'S PLAYHOUSE (NBC radio). November 16. *Lifeboat.* Produced by Howard Wiley. Directed by Bill Karn, with Alfred Hitchcock as guest director. Written by Jack Ruben, adapted from John Steinbeck's short story and Jo Swerling's screenplay. Tallulah played Connie Porter; others in the cast were Jeff Chandler, William Wilms, Sheldon Leonard, Barbara Eiler, Bob Glen, Henry Rowland, and Ann Diamond.

THE BIG SHOW (NBC radio)
November 19. Guests were Eddie Cantor, Perry Como, Bob Hope, and Ray Middleton. *"May the Good Lord Bless and Keep You," by Meredith Willson, was introduced on this broadcast; it became the show's closing theme.*

November 26. Guests were Fred Allen, Jack Carson, Ed "Archie" Gardner, Portland Hoffa, Lauritz Melchior, and Ed Wynn.

Directed by Mitch Miller and accompanied by Joe Bushkin, Tallulah recorded "I'll Be Seeing You" and "You Go to My Head" (Columbia, Number 39109), on November 27.

THE BIG SHOW (NBC radio)
December 3. Guests were Fred Allen, Joan Davis, Douglas Fairbanks, Jr., Portland Hoffa, Phil Silvers, and Margaret Truman.

Making her debut on the Lyceum circuit, at a fee of $1,500 for each of three performances, Tallulah addressed an audience

of 2800 in the McFarlin Auditorium at Southern Methodist University in Dallas, Tex., on December 5. The next day she appeared in Chicago, and the following evening she was in Wilmington, Del. She returned to New York on Saturday for rehearsals for The Big Show, *and, exhausted by the "treadmill that never stopped," resigned from the lecture loop of the Columbia Lecture Bureau.*

THE BIG SHOW (NBC radio)
December 10. Guests were Eddy Arnold, Charles Boyer, Joe Bushkin, Imogene Coca, and Clifton Webb. *"Portrait of Tallulah," written by Joe Bushkin and arranged by Alan Shulman, was dedicated to Tallulah in its radio premiere.*

December 17. Guests were Louis Armstrong, Bob Hope, Deborah Kerr, Frankie Laine, Dean Martin and Jerry Lewis, and Dorothy McGuire.

THE BOB HOPE SHOW (NBC radio). December 19. Tallulah appeared with Gordon MacRae.

THE BIG SHOW (NBC radio)
December 24. Guests were Jimmy Durante, Bert Lahr, Robert Merrill, Margaret O'Brien, Edith Piaf, and Fran Warren.

December 31. Guests were Vivian Blaine, Sam Levine, Ken Murray, and Gloria Swanson.

1951

THE BIG SHOW (NBC radio)
January 7. Guests were Fred Allen, Phil Baker, Marlene Dietrich, Portland Hoffa, Edward G. Robinson, and Danny Thomas.

January 14. Guests were Louis Calhern, Jack Carter, Florence Desmond, Jimmy Durante, Martha Raye, and Fran Warren.

January 21. Guests were Fred Allen, Eddie Cantor, Porltand Hoffa, Judy Holliday, Gypsy Rose Lee, Vaughn Monroe, and Patrice Munsel.

January 28. Guests were Ray Bolger, Gary Cooper, the Delta Rhythm Boys, Danny Kaye, "Slapsy" Maxie Rosenbloom, Rudy Vallee, and Julie Wilson.

February 4. Guests were Fred Allen, Robert Cummings, Laraine Day, Jimmy Durante, Leo Durocher, Judy Holliday, and Jane Pickens.

February 11. Geusts were the Andrews Sisters, Joan Davis, Judy Garland, Gordon MacRae, Dean Martin and Jerry Lewis, and Groucho Marx.

SCREEN DIRECTOR'S PLAYHOUSE (NBC radio). February 15. Tallulah played Judith Traherne in *Dark Victory.* David Brian was her co-star; Edmund Goulding was the director.

THE BIG SHOW (NBC radio)
February 18. Guests were Jack Carson, Dennis King, Beatrice Lillie, Lauritz Melchior, the West Point Choir, and Ed Wynn.

February 25. Guests were Uta Hagen, Jack Haley, Judy Holliday, Paul Kelly, Robert Merrill, Ole Olsen and Chick Johnson, and Monty Woolley.

March 4. Guests were Fred Allen, Clive Brooks, Portland Hoffa, Frankie Laine, Ethel Merman, Margaret Phillips, Hugh Reilly, Herb Shriner, and Margaret Truman.

March 11. Guests were Bob Burns, Jimmy Durante, Billy Eckstine, Celeste Holm, Eddie Jackson, Evelyn Knight, Jack Pearl (Baron Munchausen) and Cliff Hall (Sharlie), and Joe Smith and Charlie Dale.

March 18. Guests were Fred Allen, Phil Baker, Johnny Burke, Eddie Cantor, Eddie Fisher, Ella Fitzgerald, Portland Hoffa, Jan Peerce, and Ethel Waters.

March 25. Guests were Don Cornell, Jimmy Durante, Rex Harrison, Judy Holliday, Eddie Jackson, Jackie Miles, Carmen Miranda, and Lilli Palmer.

April 1. Guests were Ethel Barrymore, Joan Davis, Judy Holliday, Bob Hope, Van Johnson, Groucho Marx, and Ezio Pinza.

April 8. Guests were Fred Allen, Vivian Blaine, Alonzo Bozan, Dr. Ralph Bunche, John Crosby, Ossie Davis, Portland Hoffa, William Marshall, Jane Morgan, and Rudy Vallee.

On April 9, Tallulah was presented the Honorary Fellowship Award of Merit conferred by the George Washington Carver Memorial Institute for her "Contribution to the Theatre Arts, Americanism, and Human Welfare." The presentation was made in Town Hall, in New York; among previous recipients were Eleanor Roosevelt, and Jackie Robinson.

THE BIG SHOW (NBC radio)
April 15. Guests were Eddy Arnold, Eddie Cantor, Jack Carson, Olivia de Havilland, Phil Foster, Tommy Henrich, and Martha Raye.

SCREEN DIRECTOR'S PLAYHOUSE (NBC radio). April 19. Directed by Jean Negulesco, Tallulah and Stephen Cochran appeared in a dramatization of Fanny Hurst's *Humoresque.*

THE BIG SHOW (NBC radio)
April 22. Guests were Fred Allen, Joan Davis, Portland Hoffa, Judy Holliday, Dennis King, Lisa Kirk, Herb Shriner, and Fran Warren.

April 29. Guests were Milton Berle, Rosemary Clooney, Matt Cvetic, Jimmy Durante, Frank Lovejoy, Gordon MacRae and Ethel Merman.

May 6. Guests were Fred Allen, Lucienne Boyer, Portland Hoffa, George Jessel, Groucho Marx, Ginger Rogers, and Margaret Truman.

ANTA ALBUM (P)
Produced by Robert C. Schnitzer and Jean Dalrymple for the American National Theatre and Academy at the Ziegfeld Theatre, New York, May 6. 1 performance. Production supervised by Ben Krantz and Herman Shapiro. Music directed by Max Meth. Sets and lighting by Peggy Clark. In this tribute to ANTA, Tallulah served as mistress of ceremonies, sharing the lights with Faye Emerson, Margaret Webster, and Hedda Hopper. Others who appeared were Helen Gallagher, Harold Lang, Shirley Booth, Ella Logan, Phil Baker, Gloria Swanson, Lee Tracy, Geraldine Page, and Eva Le Gallienne.

Album of Stars: Great Moments from Great Plays (Decca, Number DL 9009—MG2224, MG2225) was released on June 4; in the album are two scenes from The Little Foxes, *with Tallulah, Eugenia Rawls, Kent Smith, Paul Byron, and Howard Smith.*

Upon her arrival in London, in September, where the second season of The Big Show *was to be launched, Tallulah held a lengthy press conference at the Ritz Hotel. She drank champagne from her slipper ("Size four, dahlings!"), saluted Britain, toasted Churchill, posed for photographers, answered and asked questions, recited Juliet's balcony speech, and danced the Charleston. "Nothing like this has ever happened here before," said a waiter.*

THE BIG SHOW (NBC radio)
September 30 (broadcast on the BBC on September 16). The program originated from the London Palladium; the guests were Fred Allen, Jack Buchanan, Portland Hoffa, Michael Howard, Vivien Leigh, Beatrice Lillie, the George Mitchell Choir, Laurence Olivier, George Sanders, and Robb Wilton; Leslie Mitchell was the announcer.

October 7. The program originated from the Empire Theatre, in Paris, where it was recorded on September 24. The guests were Josephine Baker, Gracie Fields, Joan Fontaine, William Gargan, Fernand Gravat, Georges Guitary, Françoise Rosay, and George Sanders; Paul Durand was the associate orchestral conductor. France Soir *praised Tallulah as "truly irresistible," adding that "she looks a lot like a Sunday school teacher," and "this astonishing woman in America is something of a national institution."*

October 14. Guests were Fred Allen, Shirley Booth, Jimmy Durante, Ethel Merman, Portland Hoffa, and George Sanders.

October 21. Guests were the Andrews Sisters, Marlene Dietrich, Phil Foster, Benny Goodman, Frankie Laine, and Margaret Truman.

October 28. Guests were Jack Carson, Jimmy Durante, Ed "Archie" Gardner, the Ink Spots, James and Pamela Mason, Dorothy Sarnoff, and Herb Shriner.

November 4. Guests were Joan Davis, Herb Jeffries, Evelyn Knight, Groucho Marx, George Sanders, and Lurene Tuttle.

November 11. Guests were Morton Downey, Jerry Lester,

Jackie Miles, Ken Murray, Ann Sheridan, Sophie Tucker, and June Valli.

November 18. Guests were Fred Allen, Gertrude Berg, Shirley Booth, Yul Brynner, Cliff Hall (Sharlie), Portland Hoffa, Jack Pearl (Baron Munchausen), and Maxine Sullivan.

November 25. Guests were Dane Clark, Graham Forbes, Phil Foster, Mary McCarty, George Sanders, Martha Scott, and Martha Wright.

December 2. Guests were Fred Allen, Wally Cox, Dolores Grey, Portland Hoffa, Paul McGrath, Lauritz Melchior, Ginger Rogers, and George Sanders.

December 9. Guests were Eddy Arnold, Jean Carroll, Robert Cummings, Ed "Archie" Gardner, Hildegarde, and Ann Sothern.

December 16. Guests were Jack Carson, Merv Griffin, Rosalind Russell, Phil Silvers, Sarah Vaughan, and Henny Youngman.

December 23. Guests were Milton Berle, Robert Merrill, Ozzie and Harriet Nelson, Alec Templeton, and Margaret Truman.

December 30. Guests were Fred Allen, Gertrude Berg, Joan Davis, Portland Hoffa, Georgia Gibbs, Johnny Johnston, and Jackie Miles.

1952

THE BIG SHOW (NBC radio)
January 6. Guests were Bob Carroll, Joan Davis, Vera Lynn, Jimmy Nelson, Claude Rains, and Herb Shriner.

The radio editors of America announced in Radio and Television Daily *on January 7 that Tallulah was named "Woman of the Year in Radio."*

THE BIG SHOW (NBC radio)
January 13. Guests were Fred Allen, Tony Bennett, Phil Foster, June Havoc, Portland Hoffa, Betty Hutton, Vera Lynn, and Sheppard Strudwick.

On January 17, the Philharmonic Symphony Orchestra, under the direction of Guido Cantelli, played the premiere performance of A Laurentian Overture; *it was composed by Alan Shulman, a cellist, and dedicated to Tallulah.*

THE BIG SHOW (NBC radio)
January 20. Guests were Shirley Booth, Phil Foster, Vera Lynn, Jack Pearl (Baron Munchausen) and Cliff Hall (Sharlie), Dick Powell, and Earl Wrightson.

January 27. Guests were James Barton, Tony Bavaar, Victor Borge, Jack Carson, Bob (Elliot) and Ray (Goulding), and Vera Lynn.

February 3. Guests were Fred Allen, Jerry Colonna, Portland Hoffa, Vera Lynn, Ethel Merman, Jan Murray, and Cathleen Nesbitt.

February 10. Guests were Joan Davis, Phil Foster, Vera Lynn, Jan Miner, Claude Rains, and Jean Sablon.

February 17. Guests were Fred Allen, Hoagy Carmichael, Joan Davis, Portland Hoffa, Vera Lynn, and Jane Pickens.

February 24. Guests were Kay Armen, Gertrude Berg, Victor Borge, Phil Foster, Ed "Archie" Gardner, and Robert Merrill.

March 2. Guests were Fred Allen, Connee Boswell, Clark Dennis, Rex Harrison, Portland Hoffa, Lilli Palmer, and Henny Youngman.

March 9. Guests were Richard Eastham, Joe Frisco, Peter Lorre, Fibber McGee and Molly (Jim and Marian Jordan), Ethel Merman, and Sheppard Strudwick.

March 16. Guests were Fred Allen, Peter Donald, William Gargan, Portland Hoffa, Helen O'Connell, and Frank Sinatra.

March 23. Guests were Victor Borge, Rosemary Clooney, Marlene Dietrich, Paul Douglas, Jack Pearl (Baron Munchausen) and Cliff Hall (Sharlie), and Earl Wrightson. *For "public service through radio programs" Tallulah and* The Big Show *received awards from the John Guedel Dinky Foundation.*

March 30. Guests were Fred Allen, Vivian Blaine, Judy Canova, Phil Foster, Portland Hoffa, Johnny Johnston, and Jan Murray.

April 6. Guests were Toni Arden, Dorothy Claire, Judy Canova, the Continental (Renzo Cesana), Herb Jeffries, Oscar Levant, Jane Russell, and Paul Winchell and Jerry Mahoney.

THE JANE PICKENS SHOW (NBC radio). April 7. Tallulah and Jane Pickens discussed the demands of radio careers.

THE BIG SHOW (NBC radio)
April 13. Guests were Fred Allen, Portland Hoffa, Peggy Lee, Groucho Marx, Jackie Miles, and George Sanders.

April 20. Guests were Fred Allen, Phil Foster, Gilbert W. Gabriel, Julie Harris, Portland Hoffa, Groucho Marx, Ethel Merman, William Prince, George Sanders, John Van Druten, and Earl Wrightson.

HY GARDNER CALLING (NBC radio). September 24. Mr. Gardner called on Tallulah, and they talked about the theater in America, the "wealth of talent on Broadway," and, of course, about *The Big Show.*

MEREDITH WILLSON'S MUSIC ROOM (NBC radio). The topic was the music Meredith provided for *The Big Show,* particularly the theme song; Tallulah said that to her, it was "almost like a hymn."

On September 29, Harper & Brothers published Tallulah *(335 pages, 48 photographs, $3.95); her autobiography became an immediate best seller, 40,000 copies of the first printing of 100,000 having been sold prior to publication.*

Tallulah decided on Tallulah *as the title after eliminating* Hew and Cry *and* Ah, My Foes, and Oh, My Friends. *The book was on most best-seller lists for more than six months; it was in print for seven years.*

ALL-STAR REVUE (NBC-TV). October 11. Produced and directed by Dee Engelbach. Executive production by Sam Fuller. Television direction by Hal Keith. Written by Mort Green and George Foster. Orchestra and chorus directed by Meredith Willson. Choreography by Ron Fletcher. Sets by Richard Day. Tallulah's costumes by Hattie Carnegie. Appearing with Tallulah in this show, her television debut, were Ethel Barrymore, Ben Grauer, Meredith Willson, and Groucho Marx.

THE AUTHOR SPEAKS (NBC radio). October 11. Tallulah, of course, was talking about *Tallulah.*

ALL-STAR REVUE (NBC-TV). November 8. Guests were David Niven, Paul Hartman, Vaughn Monroe, Patsy Kelly, Phil Foster, and Meredith Willson.

Variety announced on November 12 that Tallulah might return to Broadway the following season in a one-woman show entitled A Night with Tallulah. *Charles Barry was named as the producer, Dee Engelbach as the director.*

THEATRE GUILD OF THE AIR (NBC radio). November 16. Playing herself (alias Margo Channing) in *All About Eve,* Tallulah appeared with Kevin McCarthy and Beatrice Pearson.
    November 23. Tallulah starred in a one-hour version of *Magnificent Obsession.*

RADIO CITY PREVIEWS (NBC radio). November 28. Tallulah talked about her recent performance in *All About Eve.*

ALL-STAR REVUE (NBC-TV). December 20. Guests were Louis Armstrong, Jack Carson, Patsy Kelly, and Phil Foster.

1953

ALL-STAR REVUE (NBC-TV). January 10. Guests were Milton Berle, Dennis King, Phil Foster, Patsy Kelly, and Billy Daniels.
    February 7. Guests were Bert Lahr, Dolores Martin, and Patsy Kelly.

ANSWER THE CALL (WNBT-TV). March 2. Tallulah appeared, on tape, with President Eisenhower in this Red Cross appeal.

ALL-STAR REVUE (NBC-TV). March 14. Guests were Wally Cox, Fred MacMurray, Cab Calloway, and Patsy Kelly.
    April 18. Guests were Jimmy Durante, George Jessel, Ben Blue, and Connie Russell.

THE SANDS, LAS VEGAS (N)
Tallulah made her American nightclub debut on May 20; she was engaged for three weeks. She performed a 32-minute routine of jokes, songs, and dramatic monologues. Appearing on the same bill with her were the Clark Brothers, Dick Beaver, Virginia Hall, Bill Damian, Joy Healey, and a group known as Hi, Lo, Jack, and the Dame. Ray Sinatra's Orchestra accompanied Tallulah ("The microphone's flat, dahlings."). *"Bankhead is banknite for the Sands in Vegas," wrote the* Variety *stringer. Tallulah's "a top attraction for any class boite in this country—and all other English-speaking countries where she's known—and she has probably opened an income field for herself that will surpass anything that she has yet experienced."*

THE MILTON BERLE SHOW (NBC-TV). September 29. Tallulah and Frank Sinatra sang, but not together, and Tallulah dressed as "Uncle Miltie."

MAIN STREET TO BROADWAY (MP)
Produced by Lester Cowan for M-G-M. Opened at the Astor Theatre, New York, October 13. Screenplay by Samson Raphaelson, adapted from a story by Robert E. Sherwood. Directed by Tay Garnett. Tallulah played herself; others in the cast were Ethel Barrymore, Lionel Barrymore, Leo Durocher, Agnes Moorehead, Shirley Booth, Gertrude Berg, Mary Martin, John Van Druten, Louis Calhern, Richard Rodgers, Oscar Hammerstein II, Rex Harrison, Lillie Palmer, Helen Hayes, Cornel Wilde, and Faye Emerson.

THE MILTON BERLE SHOW (NBC-TV). November 3. Tallulah appeared with Wally Cox in a sketch about rowdy high school students. She then read, "dramatically," a Chinese menu.

On November 10, Tallulah was named chairman of a committee established to raise $10,000 for the W. C. Handy Foundation for the Blind in honor of the composer's eightieth birthday. Serving with her were Stanley Adams, Noble Sissle, Arthur Spingarn, and Carl Van Vechten.

PERSON TO PERSON (CBS-TV). November 20. Edward R. Murrow called on Tallulah in her town house on East Sixty-second Street, in New York. He saw some of the rooms and all of the pets.

1954

THE UNITED STATES STEEL HOUR (ABC-TV). January 5.

Tallulah played the title role in her first full-length television drama, *Hedda Gabler*. The play was produced by the Theatre Guild. Appearing with her were Luther Adler, Eugenia Rawls, John Baragrey, and Alan Hewitt.

The paperback edition of Tallulah *was published by Dell on January 5. The first printing was 400,000 copies.*

THE COLGATE COMEDY HOUR (NBC-TV). February 7. Jimmy Durante was the host; Tallulah and Carol Channing were his guests. Tallulah wanted to learn "all about diamonds from an expert."

WEEKEND (NBC radio). August 1. Tallulah was interviewed on the "Women's Page" segment of the program.

THE SANDS, LAS VEGAS (N)
Tallulah opened in a return engagement, this time for four weeks, on August 6. Appearing with her were George Shaw, Bobby Brandt, and Chuck Nelson.

SUNDAY WITH GARROWAY (NBC radio). September 12. The conversation ranged from jazz to home furnishings, from politics and baseball to acting and "earning a living."

DEAR CHARLES (P)
Produced by Robert Aldrich and Richard Myers, in association with Julius Fleischman, at the Morosco Theatre, New York, September 15. 155 performances. A comedy by Alan Melville, adapted from *Les Enfants d'Edouard* by Marc-Gilbert Sauvajon and Frederick Jackson, who adapted it from *Slightly Scandalous* by Frederick Jackson. Directed by Edmund Baylies (after Arthur Penn). Sets by Donald Oenslager. Tallulah's costumes by Gene Coffin. Tallulah played Dolores Darvel; others in the cast were Robert Coote, Norah Howard, Fred Keating, Tom Raynor, Grace Raynor, Hugh Reilly, Larry Robinson, Alice Pearce, Werner Klemperer, Mary Webster, and Peter Pell.

TODAY (NBC-TV). September 16. Tallulah was heard but not seen as she discussed the excitement of an opening night, reviewing the critics' opinions of *Dear Charles*.

WEEKEND (NBC radio). September 26. Interviewed by Tex McCrary, Tallulah talked about *Dear Charles* and the "marvelous clothes Mr. Gene Coffin has designed for me."

A TRIBUTE TO LIONEL BARRYMORE (NBC radio). November 21. Tallulah reminisced about the actor and read a poem; others on the program were Gene Fowler, Edward Arnold, Helen Hayes, and Norman Vincent Peale.

A CALL FOR FOSTER PARENTS (NBC radio). November 28. Tallulah, Tex, and Jinx McCrary discussed the importance of placing children in foster homes; Tallulah talked about the value of a "proper environment, with beauty and books and poetry and music."

FRIDAY WITH GARROWAY (NBC radio). December 31. She and Dave Garroway agreed it had been a good year and wished everyone the happiest of New Year's greetings.

1955

THE MARTHA RAYE SHOW (NBC-TV). September 20. Among the guests were Rocky Graziano, Gloria Lockerman, and Dennis King. Tallulah, Martha Raye, and Rocky Graziano did a satirical sketch on television quiz shows.

THE MILTON BERLE SHOW (NBC-TV). November 29. Frank Sinatra and Tallulah were the "special" guests; among others were Gale Storm, Vic Damone, Dick Contino, Rudy Vallee, Fred Clark, and Charles Farrell. Music was by Victor Young and his Orchestra.

THIS IS NEW YORK (CBS radio). November 30. With Walter Winchell and Edward R. Murrow, Tallulah discussed New York, telling why it was her "almost favorite" place.

HOLIDAY TIME (ABC radio). December 21. Estelle Winwood and Tallulah talked about childhood Christmases.

1956

PRESENTING ALFRED HITCHCOCK (NBC radio). January 25. Tallulah appeared in scenes from *Lifeboat* as Alfred Hitchcock talked about his films; he played excerpts from several soundtracks, including *39 Steps* and *Rebecca*.

A STREETCAR NAMED DESIRE (P)
Tryout: Miami, Palm Beach. Produced by the New York City Center Company at the City Center, February 15. 16 performances. A play by Tennessee Williams. Directed by Herbert Machiz. Sets by Watson Barratt, based on original designs by Jo Mielziner. Tallulah played Blanche DuBois; others in the cast were Jean Ellyn, Frances Heflin, Gerald O'Laughlin, Rudy Bond, Sandy Campbell, and Bruno Damon.

ZIEGFELD FOLLIES (P)
Produced by Richard Kollmar and James Gardiner, *Ziegfeld Follies* was scheduled to open at the Winter Garden Theatre, New York, on May 26. The show opened in Boston on April 16 and played 16 performances, and then ran in Philadelphia for 16 performances, after which it closed. Director of dances and musical numbers was Jack Cole. Tallulah headed a cast of 61; others in the cast were David Burns, Elliott Reid, Herbert Banks, and Mort Marshall.

BIOGRAPHIES IN SOUND (NBC radio). May 29. Tallulah discussed Fred Allen, his career, and his "great, great talent," in a radio biography entitled *Mr. Allen—Mr. Allen*. Also on the program were Dorothy Kilgallen and Meredith Willson.

WELCOME, DARLINGS (P)
Produced by Philip Langner and Peter Turgeon. A revue in 2 acts, with 26 sketches. Written by Paul Keyes, Hugh Martin, Timothy Gray, Marshall Barer, Dean Fuller, Jerry Herman, Jerry de Bono, and Sheldon Harnick. Advance director was Jay Harnick. Musical directors were Peter Howard and Ted Graham. Sets and lighting by Marvin Reiss. Production consultant, Gus Schirmer, Jr. Tallulah's costumes by Manhattan Costume, Robert McIntosh, Brooks Costume, and Benn Mandel. In the cast were James Kirkwood, Sheila Smith, Don Crichton, Bob Bakanic, the Martins, Timothy Gray, Don McKay, Gwen Harmon, and Preshy Marker. The revue opened in Westport, Conn., on July 16, and then moved on to Ivoryton, Dennis, and other theaters on the Eastern seaboard.

THE KATHY GODFREY SHOW (CBS-TV). August 20. Talking about summer theater in general and the general theater in particular, Tallulah stated that "things are pretty good, y'know, the audiences and all, I mean they're always nice to me. Conditions could be better in some places. That's life in this business, and I'm so lazy. Everyone wants a nice, steady job like acting."

1957

EUGENIA (P)
Produced by John C. Wilson and the Theatre Corporation of America at the Ambassador Theatre, New York, January 30. 12 performances. A play by Randolph Carter, adapted from *The Europeans* by Henry James. Directed by Herbert Machiz. Sets by Oliver Smith. Costumes by Miles White. Tallulah played the title role; others in the cast were Scott Merrill, Anne Meacham, Irma Hurley, Tom Ellis, June Hunt, Reynolds Evans, Jay Barney, Robert Duke, and Therese Quadri.

SHOWER OF STARS (CBS-TV). April 11. A television spectacular produced and directed by Ralph Levy. Written by Hugh Wedlock and Howard Snyder. Sets by Dwight Gibson. Costumes by George Whittaker. Musical supervision by Lud Gluskin and Lyn Murray. John F. Myers was associate producer. William Lundigan was host; appearing with Tallulah were Jack Benny, Ed Wynn, Tommy Sands, and Julie London.

THE STEVE ALLEN SHOW (NBC-TV). May 12. Guests were Tallulah, Pearl Bailey, Billy Graham, and Dean Jones.

CAFE DE PARIS, LONDON (N)
Tallulah was engaged for six weeks; she opened on May 27. With Ted Graham at the piano and the orchestras of Arthur Coppersmith and Harry Roy, she performed a series of songs and sketches, among the latter Dorothy Parker's monologue "The Waltz." *Her reviews were all raves;* Variety *reported, "This is fine comedy, beautifully acted."* Adlai Stevenson was in the opening-night audience.

"Gallantry, courage and chivalry, the three most complex, beautiful words in the English language. A moral man has at least one of these qualities. An immoral man lacks all three." Thus wrote Tallulah in an article entitled "The Trouble with American Morals," in which she also stated, "I'd rather be right than righteous" and, "Righteousness is unspeakable. It's the weapon of weak people." The article appeared in the July issue of Esquire.

CO-STAR (LP recording)
Produced by Hugo and Luigi. Conceived by Ray Shaw and Jack I. Astor. Released June 15. A recording (Roulette, Number CS109) of Tallulah acting scenes from *The Lady of the Camellias, Hedda Gabler, Lady Windermere's Fan, The Importance of Being Earnest, Mr. Chumley and the Giants, Two in a Boat,* and *The Truth, Miss Angela.* With the album came scripts for each play; the listener was thus able to read his lines and "act" with a star.

THIS IS NEW YORK (CBS radio). July 29. Tallulah was interviewed by Jim McKay and Dave Dugan.

THE ARTHUR MURRAY PARTY (NBC-TV). July 29. Among the contestants were Tallulah, Raymond Massey, and José Iturbi. Tallulah waltzed with Rod Alexander, and they won.

THE TEX AND JINX SHOW (NBC-TV). August 12. In a special segment of the broadcast, Tallulah interviewed Willie Mays.

FAMILY LIVING, '57 (NBC radio). With Helen Hall as moderator, Tallulah and Ben Gross, radio critic of *The Daily News,* talked about growing up in the South; Mr. Gross and Tallulah lived a few miles from each other when they were children in Alabama, and Mr. Gross remembered meeting Tallulah when, as a child, she was campaigning for her father.

JOE FRANKLIN'S MEMORY LANE (WOR-TV) October 2. Tallulah was interviewed by Joe Franklin; she talked about music with the other guests, Benny Benjamin and George Weiss, song writers.

THE GEORGE GOBEL SHOW (NBC-TV). October 8. Tallulah and George Gobel appeared in a sketch in which they were movers, always unemployed because they "broke up housekeeping." Jeff Donnell was the other guest.

THE SCHLITZ PLAYHOUSE OF STARS (CBS-TV) November 8. Tallulah starred in *The Hole Card*, the story of a woman who gambled and won. Appearing with her were Isobel Elsom, John Bryant, Ottola Nesmith, George O'Hanlon, and Jesslyn Fox. The program was rebroadcast on July 18, 1958.

THE POLLY BERGEN SHOW (NBC-TV) November 30. Tallulah sang "Give Me the Simple Life."

THE MITCH MILLER SHOW (NBC radio) December 1. Peggy Wood, Dennis King, and Tallulah told the story of "The Little Church Around the Corner," in New York.

THE LUCILLE BALL—DESI ARNAZ SHOW (CBS-TV) December 3. In a sketch entitled "The Celebrity Next Door," written by Bob Carroll, Jr., Madelyn Martin, Bob Schiller, and Bob Weiskopf, Tallulah was persuaded to star in a play sponsored by the PTA ("Who *wrote* this thing?" she asked. "And what, dahlings, is a PTA?").

THE GENERAL ELECTRIC THEATRE (CBS-TV). December 8. Tallulah played Katherine Belmont in *Eyes of a Stranger*, an original teleplay by Jameson Brewer. The show was produced by William Frye and directed by Ray Milland. Others in the cast were Richard Denning, Dan Tobin, Gavin Gordon, Cynthia Leighton, and Joan Warner.

THE ARTHUR MURRAY PARTY (NBC-TV). December 28. Among the dancing contestants were Paul Hartman, June Havoc, Hedy Lamarr, Larry Parks, Betty Garrett, Walter Slezak, Sarah Vaughan, Paul Winchell, and Bill and Cora Baird. Tallulah danced the Charleston with Rod Alexander. They won.

1958

In The New York Herald Tribune *of April 11, Bert McCord reported that Jean Dalrymple, Coordinator of the American Performing Arts Program for the Brussels World's Fair, had announced that Tallulah had been invited to portray Amanda Wingfield in* The Glass Menagerie. *Mr. McCord assumed that Tallulah would accept ("The star's answer should be forthcoming shortly and it's a good bet that it will be in the affirmative."). Tallulah declined.*

HOUSE ON THE ROCKS (P)
A comedy-mystery by George Batson. Tallulah appeared in it on the summer circuit, with plans to bring it to Broadway if its reception was favorable. It was not. The play was presented in Kennebunkport, Me., Harrisburg, Pa., Binghamton, N.Y., Laconia-Gilford, N.H., and Nyack, N.Y.

CRAZY OCTOBER (P)
Produced by Walter Starcke. A comedy by James Leo Herlihy.

Directed by James Leo Herlihy. Sets by Ben Edwards. Costumes by Alvin Colt. The play opened in New Haven, then moved to Washington, Detroit, Los Angeles, and San Francisco, where it closed. Tallulah played Daisy Filbertson; others in the cast were Estelle Winwood, Joan Blondell, Jack Weston, Collin Wilcox, J. Frank Lucas, and Fred Beir.

THE JACK PAAR SHOW (NBC-TV). October 30. Other guests were Dagmar, Cliff Arquette, and Betty Johnson.
    November 18. Other guests were Dave Wilcock, Cliff Arquette, and May Williams.

1959

THE MILTON BERLE SHOW (NBC-TV). January 7. Tallulah and Jimmie Rodgers acted a parody of westerns; she sang with Milton Berle. The program was repeated on April 29.

THE JACK PAAR SHOW (NBC-TV). April 10. Other guests were Phil Ford and Mimi Hines and Coby Dijon.

THE ED SULLIVAN SHOW (CBS-TV). April 19. Tallulah performed the subway sketch and Dorothy Parker's monologue "The Waltz." Other guests were Ginny Tiu Kao, Jack Carter, Ricky Layne, Della Reese, and Toni Arden.

MONITOR (NBC radio). May 27. Shirley Eder interviewed Tallulah from bedside at New York's Flower Fifth Avenue Hospital; the conversation centered not on Tallulah's health, but on the theater.

THE BOY WHO OWNED A MELEPHANT (MP)
Produced by Gayle-Swimmer-Anthony for Universal-International Pictures. Opened at the Palace Theatre, New York, October 6. Screenplay by Saul Swimmer and Tony Anthony, adapted from a story by Malvin Wald. Tallulah narrated the film, which starred her godson, Brockman Seawell; the film won the Gold Leaf Award at the Venice International Children's Film Festival in 1959.

THE BIG PARTY (CBS-TV). October 8. With Rock Hudson as co-host, Tallulah appeared with Sammy Davis, Jr., Lisa Kirk, Mort Sahl, Esther Williams, Matt Dennis, and the Will Mastin Trio.

THE JACK PAAR SHOW (NBC-TV). December 23. Other guests were Joey Bishop, Carl Reiner, and Judy Lynn.

1961

MIDGIE PURVIS (P)
Produced by Robert Whitehead and Roger L. Stevens, in association with Robert Fryer, Lawrence Carr, and John Herman, at the Martin Beck Theatre, New York, February 1.

21 performances. A farcical comedy by Mary Chase. Directed by Burgess Meredith. Sets and lighting by Ben Edwards. Costumes by Guy Kent. Tallulah played the title role; others in the cast were William Redfield, Alice Pearce, John Cecil Holm, Nydia Westman, Kip McCardle, Jean Bruno, Paul Mace, and Russell Hardie. *Tallulah was nominated for an Antoinette Perry Award, a "Tony," for her performance in this play.*

THE JACK PAAR SHOW (NBC-TV). February 9. Other guests were Merriman Smith, Betty White, and Jack Haskell.
    March 29. Other guests were Alexander King, Buddy Hackett, and Robert Merrill; Tallulah appeared on tape on this program, the last of the nightly telecasts.

1962

THE UNITED STATES STEEL HOUR (CBS-TV). May 5. Tallulah played Lillian Throgmorton in a teleplay entitled *A Man for Oona*, written by Michael Dyne. The drama was produced by George Kondolf and directed by Tom Donovan. Appearing with her were Nancy Carroll, Murray Matheson, Astrid Wilstrud, Yoshi Naka, Patrick Horgan, Christine Pickles, Walton Butterfield, and Lucie Lancaster.

HERE TODAY (P)
A comedy by George Oppenheimer. Tallulah appeared in the play in summer and winter stock in 1962, 1963, and 1964. Among the cities in which she appeared were Ivoryton, Conn., Mountainhome, Pa., Skowhegan and Ogunquit, Me., and Fitchburg, Falmouth, and Dennis, Mass. Tallulah played Mary Hilliard; touring with her was Estelle Winwood.

THE TONIGHT SHOW (NBC-TV). October 2. Other guests were Artie Shaw, Shelley Berman, and Fran Bennett.

Tallulah went to Huntsville, Ala., on May 18, where she dedicated Bankhead Hall, named for her father and uncle. On the platform with her were relatives Walter Will Bankhead and Mr. and Mrs. W. A. Grant, all of Jasper. In proclaiming the building officially open, Colonel W. J. MacPherson said, "In the history of the state, there is no more famous name than Bankhead."

THE TONIGHT SHOW (NBC-TV). May 28. Other guests were Malcolm Muggeridge, Bob Hope, and Kitty Kallen.

ELLIOT NORTON INTERVIEWS (WNDT-TV). June 26. The Boston drama critic interviewed Tallulah when she was appearing in New England in *Here Today*; the program was telecast throughout America on the NET network.

Tennessee Williams wrote in The New York Times *on December 29 that Tallulah "loves the theatre with so much*

of her heart that, in order to protect her heart, she has to say that she hates it. But we know better when we see her onstage." He added that he had created four parts for her: *Myra Torrance in* Battle of Angels, *Blanche DuBois in* A Streetcar Named Desire, *Ariadne del Lago in* Sweet Bird of Youth, *and Flora Goforth in* The Milk Train Doesn't Stop Here Anymore, *his "last long play for Broadway."*

1964

THE MILK TRAIN DOESN'T STOP HERE ANYMORE (P)
Produced by the David Merrick Foundation at the Brooks Atkinson Theatre, New York, January 1. 5 performances. A tragedy by Tennessee Williams. Directed by Tony Richardson. Production design by Rouben Ter-Arutunian. Music by Ned Rorem. Lighting by Martin Aronstein. Tallulah's costumes by Karinska. Hair styles by Michel Kazan. Tallulah played Flora "Sissy" Goforth; others in the cast were Tab Hunter, Ruth Ford, Ralph Roberts, Bobby Dean Hooks, Konrad Matthaei, and Marian Seldes.

1965

DIE! DIE! MY DARLING! (MP)
Produced by Anthony Hinds for Columbia Pictures. Opened at Showcase Theatres (Loew's Orpheum, New Amsterdam, and 23 others), New York, May 19. Directed by Silvio Narizzano. Screenplay by Richard Matheson, adapted from Anne Blaisdell's novel, *Nightmare*. Tallulah played Mrs. Trefoile; others in the cast were Stefanie Powers, Donald Sutherland, Peter Vaughan, Maurice Kaufman, and Yootha Joyce.

THE ANDY WILLIAMS SHOW (NBC-TV). May 2. Other guests were Sid Caesar and the Beach Boys.

THE TONIGHT SHOW (NBC-TV). May 27. Other guests were Henry Morgan and George Jessel.

WHAT'S MY LINE? (CBS-TV). June 6. Tallulah appeared as the "mystery guest."

THE MIKE DOUGLAS SHOW (Group W-TV). October 11-15. Among the guests on the five programs were Lucille Ball, Vivian Vance, Connie Francis, George Gobel, Dr. Joyce Brothers, George Jessel, Bobby Rydell, and Jack Jones.

THE RED SKELTON SHOW (CBS-TV). December 14. Tallulah danced with Red Skelton and appeared with him as a cohort of Clem Kadiddlehopper's. The other guest was Horst Jankowski.

1966

THE DAYDREAMER (MP)
Produced by Arthur Rankin, Jr., for Embassy Pictures. Premiere screening at Shore's Screening Theatre in Hollywood, July 1. Directed by Jules Bass. Screenplay by Arthur Rankin, Jr., adapted from four stories by Hans Christian Andersen. Music by Maury Laws. Tallulah was the voice of the Sea Witch; among those who appeared in the film were Jack Gilford, Ray Bolger, and Margaret Hamilton. Others whose voices were heard were Burl Ives, Victor Borge, Boris Karloff, Ed Wynn, Patty Duke, Hayley Mills, Cyril Ritchard, and Sessue Hayakawa.

Roddy McDowall's Double Exposure, *"A Gallery of the Celebrated with Commentary by the Equally Celebrated," was published by Delacorte Press in October. Tallulah wrote about Estelle Winwood: "my oldest and closest friend.... She has never failed me.... Estelle is granite in a crisis. A world with more Winwoods would be a more desirable sphere on which to fret and fume."*

1967

BATMAN (ABC-TV). March 15. In *The Black Widow Strikes Again,* Tallulah's role was that of the title character. Adam West was Batman; Burt Ward was Robin.

March 16. Tallulah again played the Black Widow in the following segment, entitled *Caught in the Spider's Web.*

THE MERV GRIFFIN SHOW (Group W-TV). April 21.

Among the guests were Milt Kamen, Selma Diamond, Bob Considine, and Joe Hyams.

May 24. The guests were Erroll Garner, Henry Morgan, and George Frazier, columnist for *The Boston Globe* and social essayist for *Esquire.*

THE SMOTHERS BROTHERS COMEDY HOUR (CBS-TV). December 17. Tallulah participated in a skit on gun control ("If one out of every four Americans is carrying a gun, that means, dahlings, that one of the Lennon Sisters is packing a rod."). Other guests were the Temptations.

1968

THE MERV GRIFFIN SHOW (Group W-TV). January 23. Other guests were Dirk Bogarde, Jack Carter, Barbara Nichols, and Ted Mack.

THE TONIGHT SHOW (NBC-TV). May 14. Joe Garagiola was the host; among the guests were Tony Scotti, Soupy Sales, Lou Thesz, Jack Twyman, Paul McCartney, and John Lennon. Tallulah told again the origin of her name, chatted with the host about baseball, and persuaded the pair of Beatles to talk about their music ("My godson adores, dahlings, all your songs, but I don't think I understand all of them ... too much social significance, y'know, and I like a song I can hum cause I can't always remember all the words, in the right places, I mean."). This was her last television appearance.

PHOTO CREDITS. James Abbe: 29, 35, 40, 110, 111, 112. Richard Avedon: 212-13, 231. Hugh Beeson, Jr.: 30, 58, 85, 89, 117, 146, 147, 150, 151, 152-53, 155, 198, 228 bottom right, 230, 249, 256-57, 258-59. Bettman Archive: 40, 145. Karl Bissinger: 229. Mrs. John Mason Brown: 62. Coffee House Club: 112-13. Cole Porter Collection, Yale University: 39. Condé Nast: 163. Janet Cohn: 201, 219. Nancy Crampton: 6-7, 31, 94, 99, 225. Culver Pictures, Inc.: 32, 104-05, 162, 173, 188-89, 191. Department of Archives and History of the State of Alabama: endpapers, 2, 3, 8, 18, 20, 27, 90, 91, 92, 93, 95, 96, 167, 172, 182. Alfred Eisenstadt, Life Magazine © Time Inc.: 84. Don English: 238-39. Friedman-Abeles: 68, 86, 193, 240-41, 242, 243, 247, 248, 249. Henry Grossman, Life Magazine © Time Inc.: 256. Philippe Halsman: 236, 237. Ira Hill: 115. Horst: 190 top, 204. James Kirkwood: 244 top. David Jackson: 148, 161, 178, 189, 204, 210, 246. Jill Krementz: 256. Life Magazine © Time Inc.: 227, 254-55. Raymond Mander–Joseph Mitchenson: 116, 118, 120, 121, 122-23, 124, 125, 126, 128, 129, 130, 133, 135, 137, 138, 139, 142, 143, 158. Robert McAfee: 187. Museum of the City of New York (Theatre and Music Collection): 41, 100 top right, 116 top, 119 bottom, 122 left, 148, 150, 154 bottom left, 171, 191 top. NBC: 76, 107, 166, 220, 221, 224, 225. Players Club: 30, 34, 38, 42, 45, 46, 53, 55, 75, 77, 98, 99, 108, 109, 114, 116, 122 left, 134, 149, 158, 159, 184, 186, 195, 196-97, 202-03, 204, 213, 218, 228, 245, 251. Allen Porter : 144-45. Eugenia Rawls: 45, 61, 87, 179 bottom, 200, 201 top, 201 left, 210, 230, 251, 261. Sy Schecter: 192-93. Cal Schumann: 81, 131. Valentine Sherry: 73. Leonard Sillman: 242, 243. Frank Sullivan: 71 bottom. Josef Szalay: 206, 207, 208-09. Theatre Collection, The New York Public Library, Astor, Lenox and Tilden Foundations: 171, 245, 252. Day Tuttle: 166, 210 top. U.P.I., Inc.: 54, 64, 80, 108, 154 top right, bottom right, 156-57, 180, 224, 226, 232, 233, 253. Van Damm Photos, Theatre Collection, The New York Public Library, Astor, Lenox and Tilden Foundations: 5, 72, 160, 174, 175, 176-77, 205. Carl Van Vechten: 68. Wide World Photos, Inc.: 13, 180, 194, 207, 214, 215, 260. Dorothy Wilding: 136, 140-41. Dare Wright: 79, 87. Jerome Zerbe: 58, 158.

Acknowledgment is made to *Weekend Review,* London, and The Owners of the Copyright, for "A Tallulah First-Night" by Arnold Bennett; Warner Brothers, Inc., for lines from "Bye, Bye, Blackbird" by Mort Dixon and Ray Henderson; and Random House for the excerpt from *George* by Emlyn Williams. Copyright © 1961, by Emlyn Williams.

INDEX

The text is set in linotype Garamond #3
by Haber Typographers, Inc.
with display in Avant Garde Gothic Extra Light.
Printed by the Stonetone process by Rapaport Printing Corp.
on Warren's 80# Bookman Matte.
Bound by Haddon Bindery.

Contributors to production:
Wilson Gathings: Production Editor
James Lepper: Production Manager
Robert Reed: Art Director
Libra Graphic Services: Mechanical Preparation
Vallo Riberto: Designer's Production Assistant